Futaribeya

A ROOM FOR TWO

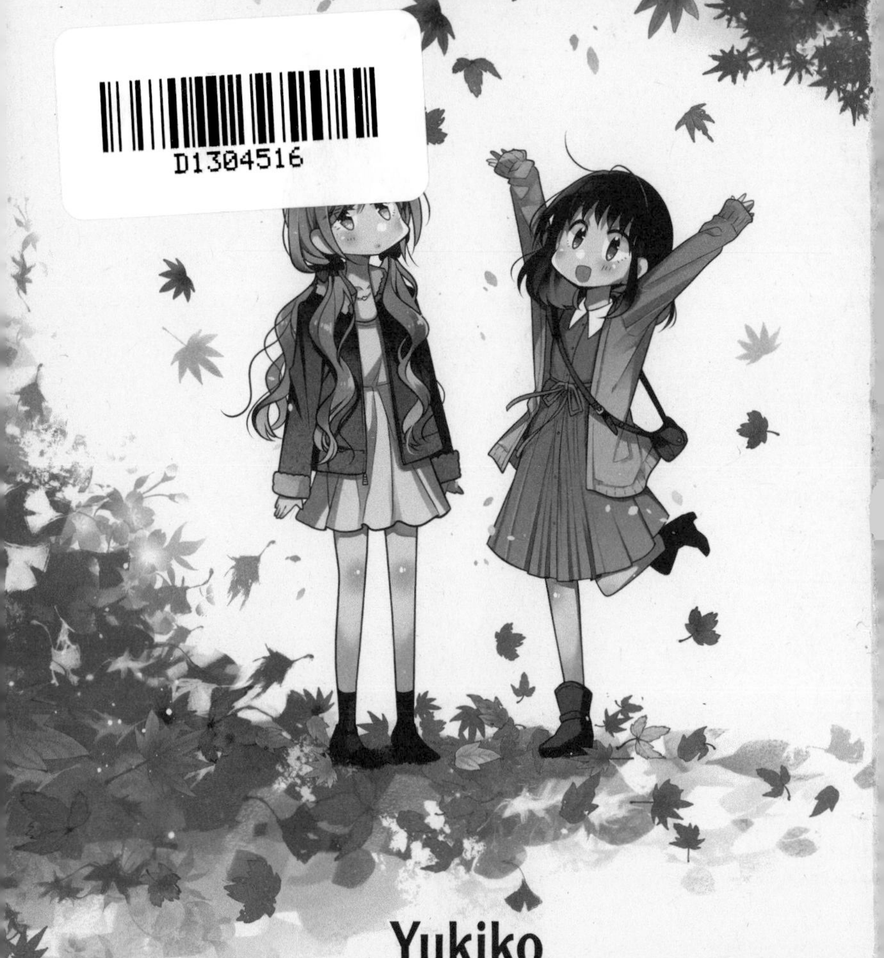

Yukiko

CHARACTER

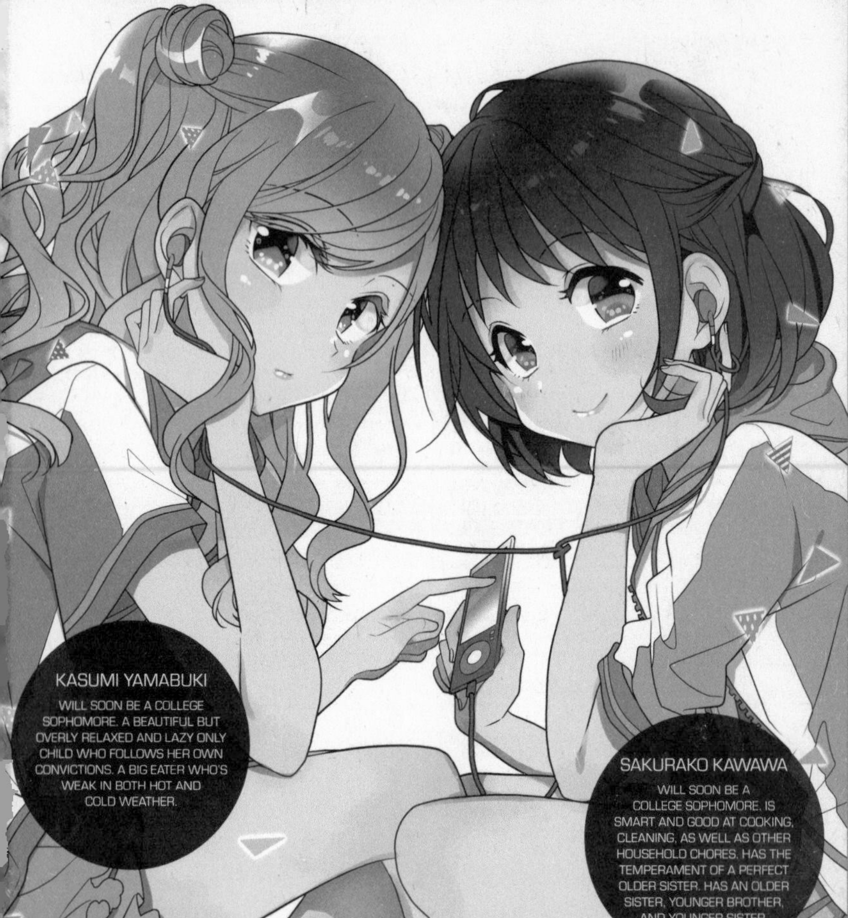
KASUMI YAMABUKI
WILL SOON BE A COLLEGE SOPHOMORE. A BEAUTIFUL BUT OVERLY RELAXED AND LAZY ONLY CHILD WHO FOLLOWS HER OWN CONVICTIONS. A BIG EATER WHO'S WEAK IN BOTH HOT AND COLD WEATHER.
SAKURAKO KAWAWA
WILL SOON BE A COLLEGE SOPHOMORE. IS SMART AND GOOD AT COOKING, CLEANING, AS WELL AS OTHER HOUSEHOLD CHORES. HAS THE TEMPERAMENT OF A PERFECT OLDER SISTER. HAS AN OLDER SISTER, YOUNGER BROTHER, AND YOUNGER SISTER.

SAKURAKO AND KASUMI BECAME ROOMMATES WHEN THEY ENTERED THEIR HIGH SCHOOL'S BOARDING HOUSE, AND NOW THEY ARE GREAT FRIENDS. THEY CONTINUE TO LIVE TOGETHER IN A ONE-ROOM APARTMENT, SHARING A BED. EVEN THOUGH THEY HAVE DIFFERENT MAJORS, BY GETTING DRIVER'S LICENSES AND GOING CAMPING THEY ENJOY LIFE ALONG WITH THEIR COLLEGE FRIENDS KORURI, MOKA, AND YUKARI.

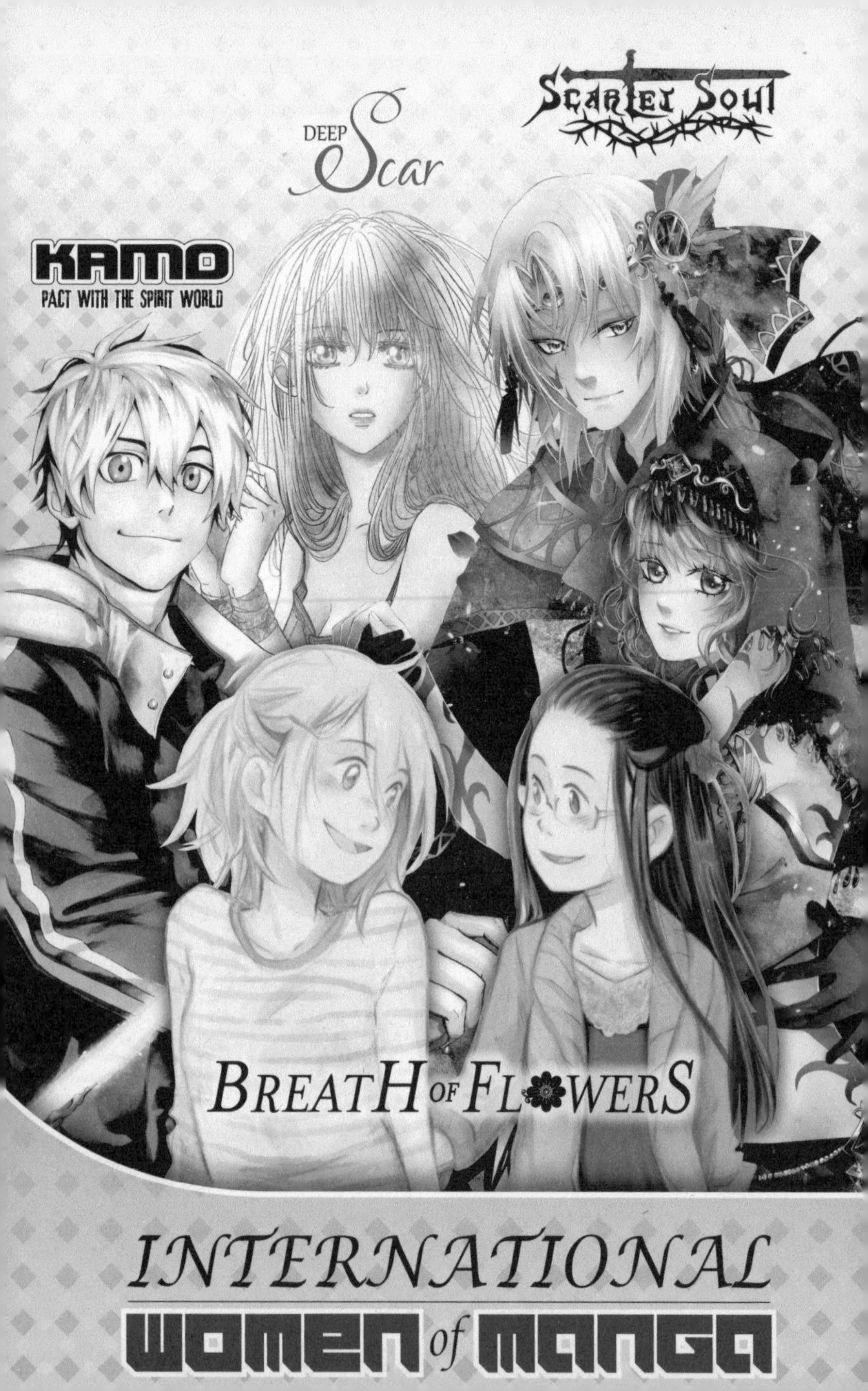
Scarlet Soul
DEEP Scar
KAMO
PACT WITH THE SPIRIT WORLD
BREATH OF FLOWERS
INTERNATIONAL
WOMEN of MANGA

STOP

THIS IS THE BACK OF THE BOOK!

How do you read manga-style? It's simple! Let's practice -- just start in the top right panel and follow the numbers below!

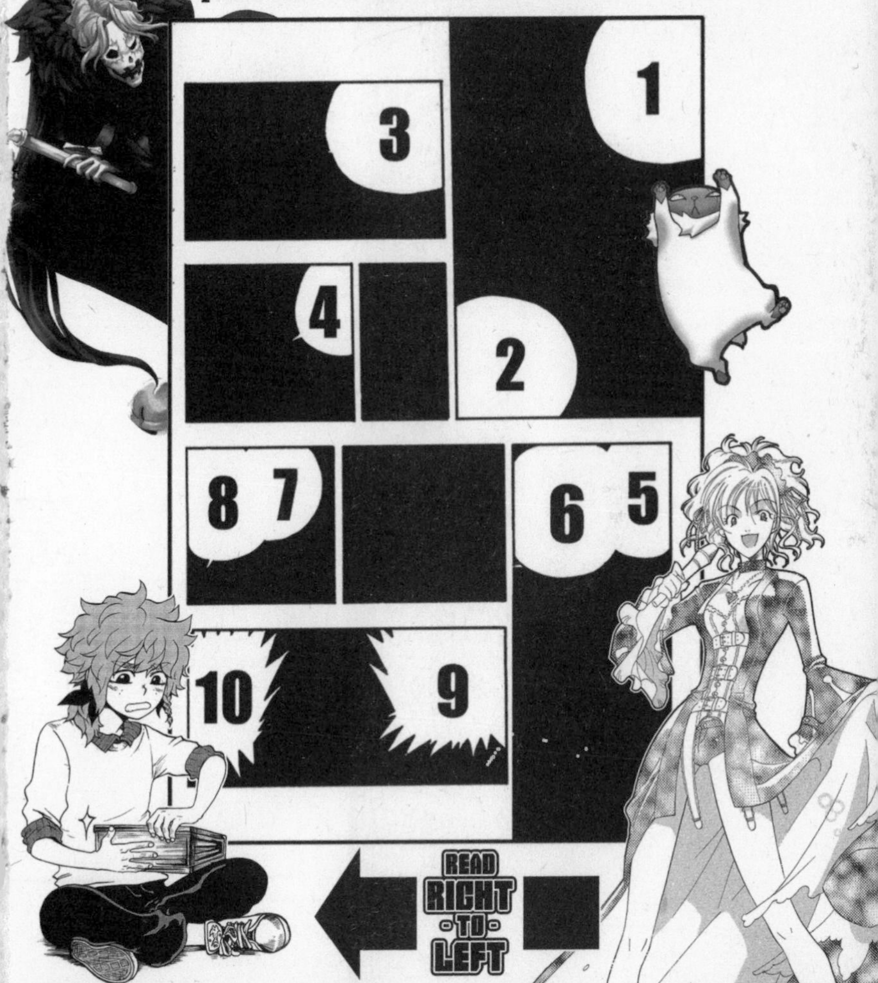

1
2
3
4
5
6
7
8
9
10
READ
RIGHT
-TO-
LEFT

Crimson from ***Kamo*** / Fairy Cat from ***Grimms Manga Tales***
Morrey from ***Goldfisch*** / Princess Ai from ***Princess Ai***

Futaribeya Volume 6
Yukiko

Editor - Lena Atanassova
Marketing Associate - Kae Winters
Technology and Digital Media Assistant - Phillip Hong
Translator - Katie McLendon
Copy Editor - Massiel Gutierrez
QC - Keisuke Ariga & Ryota Suzuki
Graphic Designer - Phillip Hong
Licensing Specialist - Arika Yanaka
Retouching and Lettering - Vibrraant Publishing Studio
Editor-in-Chief & Publisher - Stu Levy

A  Manga

TOKYOPOP and 🐾 are trademarks or registered trademarks of TOKYOPOP Inc.

TOKYOPOP inc.
5200 W Century Blvd
Suite 705
Los Angeles, CA 90045 USA

E-mail: info@TOKYOPOP.com
Come visit us online at www.TOKYOPOP.com

f www.facebook.com/TOKYOPOP
🐦 www.twitter.com/TOKYOPOP
📌 www.pinterest.com/TOKYOPOP
📷 www.instagram.com/TOKYOPOP

© 2019 TOKYOPOP
All Rights Reserved

All rights reserved. No portion of this book may be reproduced or transmitted in any form or by any means without written permission from the copyright holders. This manga is a work of fiction. Any resemblance to actual events or locales or persons, living or dead, is entirely coincidental.

Futaribeya Vol. 6
© YUKIKO, GENTOSHA COMICS 2018

All Rights Reserved. First published in 2018 by GENTOSHA COMICS Inc., Tokyo.

ISBN: 978-1-4278-6171-9
First TOKYOPOP Printing: November 2019
10 9 8 7 6 5 4 3 2 1
Printed in CANADA

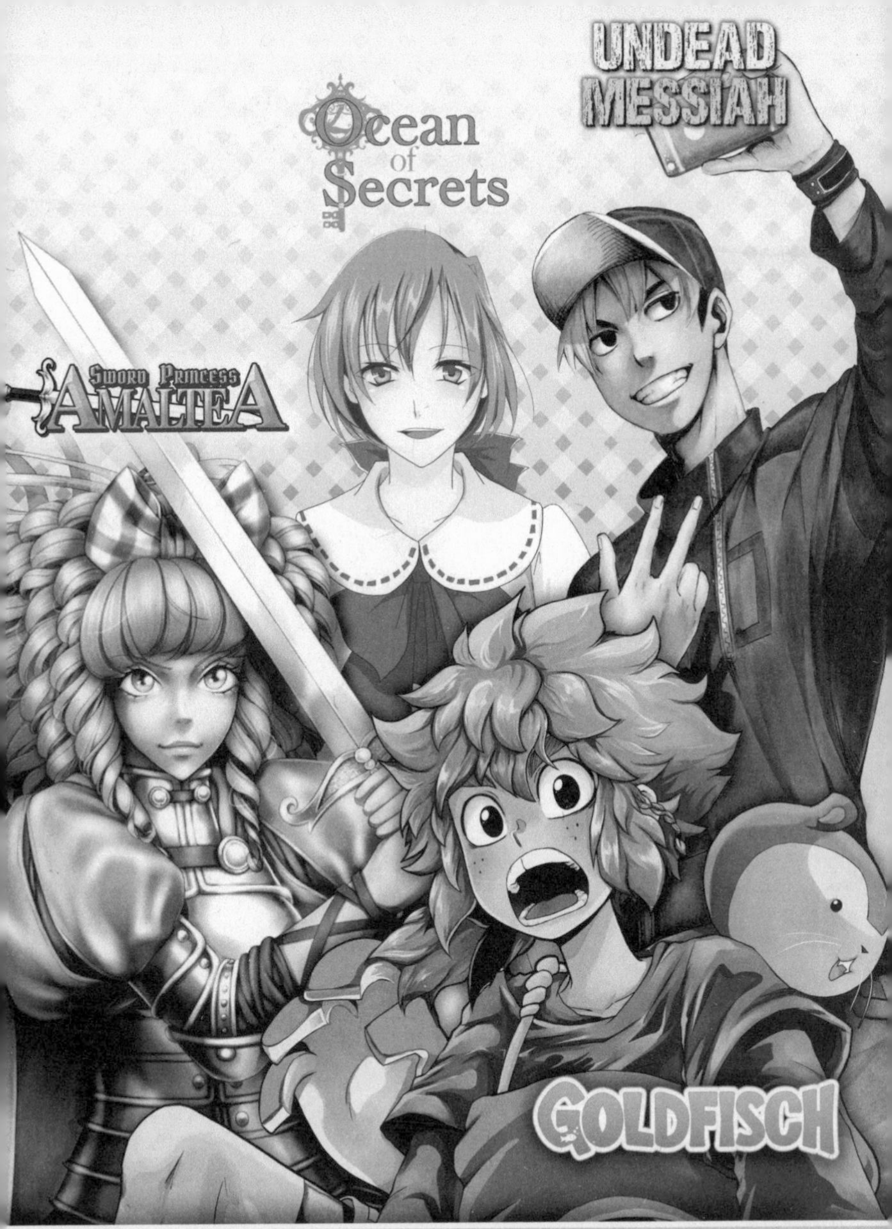
UNDEAD MESSIAH
Ocean of Secrets
SWORD PRINCESS AMALTEA
GOLDFISCH

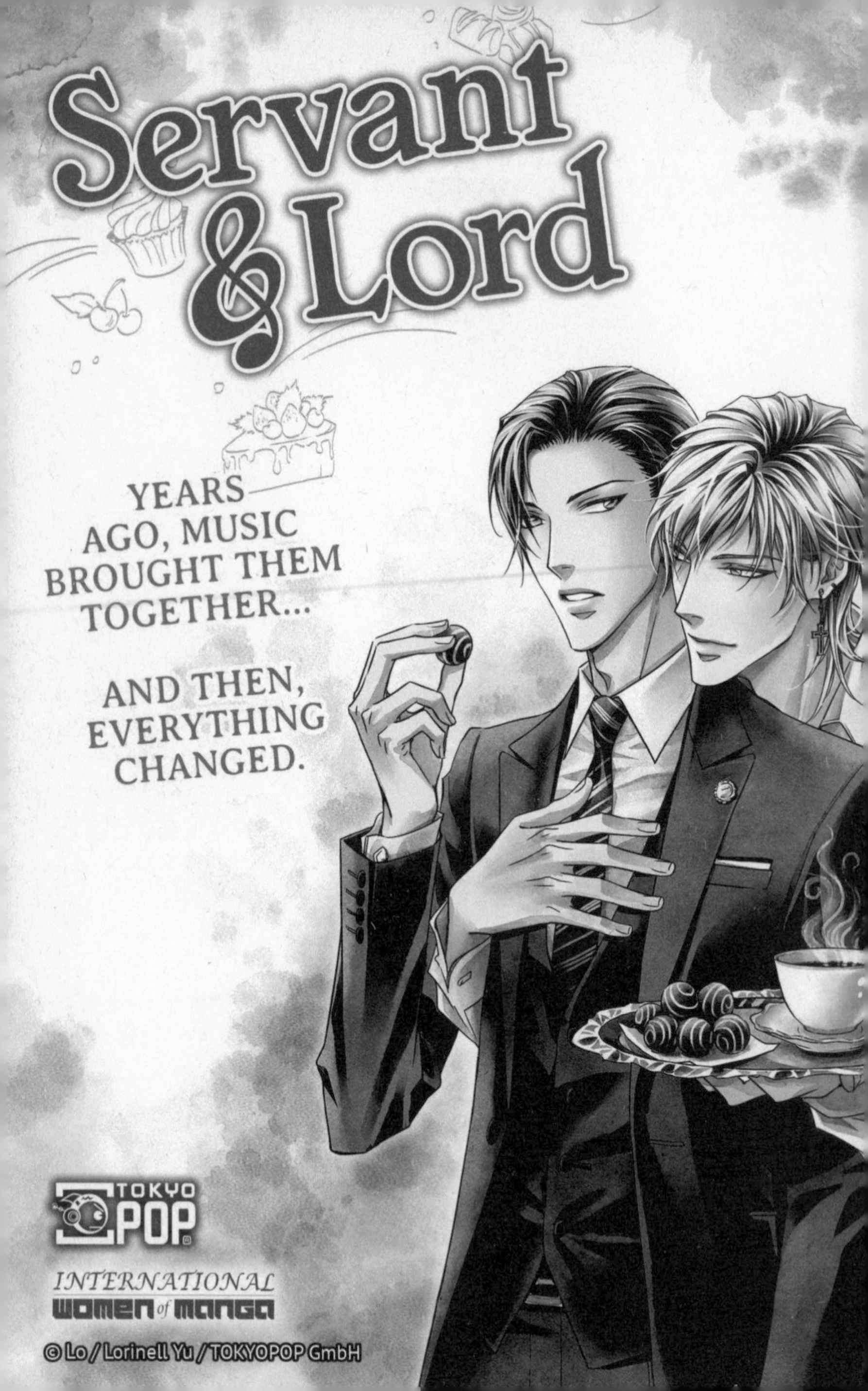

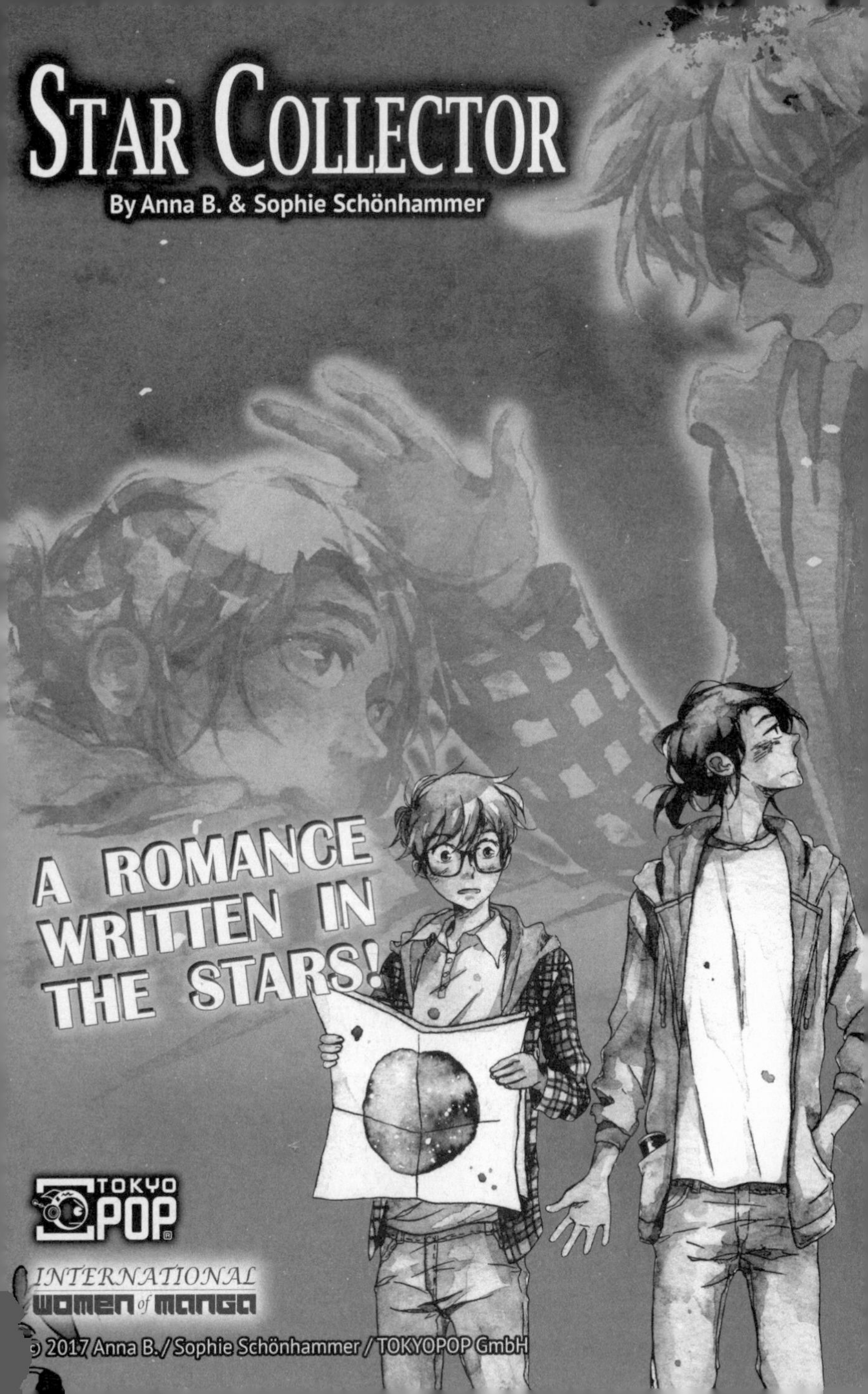
STAR COLLECTOR
By Anna B. & Sophie Schönhammer
A ROMANCE WRITTEN IN THE STARS!
TOKYO POP
INTERNATIONAL WOMEN of MANGA
© 2017 Anna B. / Sophie Schönhammer / TOKYOPOP GmbH

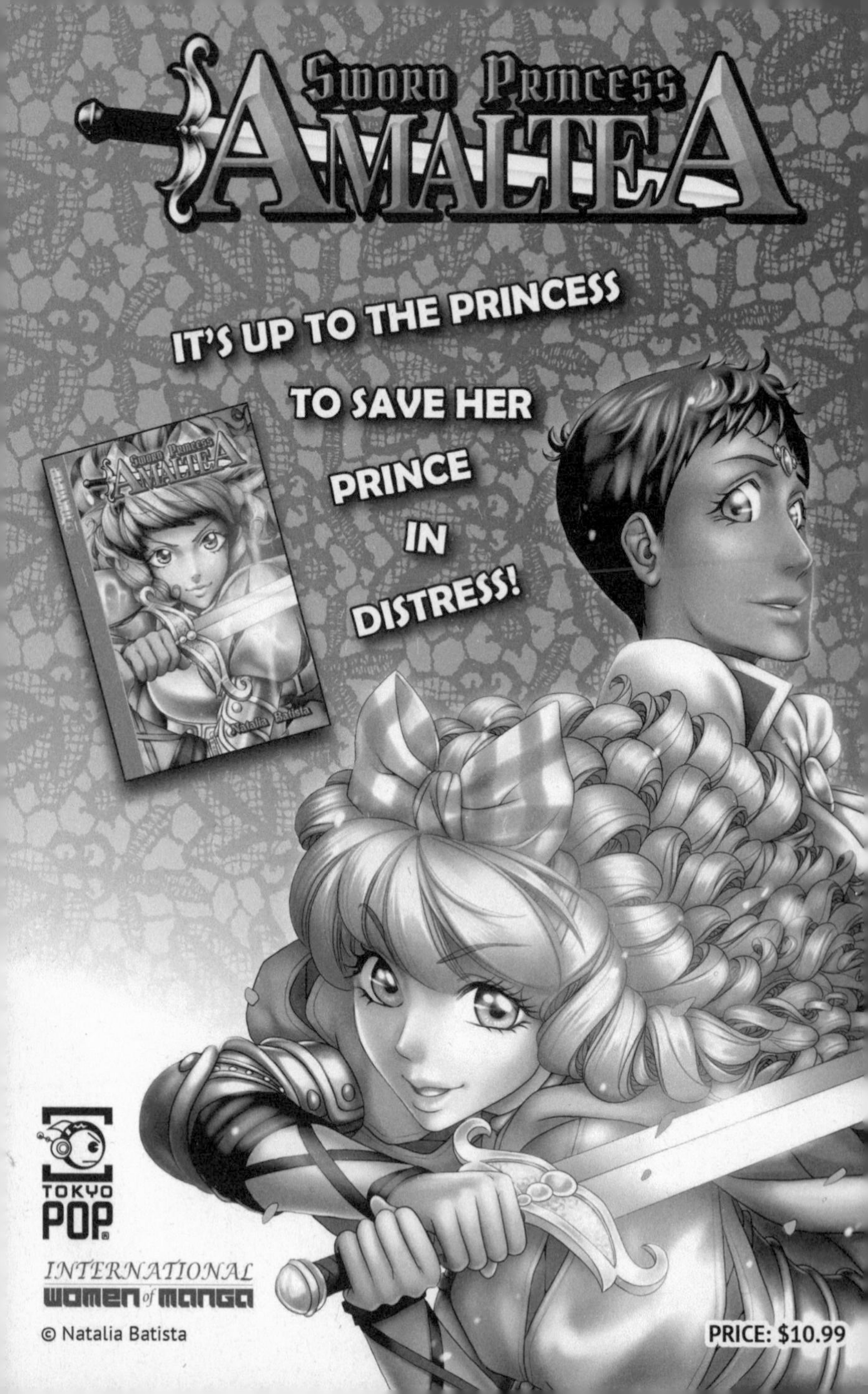
Sword Princess
AMALTEA
IT'S UP TO THE PRINCESS
TO SAVE HER
PRINCE
IN
DISTRESS!
Sword Princess Amaltea
Natalia Batista
TOKYO POP
INTERNATIONAL
women of manga
© Natalia Batista
PRICE: $10.99

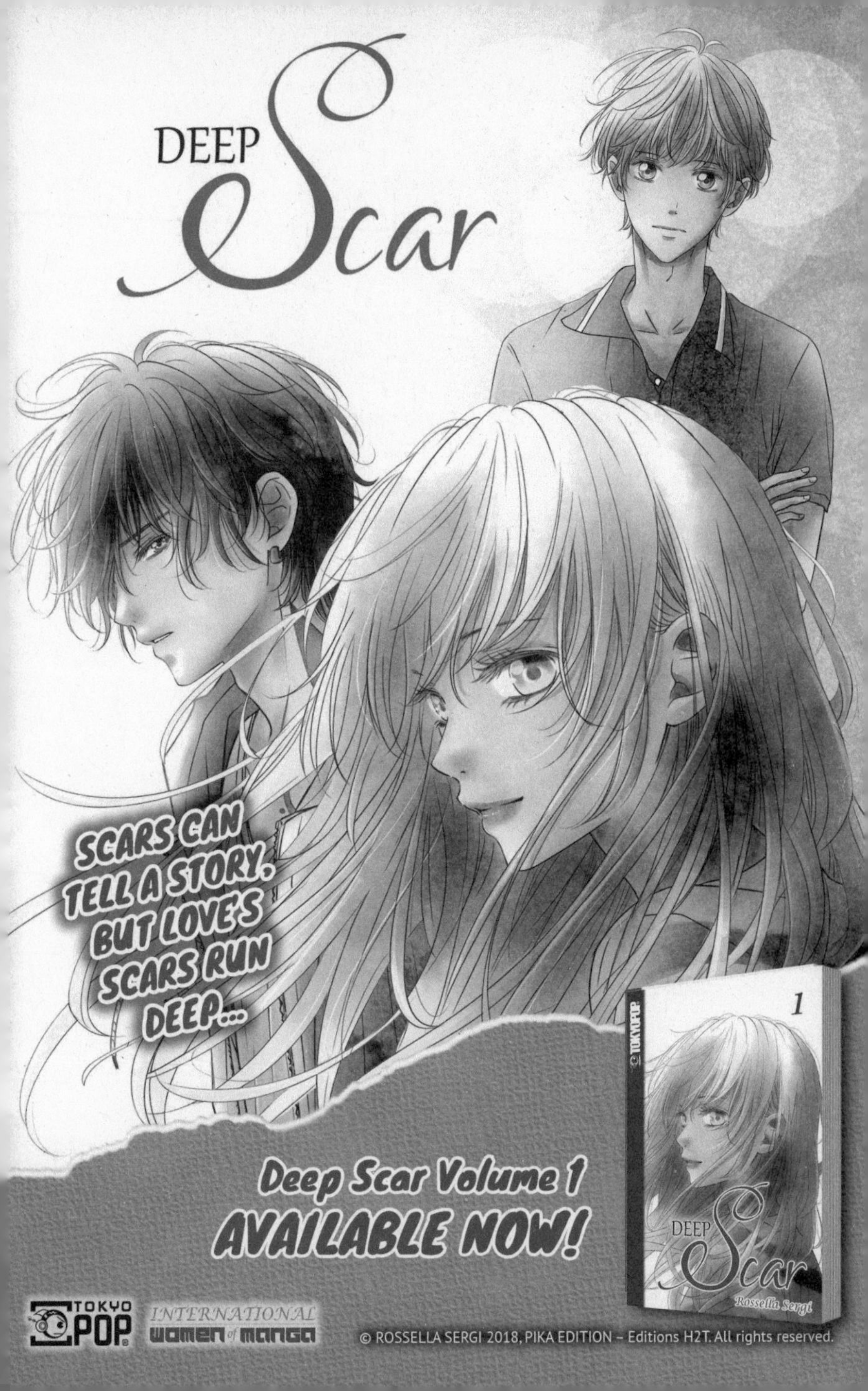
DEEP Scar
SCARS CAN TELL A STORY, BUT LOVE'S SCARS RUN DEEP...
Deep Scar Volume 1
AVAILABLE NOW!
1
TOKYOPOP
DEEP Scar
Rossella Sergi
TOKYO POP
INTERNATIONAL Women of Manga
© ROSSELLA SERGI 2018, PIKA EDITION – Editions H2T. All rights reserved.

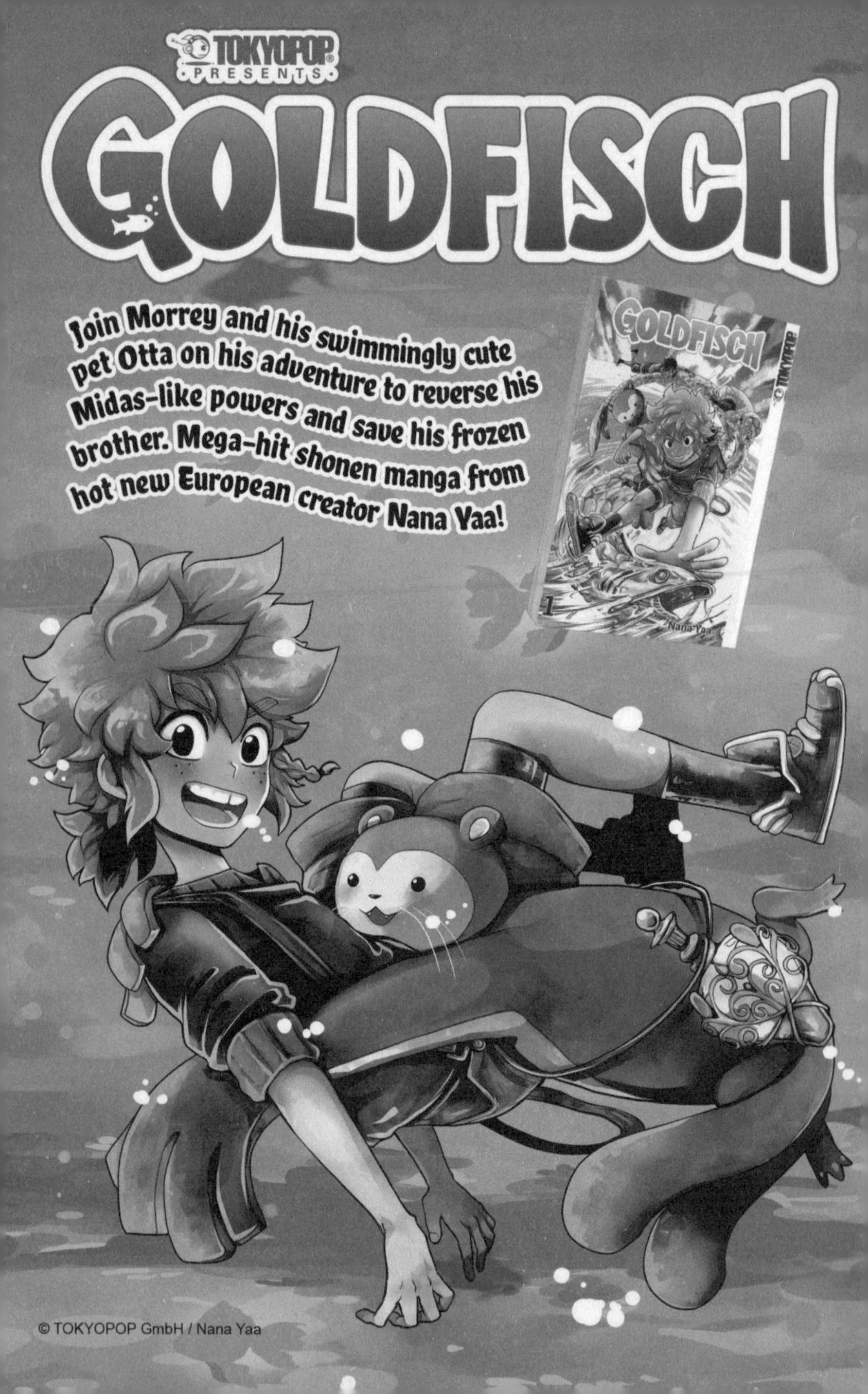
TOKYOPOP PRESENTS
GOLDFISCH
Join Morrey and his swimmingly cute pet Otta on his adventure to reverse his Midas-like powers and save his frozen brother. Mega-hit shonen manga from hot new European creator Nana Yaa!
GOLDFISCH
TOKYOPOP
1
Nana Yaa
© TOKYOPOP GmbH / Nana Yaa

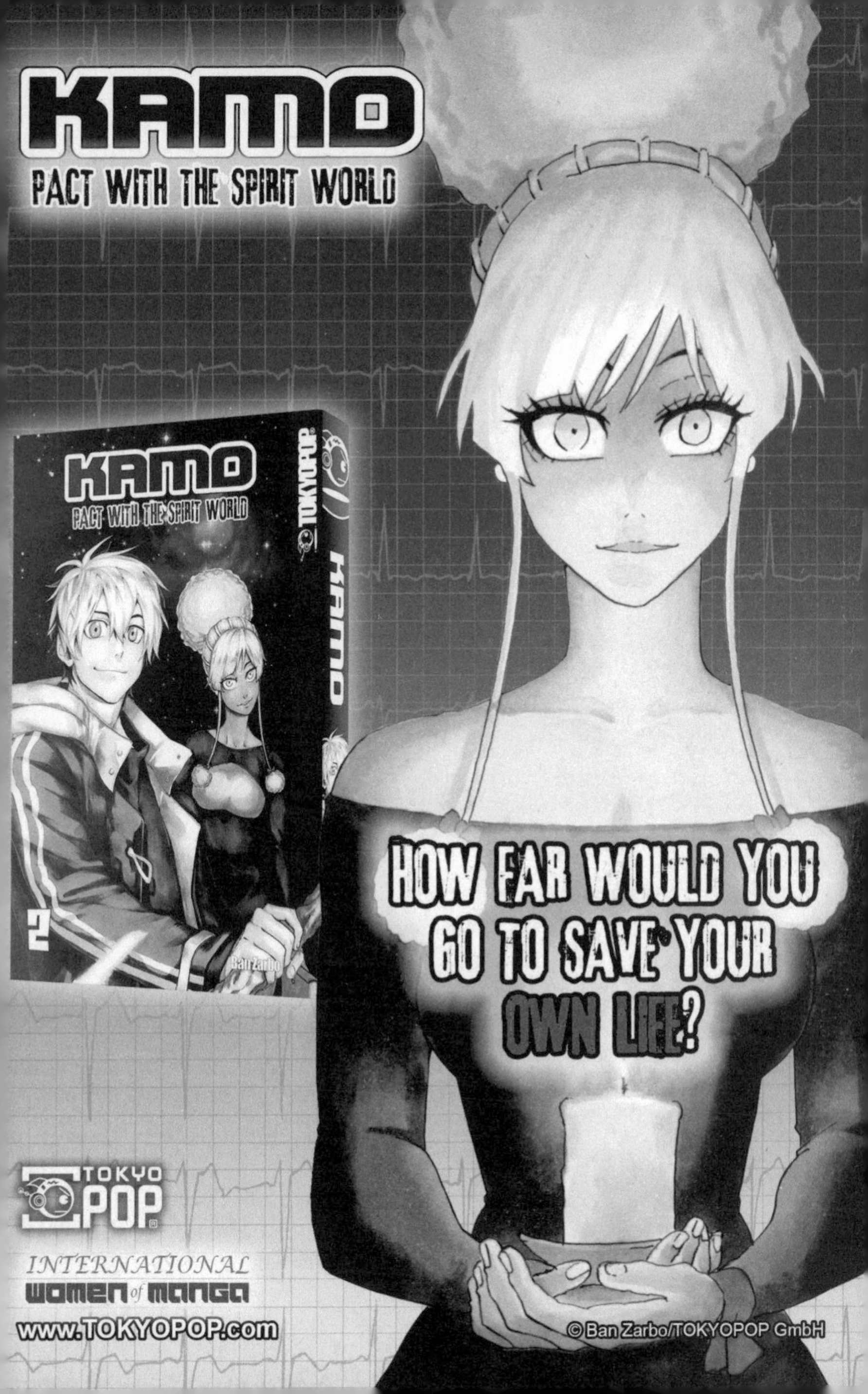
KAMO
PACT WITH THE SPIRIT WORLD
KAMO
PACT WITH THE SPIRIT WORLD
TOKYOPOP
KAMO
2
Ban Zarbo
HOW FAR WOULD YOU GO TO SAVE YOUR OWN LIFE?
TOKYOPOP
INTERNATIONAL
women of manga
www.TOKYOPOP.com
© Ban Zarbo/TOKYOPOP GmbH

A R I A The MASTERPIECE

★ DELUXE, REMASTERED 2-IN-1 EDITION
★ GORGEOUS GOLD-FOIL COVER
★ INCLUDES FULL-COLOR ILLUSTRATIONS

KOZUE AMANO

EXPERIENCE THE WORLD OF AQUA LIKE NEVER BEFORE!

© KOZUE AMANO / MAG Garden

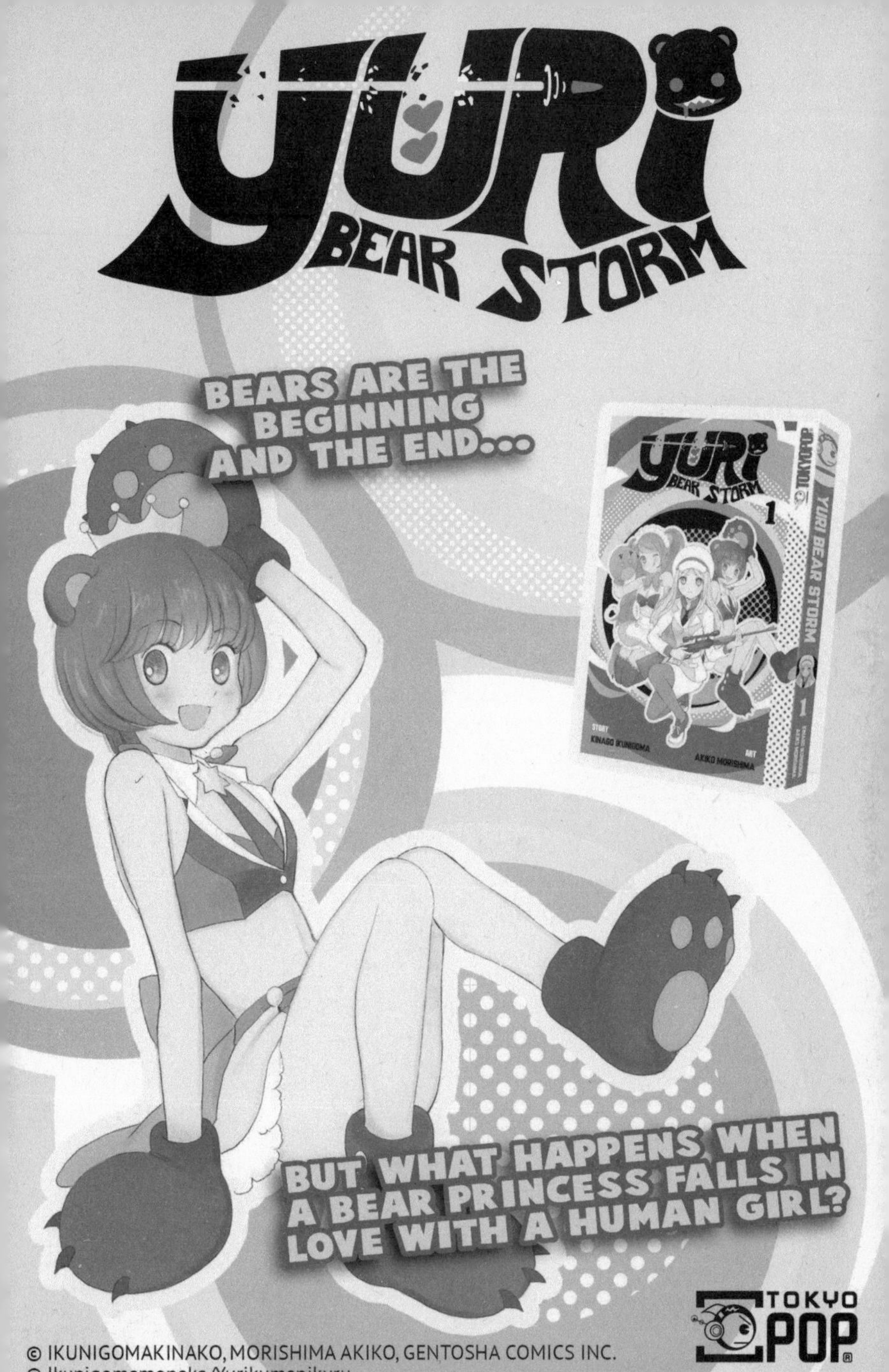
YURI BEAR STORM
BEARS ARE THE BEGINNING AND THE END...
YURI BEAR STORM 1
STORY KINAGO IKUNIGOMA
ART AKIKO MORISHIMA
TOKYOPOP
BUT WHAT HAPPENS WHEN A BEAR PRINCESS FALLS IN LOVE WITH A HUMAN GIRL?
TOKYO POP

KONOHANA KITAN

Welcome, valued guest... to Konohanatei!

WWW.TOKYOPOP.COM

© AMANO SAKUYA, GENTOSHA COMICS

PRICE: $12.99

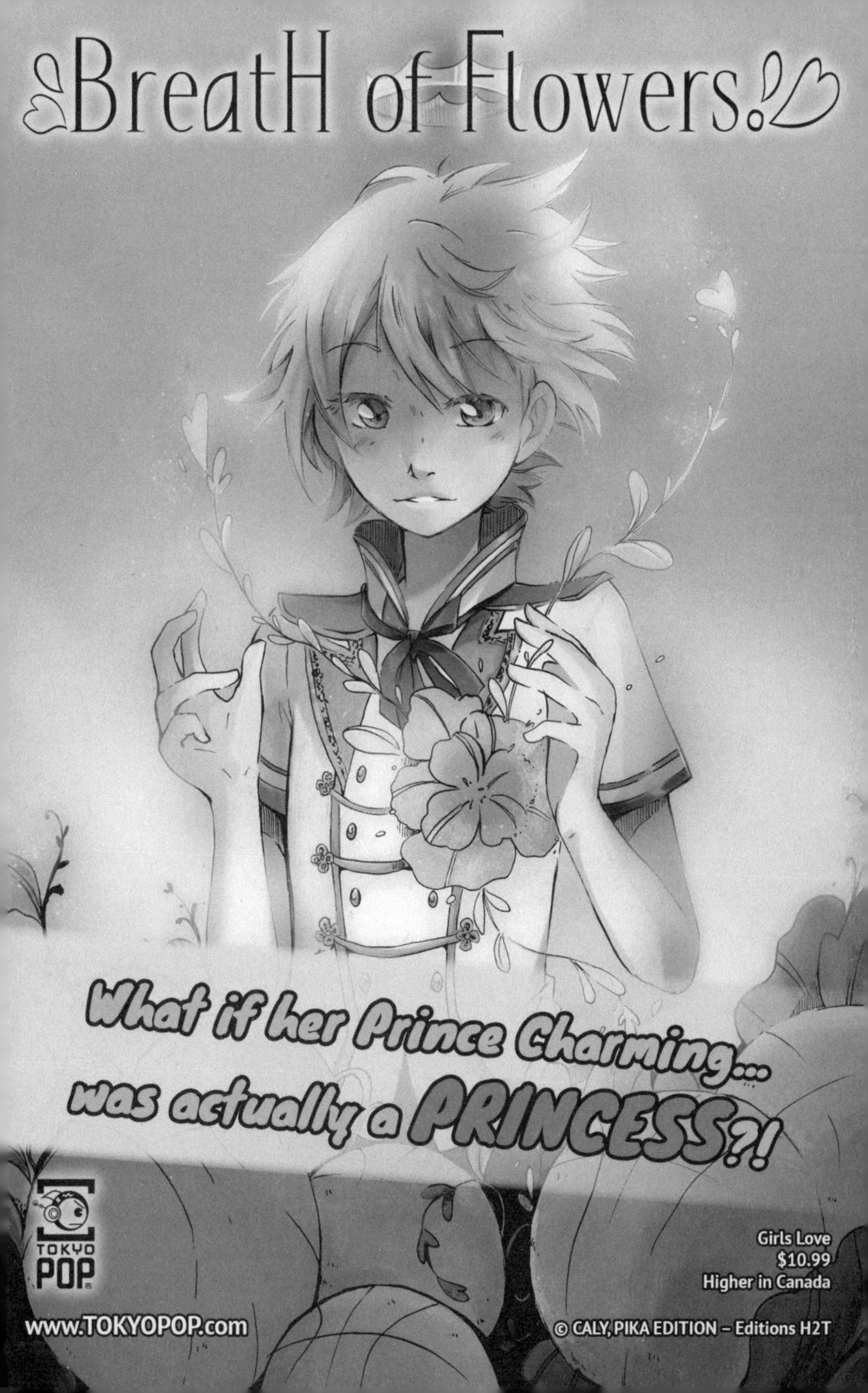
Breath of Flowers!
What if her Prince Charming... was actually a PRINCESS?!
TOKYO POP
Girls Love
$10.99
Higher in Canada
www.TOKYOPOP.com
© CALY, PIKA EDITION – Editions H2T

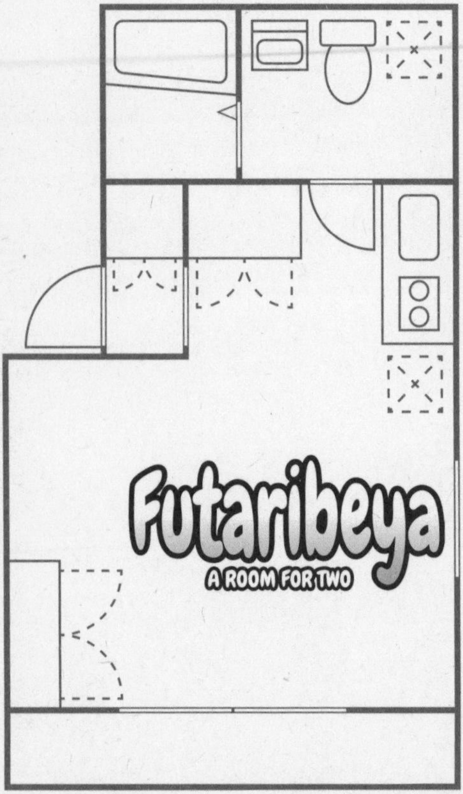
Futaribeya
A ROOM FOR TWO

STORY and

MOKA NENASHI

A PSYCHOLOGY MAJOR LIKE SAKURAKO. SHE HAS A FREE VIEW ON LOVE AND OFTEN STAYS OVER AT KORURI'S HOUSE.

KORURI MASUI

STUDIES IN THE LIFE ENVIRONMENT STUDIES DEPARTMENT WITH KASUMI. SHE HAS A BAD SENSE OF DIRECTION AND IS UNABLE TO THROW THINGS AWAY.

SHOUKO AKASHI

A HIGH SCHOOL SENIOR ROOMING WITH SERI. SHE'S A MEMBER OF THE TRACK TEAM AND HAS A FRANK PERSONALITY.

SERI FURUYASHIKI

A HIGH SCHOOL SENIOR ROOMING WITH SHOUKO. SHE'S A SHELTERED RICH GIRL WHO USES POLITE SPEECH WITH EVERYONE SHE MEETS.

YUKARII

SAKURAKO AND KASUMI'S HIGH SCHOOL CLASSMATE WHO ATTENDS THE SAME COLLEGE AS THEM. SHE EVEN JOINED THE SAME CLUB AND IS A CLOSE FRIEND.

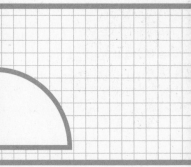

HINAKO

A HIGH SCHOOL SOPHOMORE AND SAKURAKO'S LITTLE SISTER. SHE'S SPOILED AND ABSOLUTELY LOVES SAKURAKO AND KASUMI. SHE HAS A TWIN BROTHER NAMED KAKERU.

FUJIHOI

A HIGH SCHOOL SOPHOMORE ROOMING WITH HINAKO. DESPITE HER FUTILE PROTESTS, SHE USUALLY ENDS UP GOING ALONG WITH HINAKO'S IDEAS.

Contents

Chapter 48.5

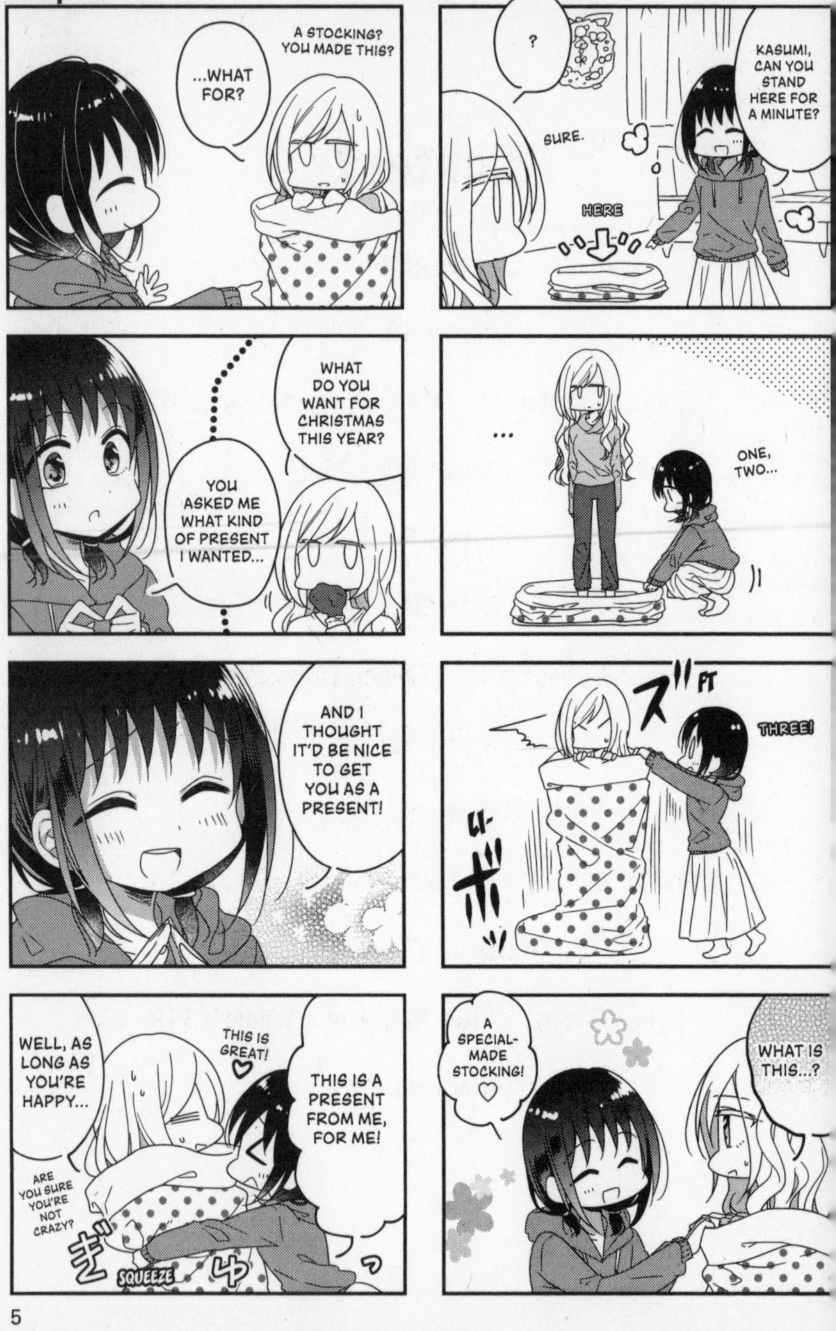
KASUMI, CAN YOU STAND HERE FOR A MINUTE?
?
SURE.
HERE
ONE, TWO...
...
PT
THREE!
WHAT IS THIS...?
A SPECIAL-MADE STOCKING! ♡
A STOCKING? YOU MADE THIS?
...WHAT FOR?
WHAT DO YOU WANT FOR CHRISTMAS THIS YEAR?
YOU ASKED ME WHAT KIND OF PRESENT I WANTED...
AND I THOUGHT IT'D BE NICE TO GET YOU AS A PRESENT!
THIS IS A PRESENT FROM ME, FOR ME!
THIS IS GREAT! ♡
WELL, AS LONG AS YOU'RE HAPPY...
ARE YOU SURE YOU'RE NOT CRAZY?
SQUEEZE

Futaribeya
A ROOM FOR TWO

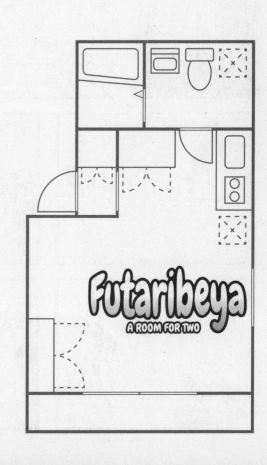

Chapter 49

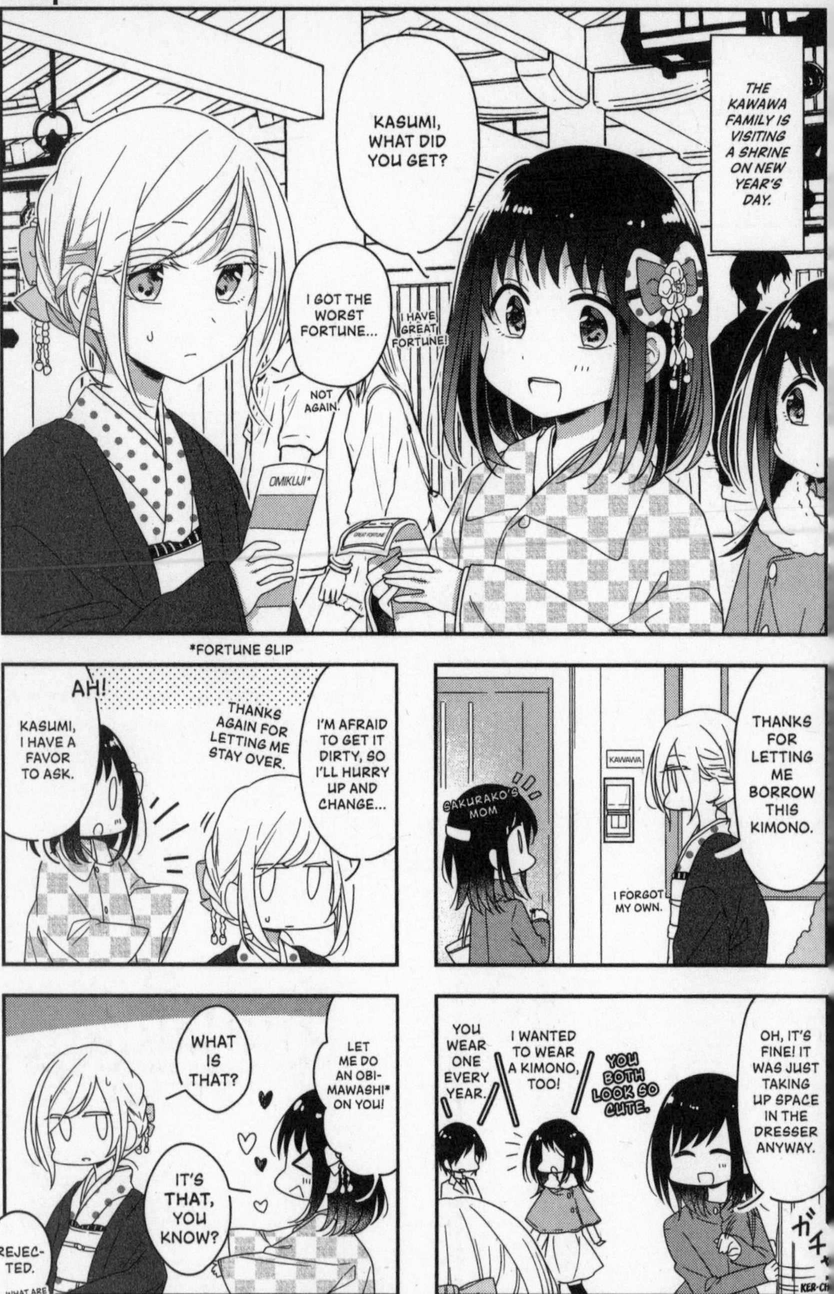
THE KAWAWA FAMILY IS VISITING A SHRINE ON NEW YEAR'S DAY.
KASUMI, WHAT DID YOU GET?
I HAVE GREAT FORTUNE!
I GOT THE WORST FORTUNE...
NOT AGAIN.
GREAT FORTUNE
OMIKUJI*
THANKS FOR LETTING ME BORROW THIS KIMONO.
KAWAWA
SAKURAKO'S MOM
I FORGOT MY OWN.
I'M AFRAID TO GET IT DIRTY, SO I'LL HURRY UP AND CHANGE...
THANKS AGAIN FOR LETTING ME STAY OVER.
AH!
KASUMI, I HAVE A FAVOR TO ASK.
OH, IT'S FINE! IT WAS JUST TAKING UP SPACE IN THE DRESSER ANYWAY.
YOU BOTH LOOK SO CUTE.
I WANTED TO WEAR A KIMONO, TOO!
YOU WEAR ONE EVERY YEAR.
KER-CH
LET ME DO AN OBI-MAWASHI* ON YOU!
WHAT IS THAT?
IT'S THAT, YOU KNOW?
REJECTED.
WHAT ARE YOU, A PERVY OLD MAN?

*FORTUNE SLIP

*PULLING ON SOMEONE'S OBI (BELT) TO MAKE THEM SPIN AROUND

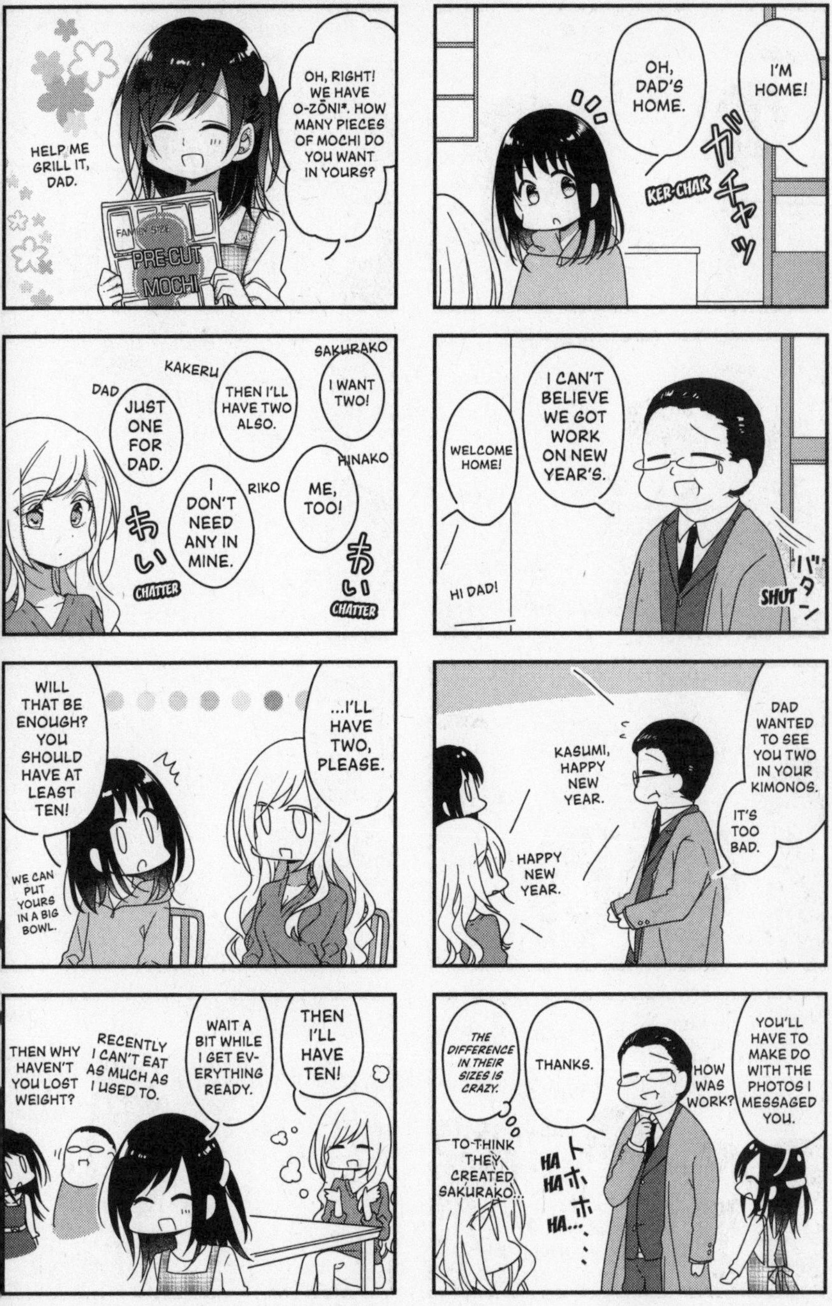
I'M HOME!
ガチャッ
KER-CHAK
OH, DAD'S HOME.
I CAN'T BELIEVE WE GOT WORK ON NEW YEAR'S.
WELCOME HOME!
HI DAD!
バタン
SHUT
DAD WANTED TO SEE YOU TWO IN YOUR KIMONOS.
IT'S TOO BAD.
KASUMI, HAPPY NEW YEAR.
HAPPY NEW YEAR.
YOU'LL HAVE TO MAKE DO WITH THE PHOTOS I MESSAGED YOU.
HOW WAS WORK?
THANKS.
トホホ…
HA HA HA...
THE DIFFERENCE IN THEIR SIZES IS CRAZY.
TO THINK THEY CREATED SAKURAKO...
OH, RIGHT! WE HAVE O-ZŌNI*. HOW MANY PIECES OF MOCHI DO YOU WANT IN YOURS?
HELP ME GRILL IT, DAD.
FAMILY SIZE
PRE-CUT MOCHI
SAKURAKO
I WANT TWO!
KAKERU
THEN I'LL HAVE TWO ALSO.
HINAKO
ME, TOO!
DAD
JUST ONE FOR DAD.
RIKO
I DON'T NEED ANY IN MINE.
わいわい
CHATTER
わいわい
CHATTER
...I'LL HAVE TWO, PLEASE.
WILL THAT BE ENOUGH? YOU SHOULD HAVE AT LEAST TEN!
WE CAN PUT YOURS IN A BIG BOWL.
THEN I'LL HAVE TEN!
WAIT A BIT WHILE I GET EVERYTHING READY.
RECENTLY I CAN'T EAT AS MUCH AS I USED TO.
THEN WHY HAVEN'T YOU LOST WEIGHT?

*NEW YEAR'S SOUP MADE WITH BROTH, VEGETABLES, AND MOCHI

*A HOUSEHOLD TALISMAN OR AMULET, BOUGHT AT A SHRINE

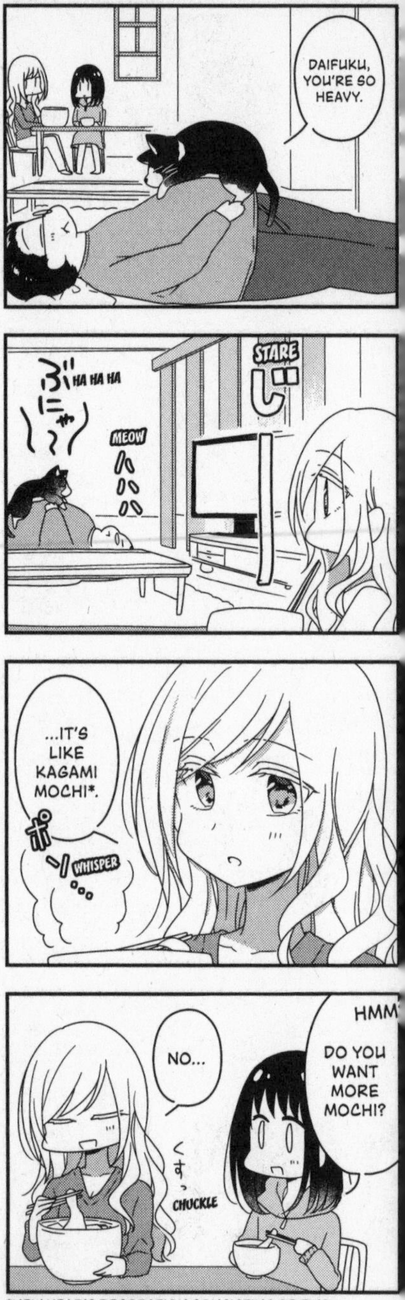
DAIFUKU, YOU'RE SO HEAVY.
STARE
じー
ぶにゃ~
HA HA HA
MEOW
ハハハ
...IT'S LIKE KAGAMI MOCHI*.
ポー
WHISPER
HMM
DO YOU WANT MORE MOCHI?
NO...
くすっ
CHUCKLE

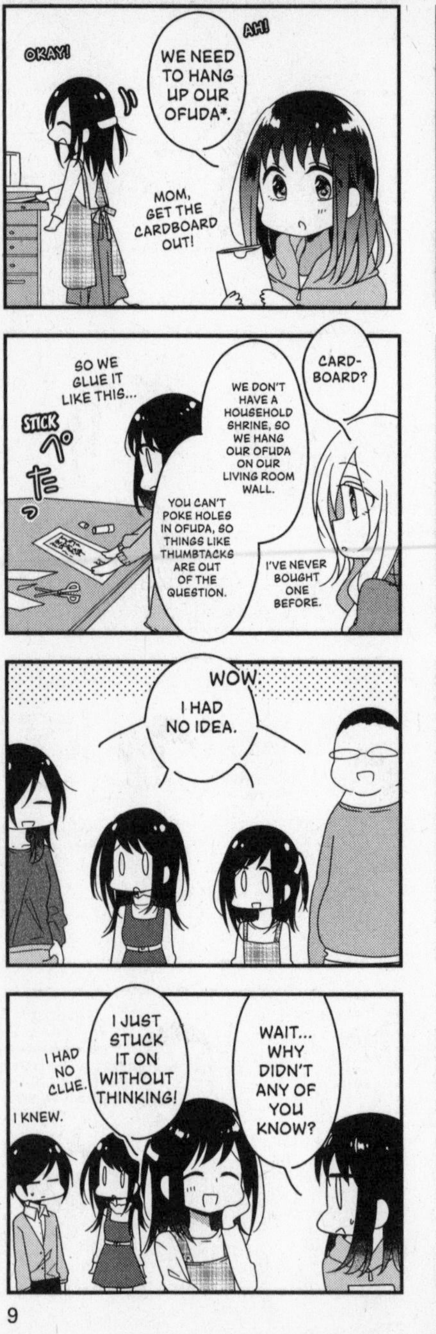
AH!
WE NEED TO HANG UP OUR OFUDA*.
OKAY!
MOM, GET THE CARDBOARD OUT!
CARD-BOARD?
WE DON'T HAVE A HOUSEHOLD SHRINE, SO WE HANG OUR OFUDA ON OUR LIVING ROOM WALL.
YOU CAN'T POKE HOLES IN OFUDA, SO THINGS LIKE THUMBTACKS ARE OUT OF THE QUESTION.
I'VE NEVER BOUGHT ONE BEFORE.
SO WE GLUE IT LIKE THIS...
STICK
ぺたっ
WOW.
I HAD NO IDEA.
WAIT... WHY DIDN'T ANY OF YOU KNOW?
I JUST STUCK IT ON WITHOUT THINKING!
I HAD NO CLUE.
I KNEW.

*NEW YEAR'S DECORATION CONSISTING OF TWO ROUND MOCHI WITH A SMALL ORANGE ON TOP

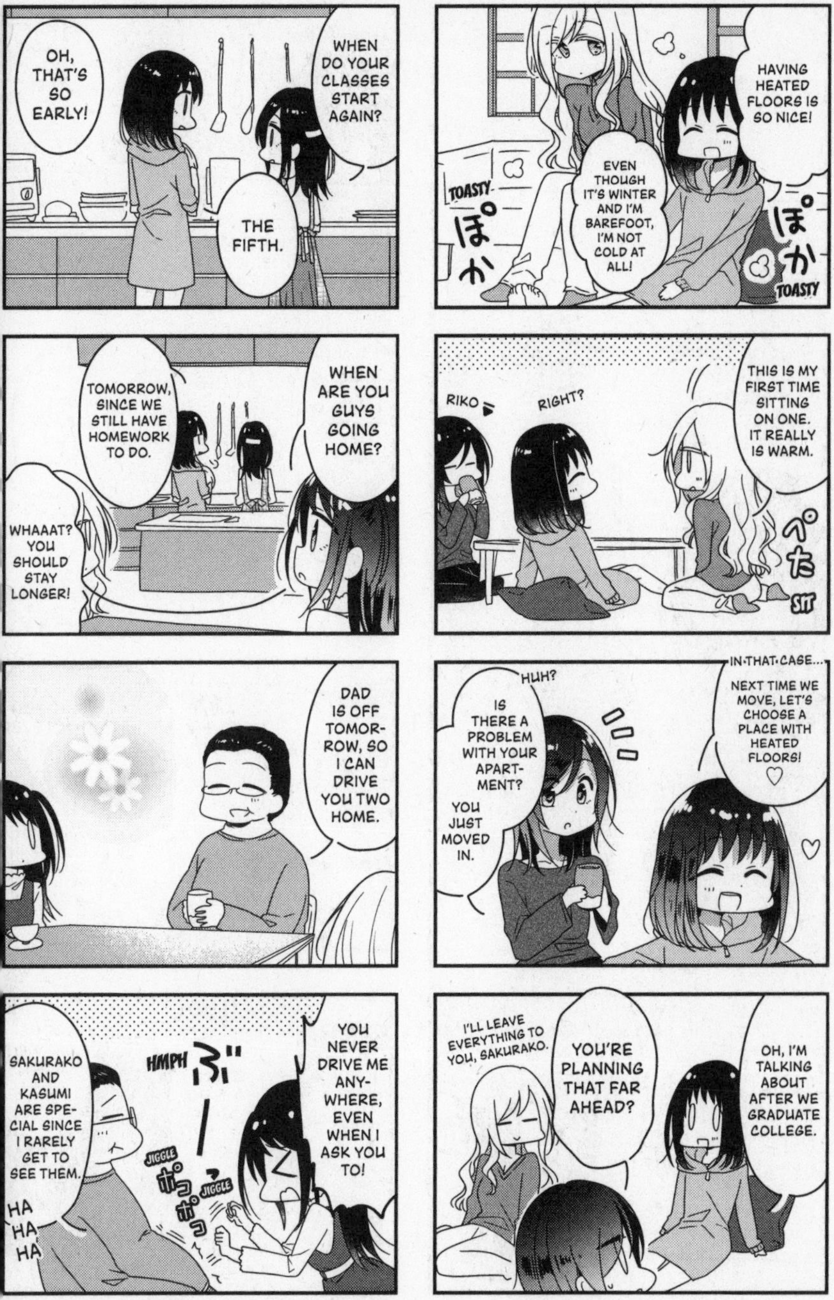
HAVING HEATED FLOORS IS SO NICE!
EVEN THOUGH IT'S WINTER AND I'M BAREFOOT, I'M NOT COLD AT ALL!
ぽか TOASTY
TOASTY ぽか
THIS IS MY FIRST TIME SITTING ON ONE. IT REALLY IS WARM.
ぺた SIT
RIGHT?
RIKO
IN THAT CASE...
NEXT TIME WE MOVE, LET'S CHOOSE A PLACE WITH HEATED FLOORS! ♡
HUH?
IS THERE A PROBLEM WITH YOUR APARTMENT?
YOU JUST MOVED IN.
OH, I'M TALKING ABOUT AFTER WE GRADUATE COLLEGE.
YOU'RE PLANNING THAT FAR AHEAD?
I'LL LEAVE EVERYTHING TO YOU, SAKURAKO.
WHEN DO YOUR CLASSES START AGAIN?
THE FIFTH.
OH, THAT'S SO EARLY!
WHEN ARE YOU GUYS GOING HOME?
TOMORROW, SINCE WE STILL HAVE HOMEWORK TO DO.
WHAAAT? YOU SHOULD STAY LONGER!
DAD IS OFF TOMORROW, SO I CAN DRIVE YOU TWO HOME.
YOU NEVER DRIVE ME ANYWHERE, EVEN WHEN I ASK YOU TO!
ぶー HMPH
ポコポコ JIGGLE JIGGLE
SAKURAKO AND KASUMI ARE SPECIAL SINCE I RARELY GET TO SEE THEM.
HA HA HA

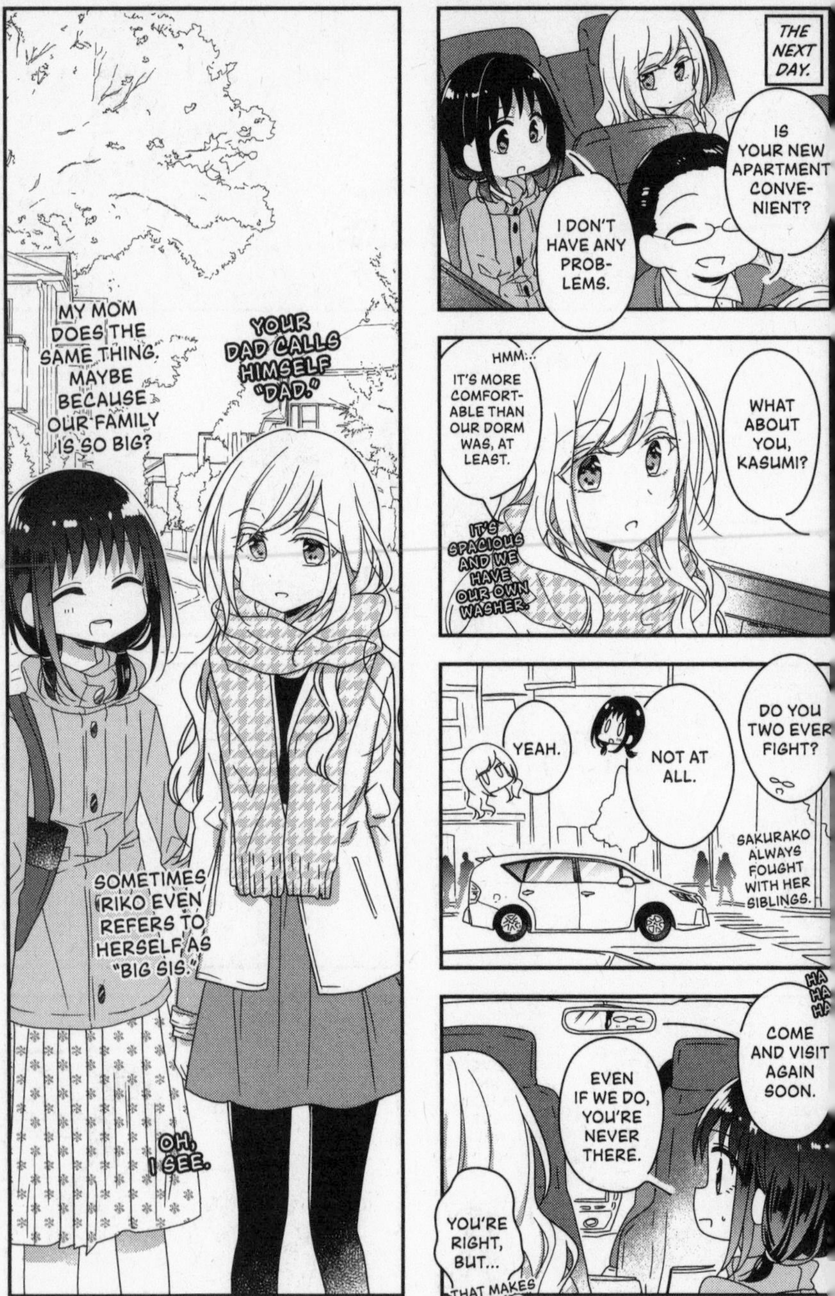
THE NEXT DAY.
IS YOUR NEW APARTMENT CONVENIENT?
I DON'T HAVE ANY PROBLEMS.
WHAT ABOUT YOU, KASUMI?
HMM...
IT'S MORE COMFORTABLE THAN OUR DORM WAS, AT LEAST.
IT'S SPACIOUS AND WE HAVE OUR OWN WASHER.
DO YOU TWO EVER FIGHT?
NOT AT ALL.
YEAH.
SAKURAKO ALWAYS FOUGHT WITH HER SIBLINGS.
HA HA HA
COME AND VISIT AGAIN SOON.
EVEN IF WE DO, YOU'RE NEVER THERE.
YOU'RE RIGHT, BUT...
THAT MAKES DAD SAD.
YOUR DAD CALLS HIMSELF "DAD."
MY MOM DOES THE SAME THING. MAYBE BECAUSE OUR FAMILY IS SO BIG?
SOMETIMES RIKO EVEN REFERS TO HERSELF AS "BIG SIS."
OH, I SEE.

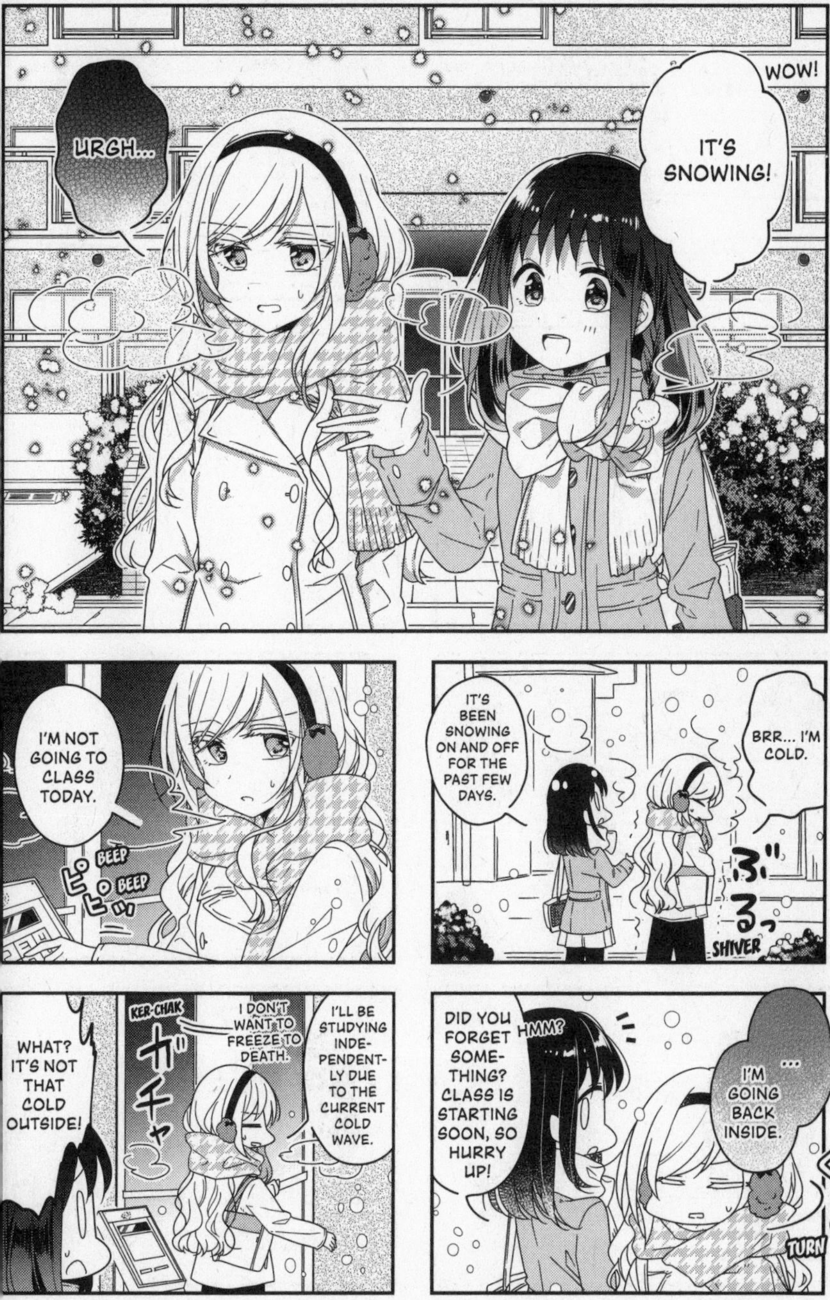
WOW!
IT'S SNOWING!
URGH...
BRR... I'M COLD.
IT'S BEEN SNOWING ON AND OFF FOR THE PAST FEW DAYS.
ぶるっ SHIVER
I'M NOT GOING TO CLASS TODAY.
ピッ BEEP
ピッ BEEP
...
I'M GOING BACK INSIDE.
HMM?
DID YOU FORGET SOMETHING? CLASS IS STARTING SOON, SO HURRY UP!
くるっ TURN
I'LL BE STUDYING INDEPENDENTLY DUE TO THE CURRENT COLD WAVE.
I DON'T WANT TO FREEZE TO DEATH.
KER-CHAK ガチャ
WHAT? IT'S NOT THAT COLD OUTSIDE!

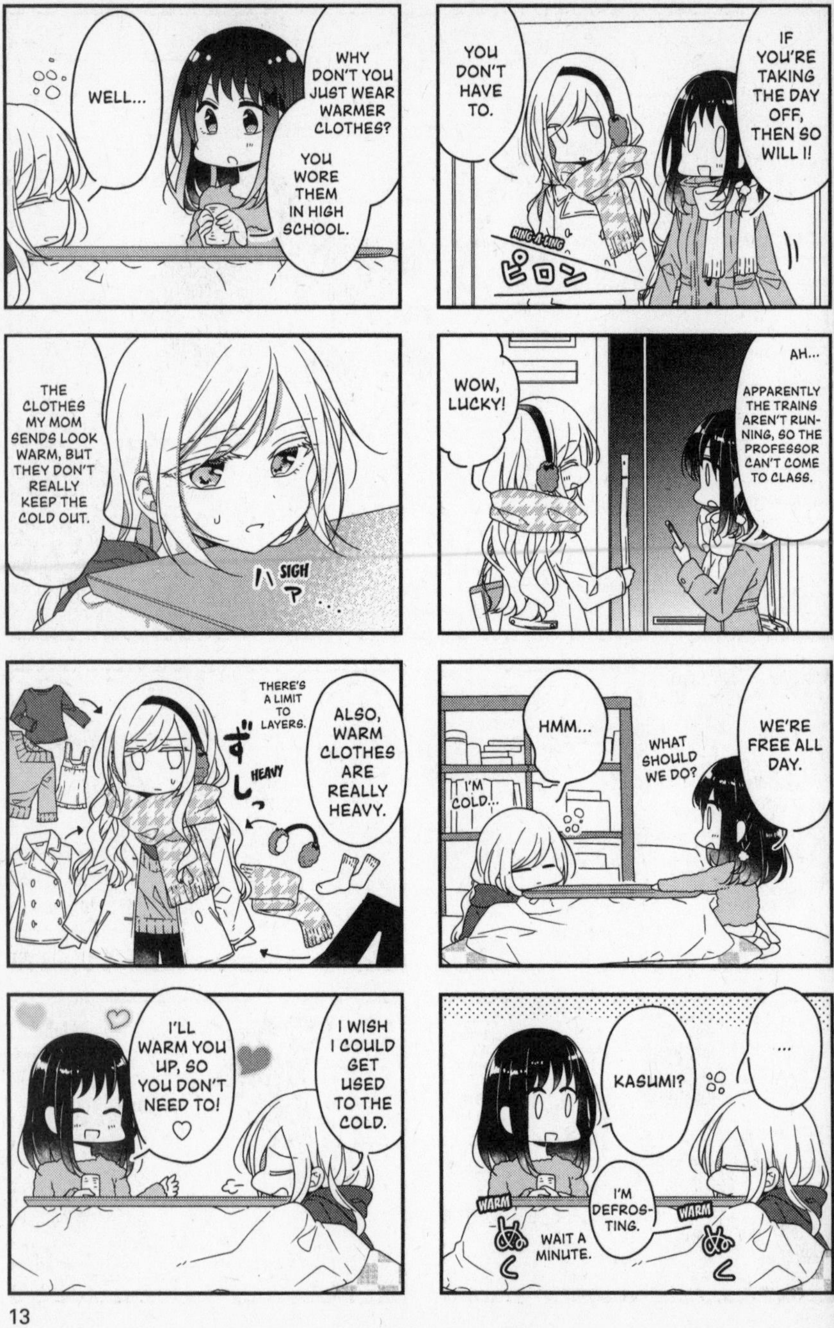
IF YOU'RE TAKING THE DAY OFF, THEN SO WILL I!
YOU DON'T HAVE TO.
RING-A-LING
ピロン
AH...
APPARENTLY THE TRAINS AREN'T RUN-NING, SO THE PROFESSOR CAN'T COME TO CLASS.
WOW, LUCKY!
WE'RE FREE ALL DAY.
WHAT SHOULD WE DO?
HMM...
I'M COLD...
...
KASUMI?
I'M DEFROS-TING.
WARM
ぬく
WARM
ぬく
WAIT A MINUTE.
WHY DON'T YOU JUST WEAR WARMER CLOTHES?
YOU WORE THEM IN HIGH SCHOOL.
WELL...
THE CLOTHES MY MOM SENDS LOOK WARM, BUT THEY DON'T REALLY KEEP THE COLD OUT.
SIGH
ハア...
ALSO, WARM CLOTHES ARE REALLY HEAVY.
THERE'S A LIMIT TO LAYERS.
HEAVY
ずしっ
I WISH I COULD GET USED TO THE COLD.
I'LL WARM YOU UP, SO YOU DON'T NEED TO!

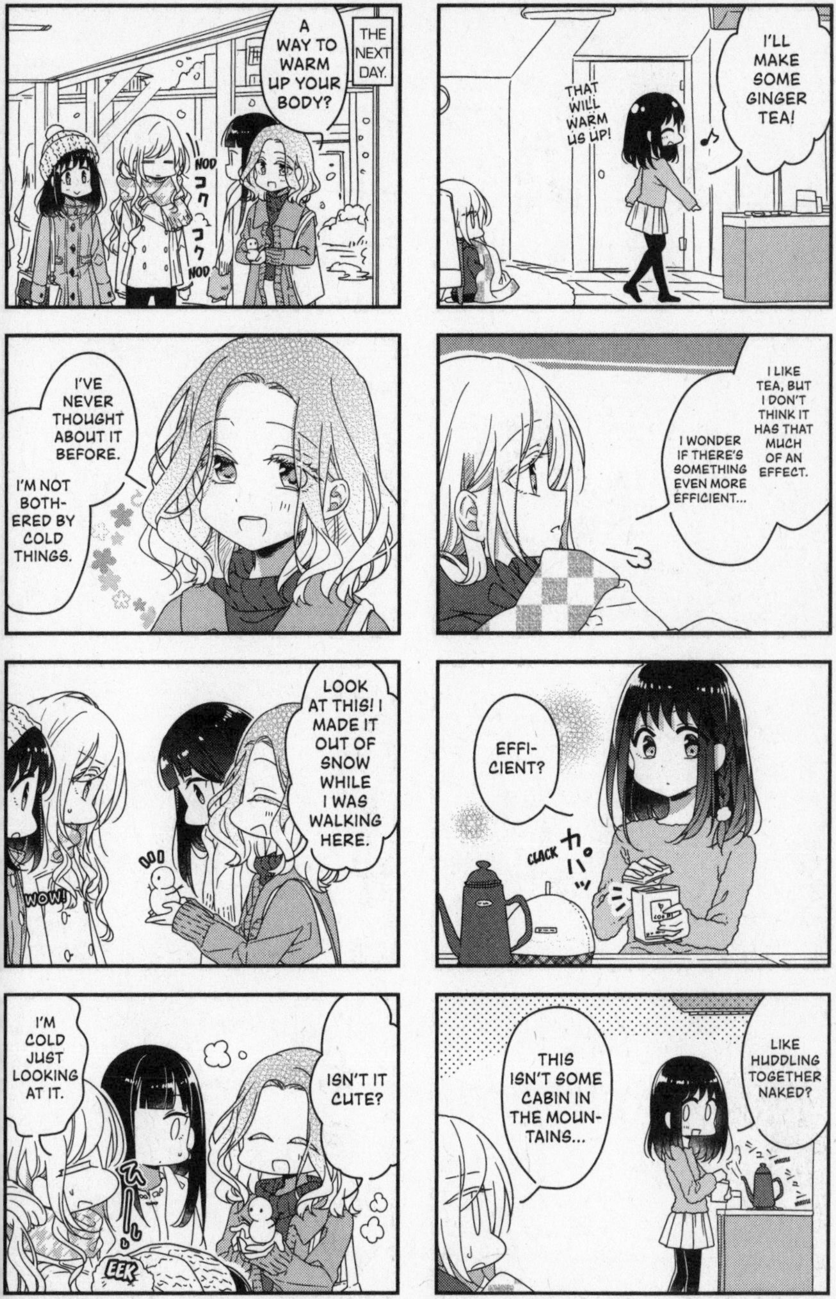
I'LL MAKE SOME GINGER TEA!
THAT WILL WARM US UP!
I LIKE TEA, BUT I DON'T THINK IT HAS THAT MUCH OF AN EFFECT.
I WONDER IF THERE'S SOMETHING EVEN MORE EFFICIENT...
EFFI-CIENT?
CLACK
カパッ
LIKE HUDDLING TOGETHER NAKED?
THIS ISN'T SOME CABIN IN THE MOUN-TAINS...
THE NEXT DAY.
A WAY TO WARM UP YOUR BODY?
NOD
コク
コク
NOD
I'VE NEVER THOUGHT ABOUT IT BEFORE.
I'M NOT BOTH-ERED BY COLD THINGS.
LOOK AT THIS! I MADE IT OUT OF SNOW WHILE I WAS WALKING HERE.
WOW!
ISN'T IT CUTE?
I'M COLD JUST LOOKING AT IT.
EEK

BARE HANDS...

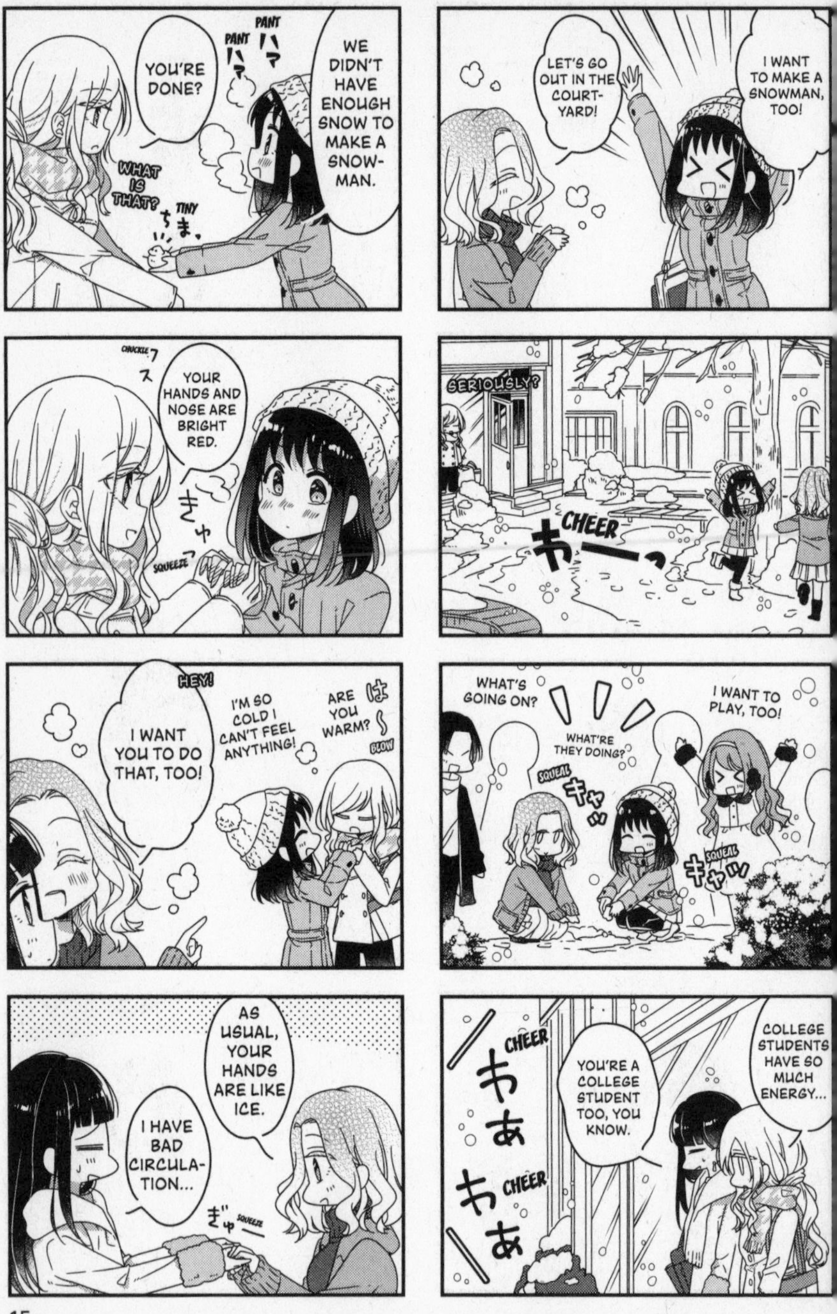
I WANT TO MAKE A SNOWMAN, TOO!
LET'S GO OUT IN THE COURT-YARD!
SERIOUSLY?
CHEER
やーっ
WHAT'S GOING ON?
I WANT TO PLAY, TOO!
WHAT'RE THEY DOING?
SQUEAL
キャッ
SQUEAL
キャッ
COLLEGE STUDENTS HAVE SO MUCH ENERGY...
YOU'RE A COLLEGE STUDENT TOO, YOU KNOW.
CHEER
やあ
CHEER
やあ
WE DIDN'T HAVE ENOUGH SNOW TO MAKE A SNOW-MAN.
PANT
ハァ
PANT
ハァ
YOU'RE DONE?
WHAT IS THAT?
TINY
ちま
YOUR HANDS AND NOSE ARE BRIGHT RED.
CHUCKLE
フス
きゅ
SQUEEZE
ARE YOU WARM?
は~
BLOW
I'M SO COLD I CAN'T FEEL ANYTHING!
HEY!
I WANT YOU TO DO THAT, TOO!
AS USUAL, YOUR HANDS ARE LIKE ICE.
I HAVE BAD CIRCULA-TION...
ぎゅ
SQUEEZE

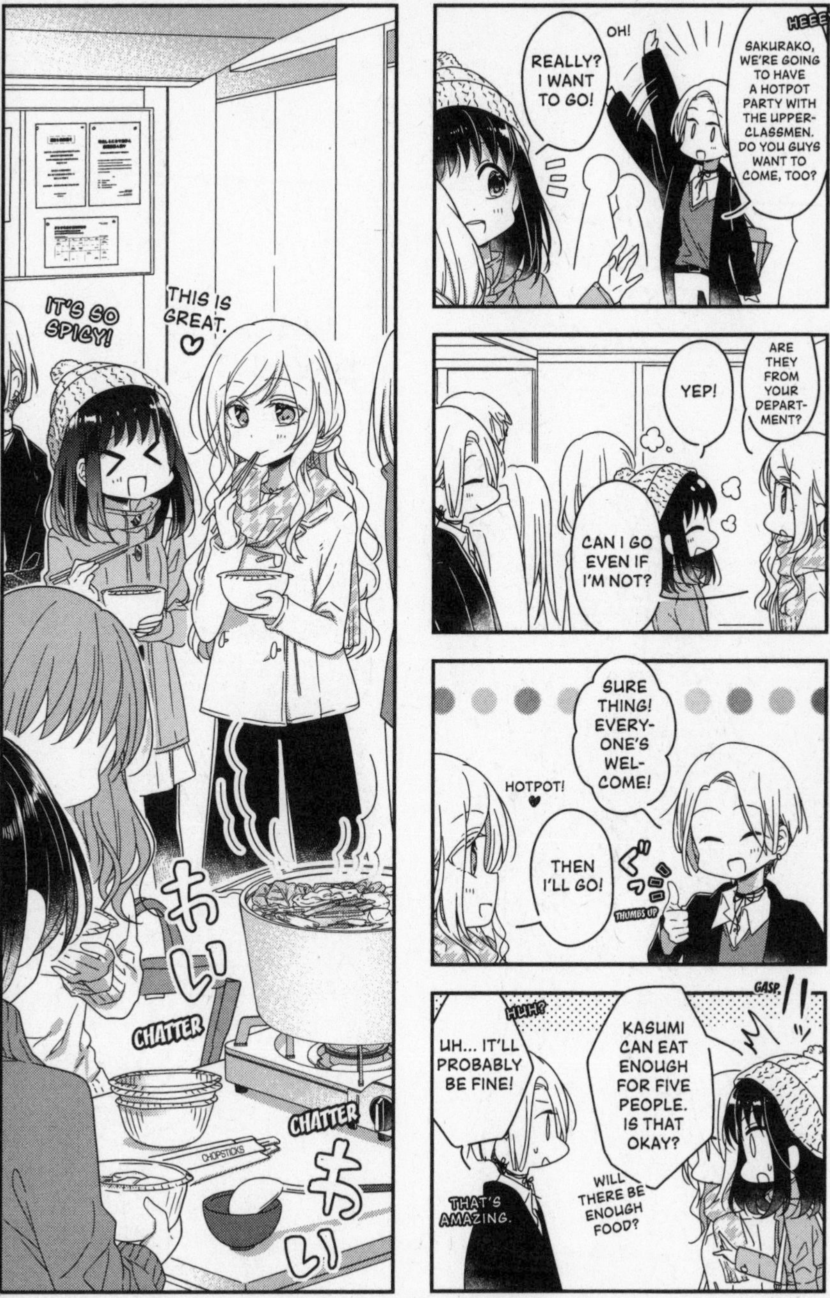
HEEEY!
SAKURAKO, WE'RE GOING TO HAVE A HOTPOT PARTY WITH THE UPPER-CLASSMEN. DO YOU GUYS WANT TO COME, TOO?
OH!
REALLY? I WANT TO GO!
ARE THEY FROM YOUR DEPART-MENT?
YEP!
CAN I GO EVEN IF I'M NOT?
SURE THING! EVERY-ONE'S WEL-COME!
HOTPOT!
THEN I'LL GO!
THUMBS UP
GASP.
KASUMI CAN EAT ENOUGH FOR FIVE PEOPLE. IS THAT OKAY?
HUH?
WILL THERE BE ENOUGH FOOD?
UH... IT'LL PROBABLY BE FINE!
THAT'S AMAZING.
THIS IS GREAT.
IT'S SO SPICY!
わい
CHATTER
CHATTER
わい
CHOPSTICKS

Illustration gallery of Yukiko

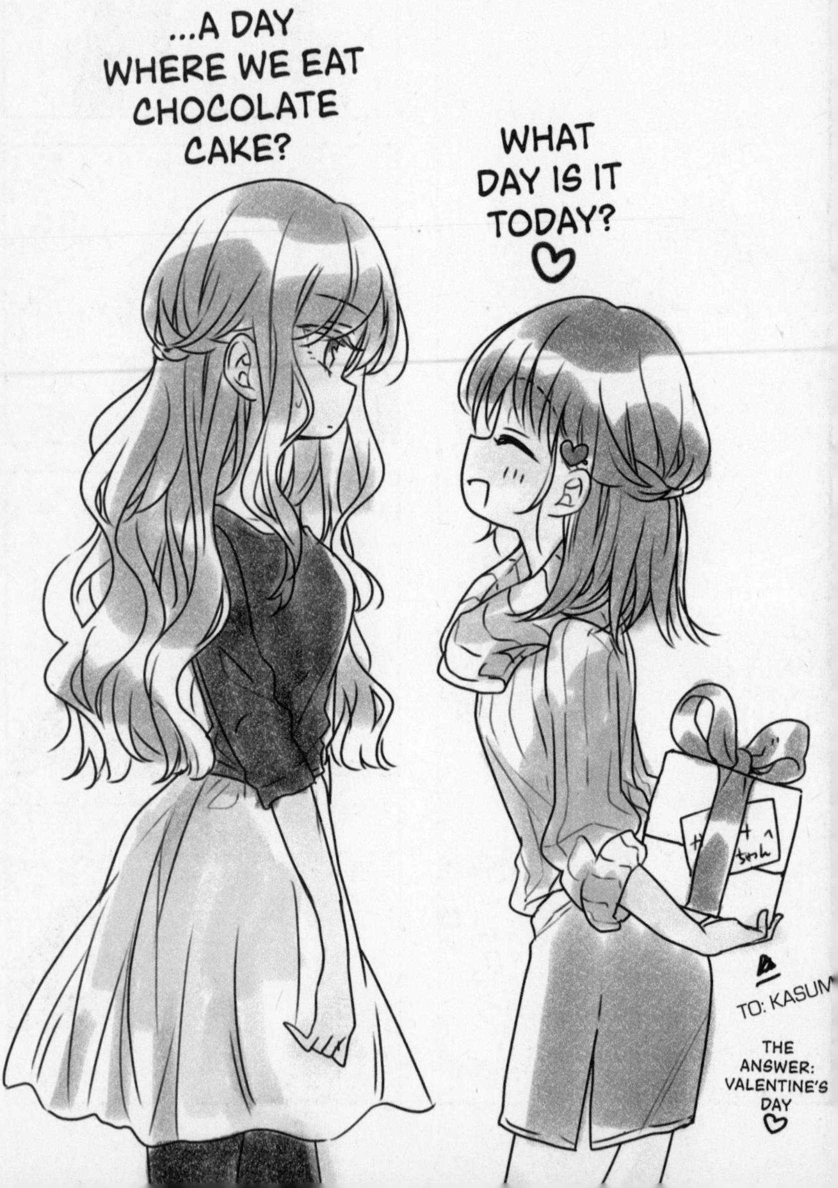
WHAT DAY IS IT TODAY?
...A DAY WHERE WE EAT CHOCOLATE CAKE?
TO: KASUM
THE ANSWER: VALENTINE'S DAY

Futaribeya
A ROOM FOR TWO

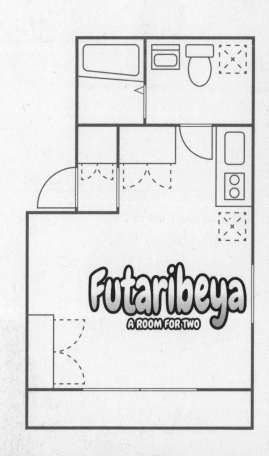

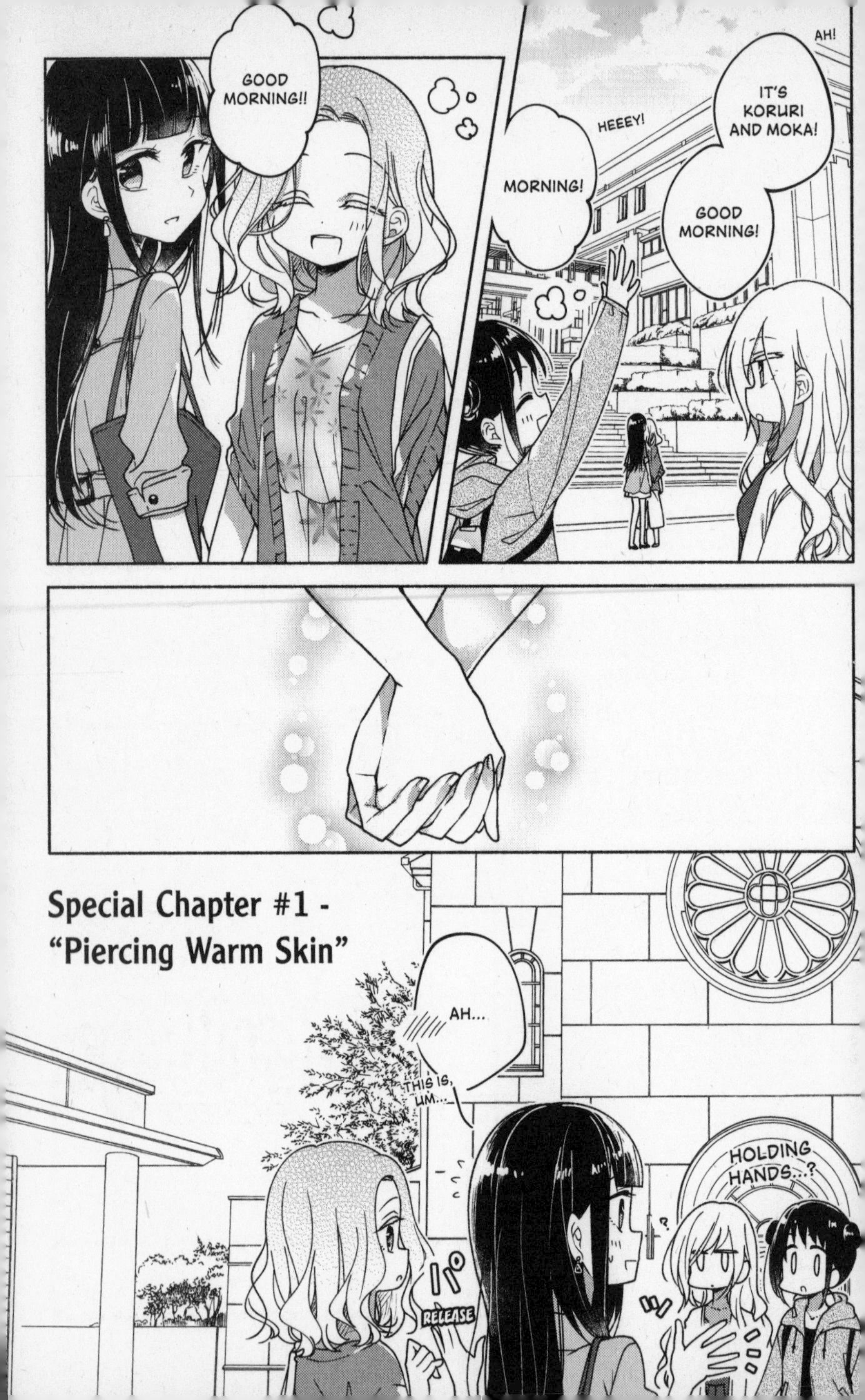
AH!
IT'S KORURI AND MOKA!
HEEEY!
GOOD MORNING!
MORNING!
GOOD MORNING!!
HOLDING HANDS...?
AH...
THIS IS, UM...
RELEASE

Special Chapter #1 - "Piercing Warm Skin"

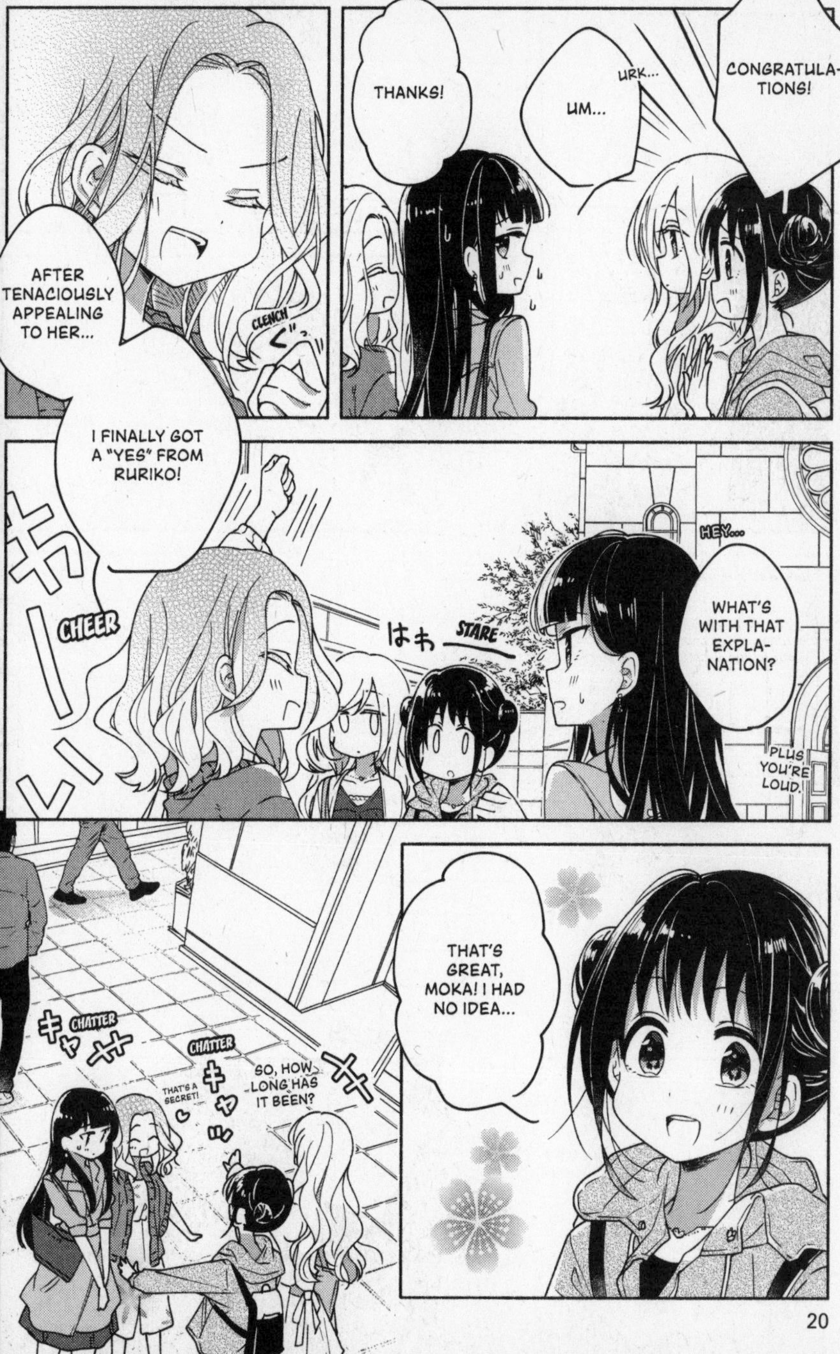
CONGRATULA-TIONS!
UM...
URK...
THANKS!
AFTER TENACIOUSLY APPEALING TO HER...
CLENCH
I FINALLY GOT A "YES" FROM RURIKO!
HEY...
WHAT'S WITH THAT EXPLANATION?
PLUS YOU'RE LOUD.
STARE
はわ
CHEER
THAT'S GREAT, MOKA! I HAD NO IDEA...
SO, HOW LONG HAS IT BEEN?
THAT'S A SECRET!
CHATTER
CHATTER

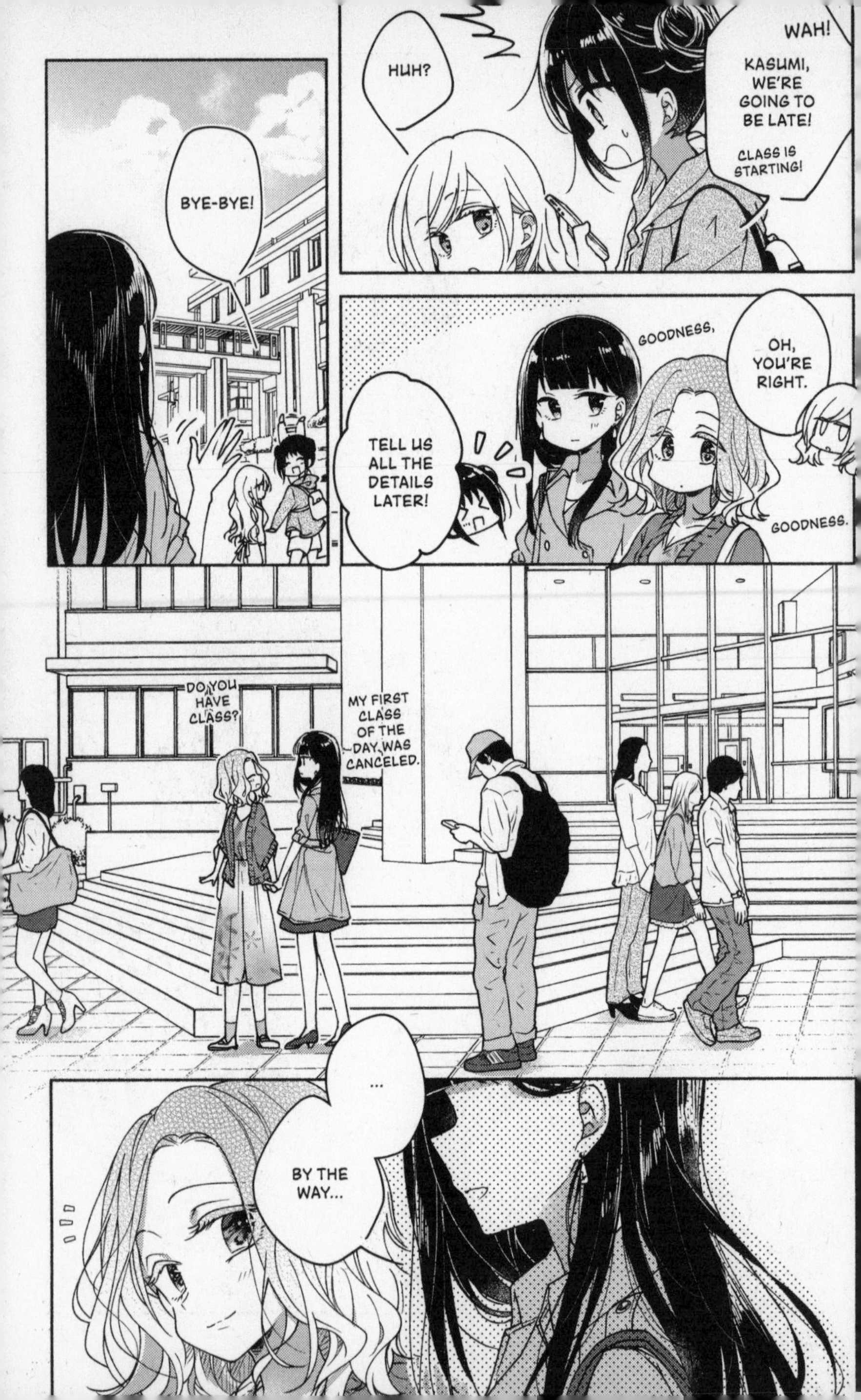

WAH!
KASUMI, WE'RE GOING TO BE LATE!
CLASS IS STARTING!
HUH?
OH, YOU'RE RIGHT.
GOODNESS,
GOODNESS.
TELL US ALL THE DETAILS LATER!
BYE-BYE!
MY FIRST CLASS OF THE DAY WAS CANCELED.
DO YOU HAVE CLASS?
...
BY THE WAY...

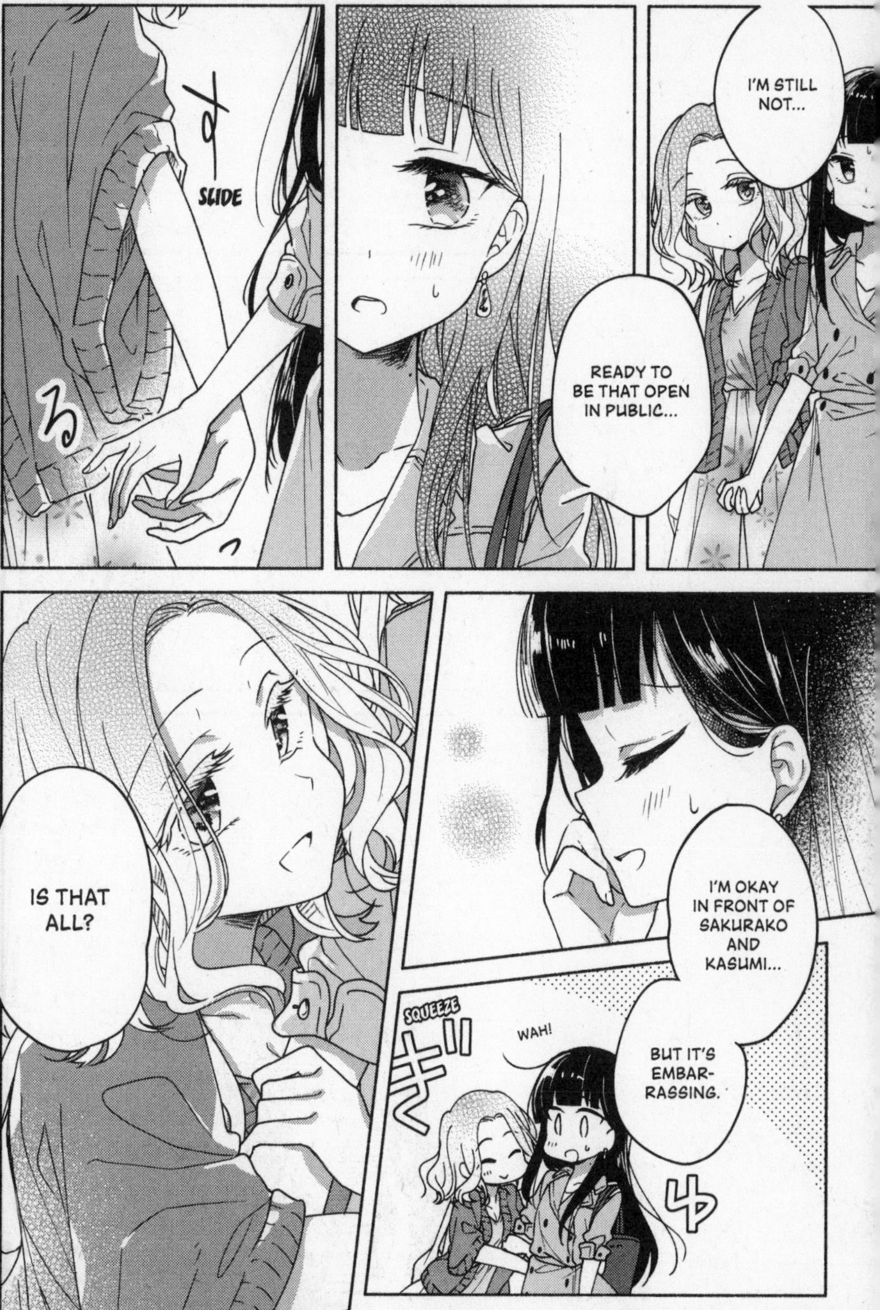
I'M STILL NOT...
READY TO BE THAT OPEN IN PUBLIC...
SLIDE
I'M OKAY IN FRONT OF SAKURAKO AND KASUMI...
BUT IT'S EMBAR-RASSING.
WAH!
SQUEEZE
IS THAT ALL?

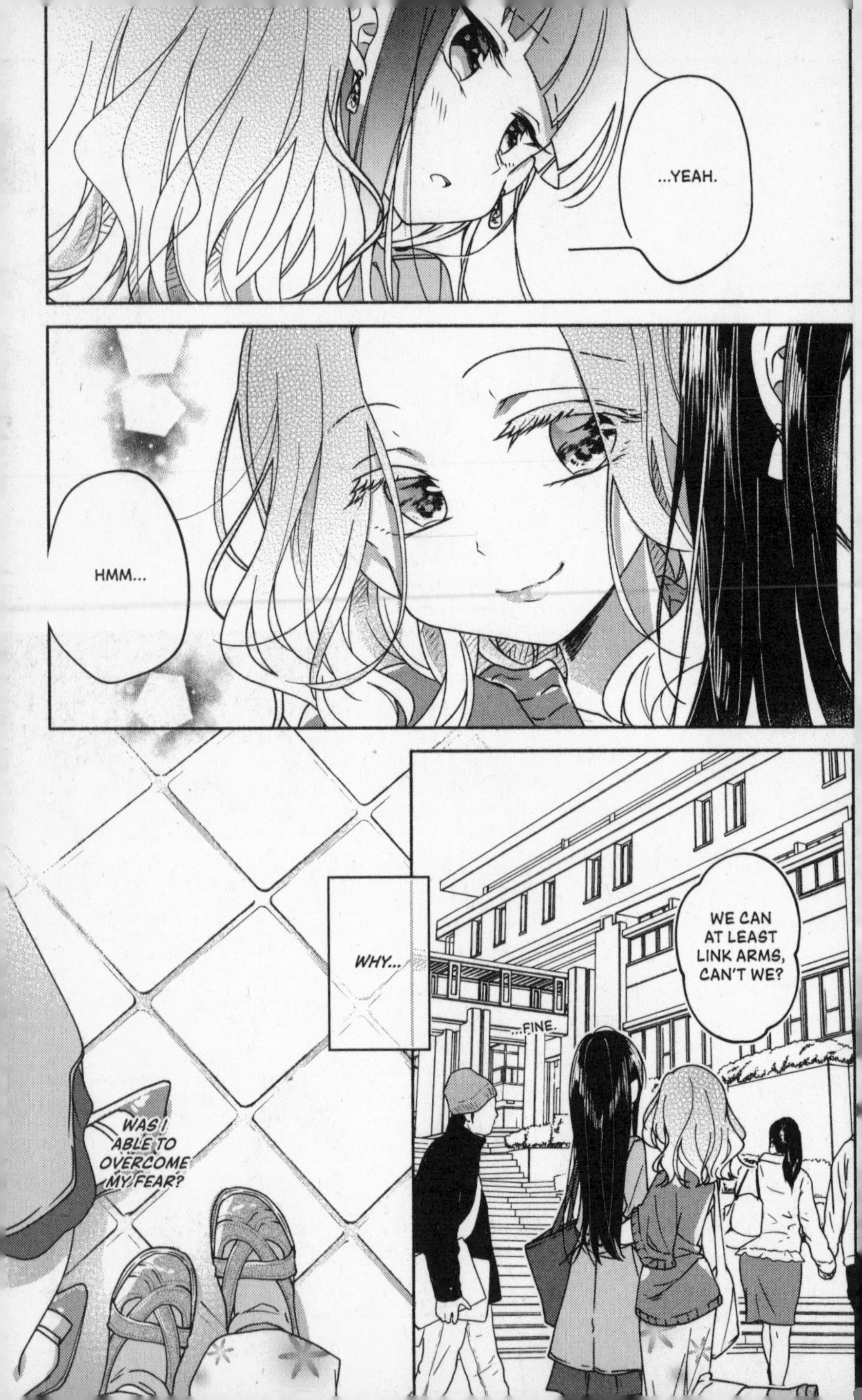
...YEAH.
HMM...
WE CAN AT LEAST LINK ARMS, CAN'T WE?
...FINE.
WHY...
WAS I ABLE TO OVERCOME MY FEAR?

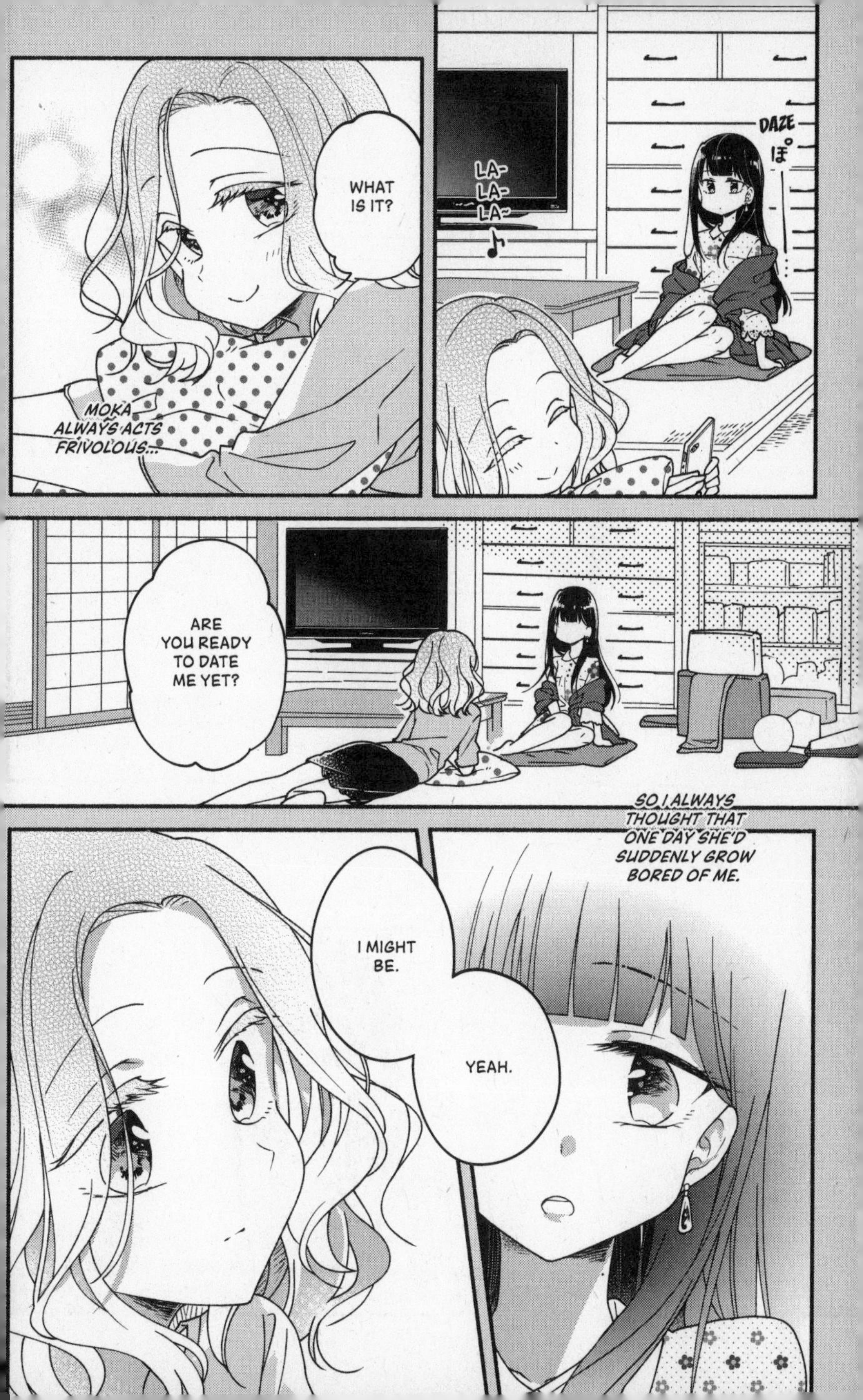
LA- LA- LA- ♪
DAZE
ぽ
WHAT IS IT?
MOKA ALWAYS ACTS FRIVOLOUS...
ARE YOU READY TO DATE ME YET?
SO I ALWAYS THOUGHT THAT ONE DAY SHE'D SUDDENLY GROW BORED OF ME.
I MIGHT BE.
YEAH.

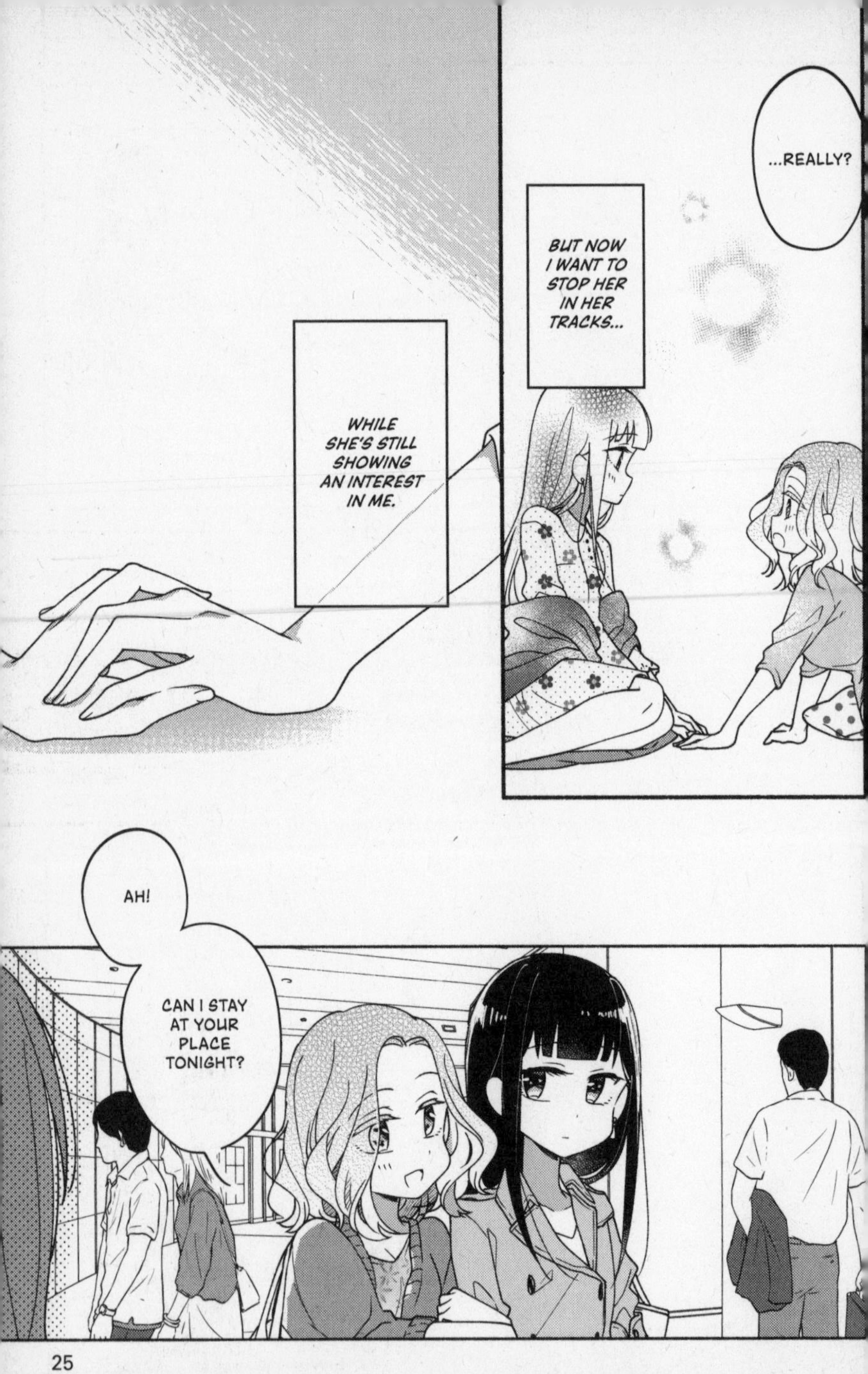
...REALLY?
BUT NOW I WANT TO STOP HER IN HER TRACKS...
WHILE SHE'S STILL SHOWING AN INTEREST IN ME.
AH!
CAN I STAY AT YOUR PLACE TONIGHT?

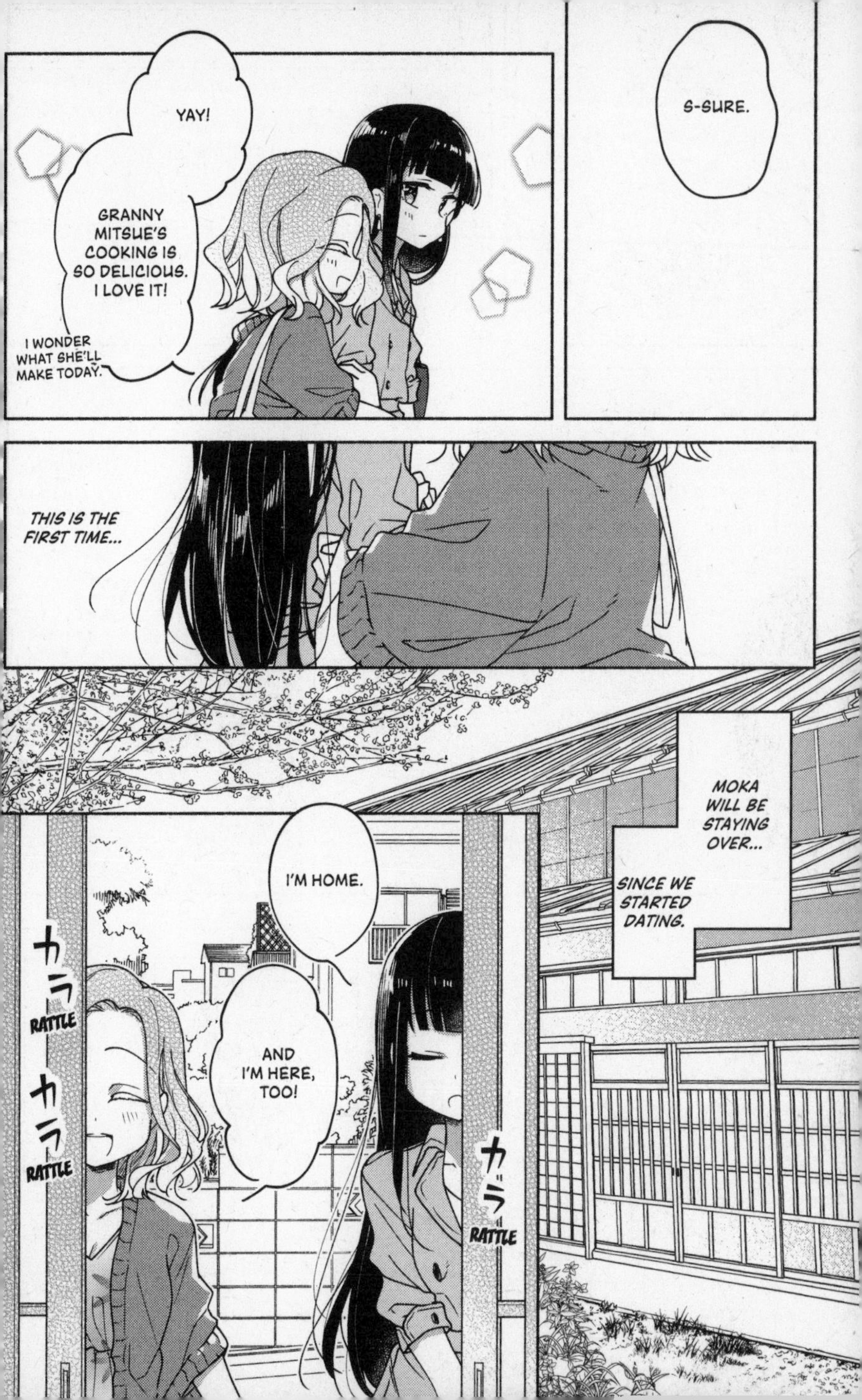
S-SURE.
YAY!
GRANNY MITSUE'S COOKING IS SO DELICIOUS. I LOVE IT!
I WONDER WHAT SHE'LL MAKE TODAY.
THIS IS THE FIRST TIME...
MOKA WILL BE STAYING OVER...
SINCE WE STARTED DATING.
ガラ
RATTLE
I'M HOME.
AND I'M HERE, TOO!
カラ
RATTLE
カラ
RATTLE

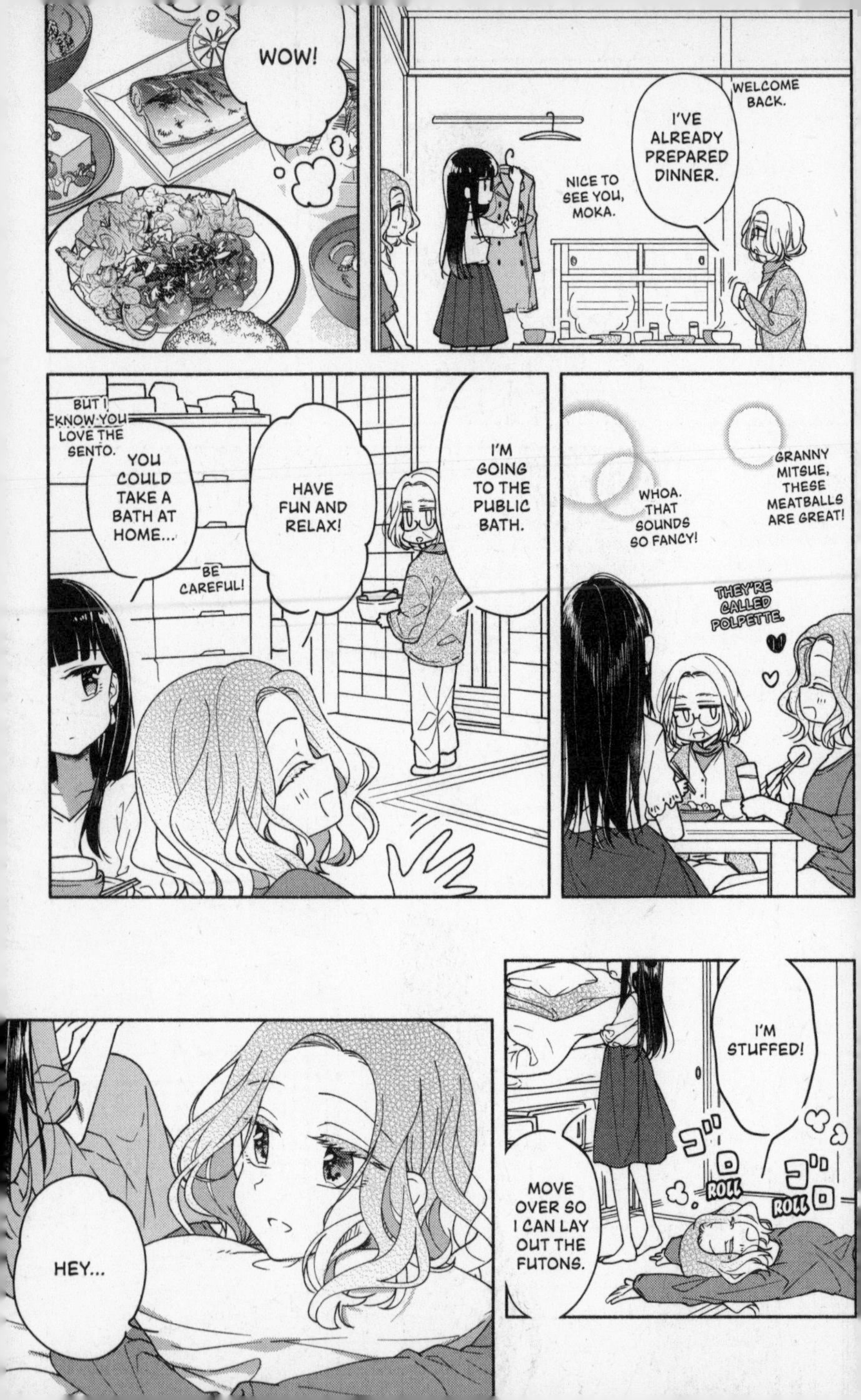
WELCOME BACK.
I'VE ALREADY PREPARED DINNER.
NICE TO SEE YOU, MOKA.
WOW!
GRANNY MITSUE, THESE MEATBALLS ARE GREAT!
WHOA. THAT SOUNDS SO FANCY!
THEY'RE CALLED POLPETTE.
I'M GOING TO THE PUBLIC BATH.
HAVE FUN AND RELAX!
YOU COULD TAKE A BATH AT HOME...
BUT I KNOW YOU LOVE THE SENTO.
BE CAREFUL!
I'M STUFFED!
ROLL
ROLL
MOVE OVER SO I CAN LAY OUT THE FUTONS.
HEY...

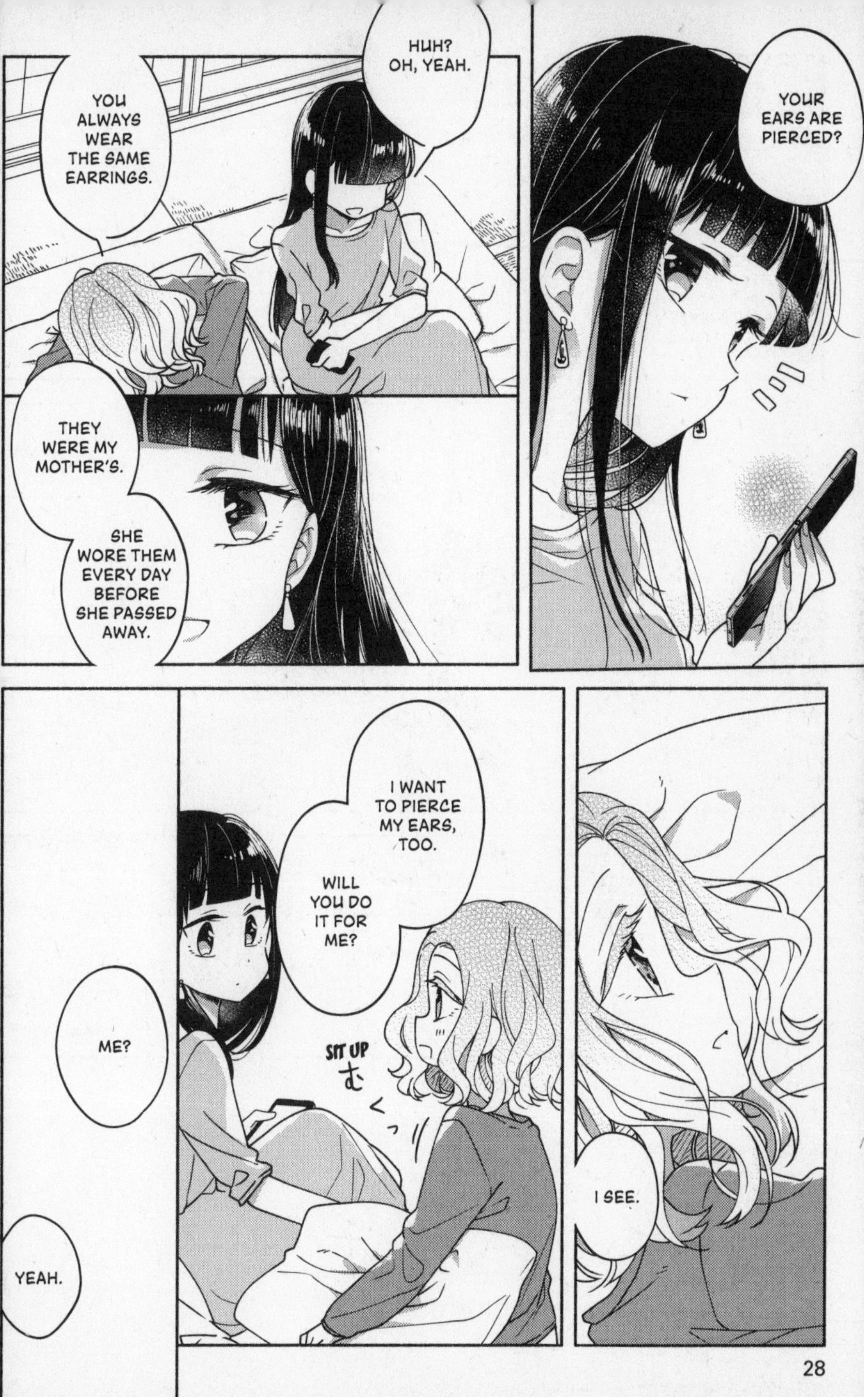
YOUR EARS ARE PIERCED?
HUH? OH, YEAH.
YOU ALWAYS WEAR THE SAME EARRINGS.
THEY WERE MY MOTHER'S.
SHE WORE THEM EVERY DAY BEFORE SHE PASSED AWAY.
I SEE.
I WANT TO PIERCE MY EARS, TOO.
WILL YOU DO IT FOR ME?
SIT UP
むくっ
ME?
YEAH.

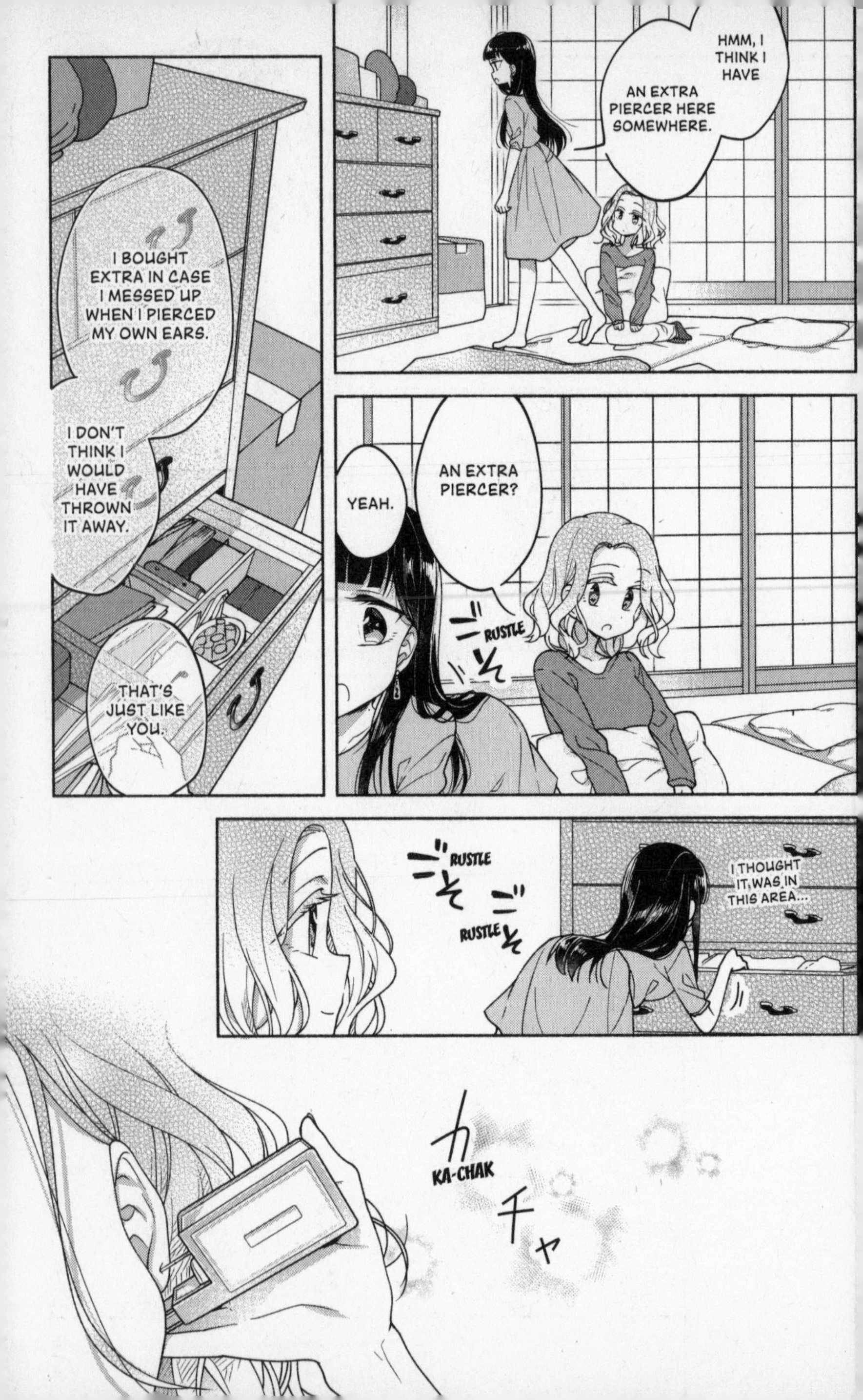
HMM, I THINK I HAVE AN EXTRA PIERCER HERE SOMEWHERE.
AN EXTRA PIERCER?
YEAH.
RUSTLE
I BOUGHT EXTRA IN CASE I MESSED UP WHEN I PIERCED MY OWN EARS.
I DON'T THINK I WOULD HAVE THROWN IT AWAY.
THAT'S JUST LIKE YOU.
I THOUGHT IT WAS IN THIS AREA...
RUSTLE
RUSTLE
KA-CHAK

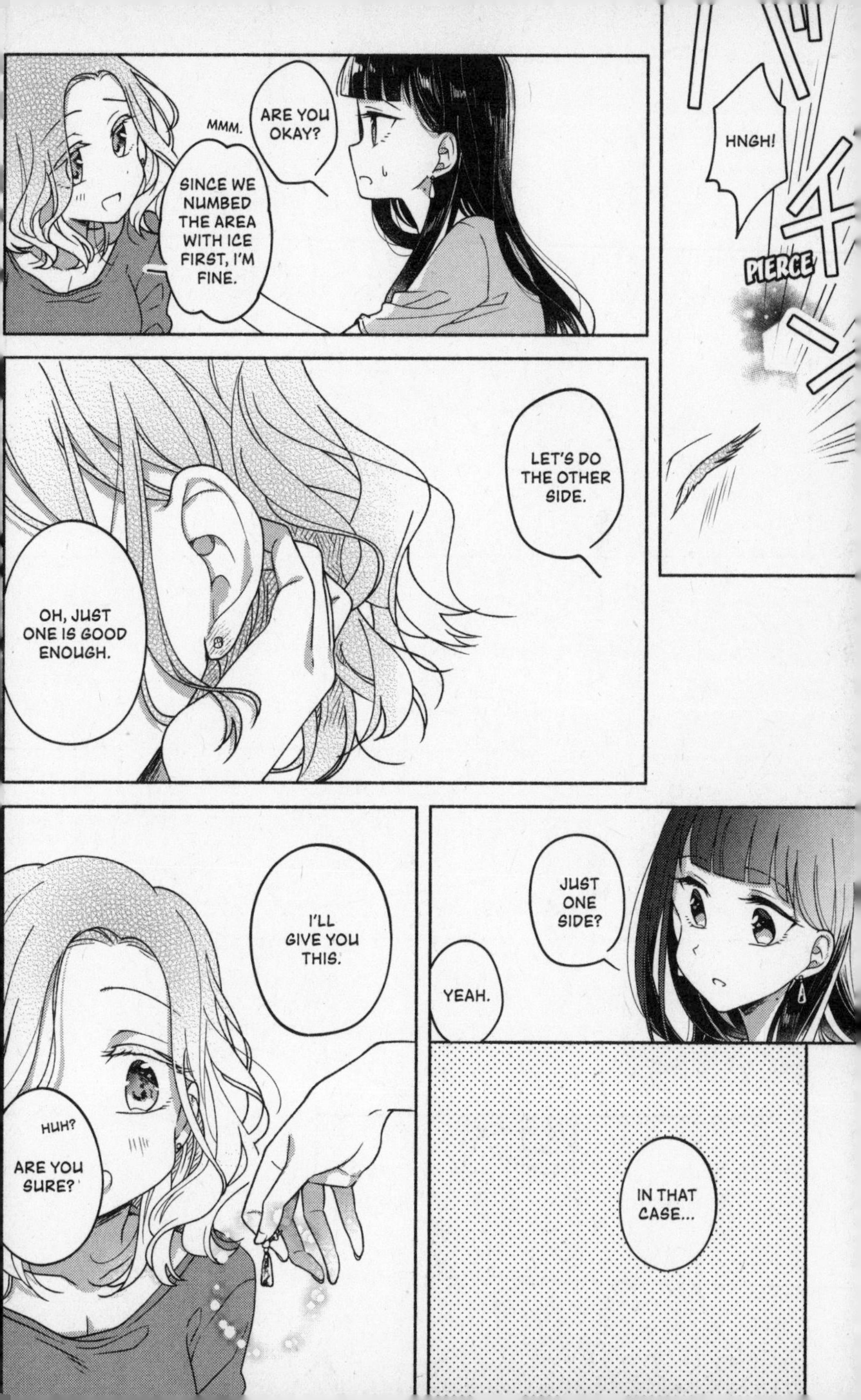
HNGH!
PIERCE
ARE YOU OKAY?
MMM.
SINCE WE NUMBED THE AREA WITH ICE FIRST, I'M FINE.
LET'S DO THE OTHER SIDE.
OH, JUST ONE IS GOOD ENOUGH.
JUST ONE SIDE?
YEAH.
IN THAT CASE...
I'LL GIVE YOU THIS.
HUH?
ARE YOU SURE?

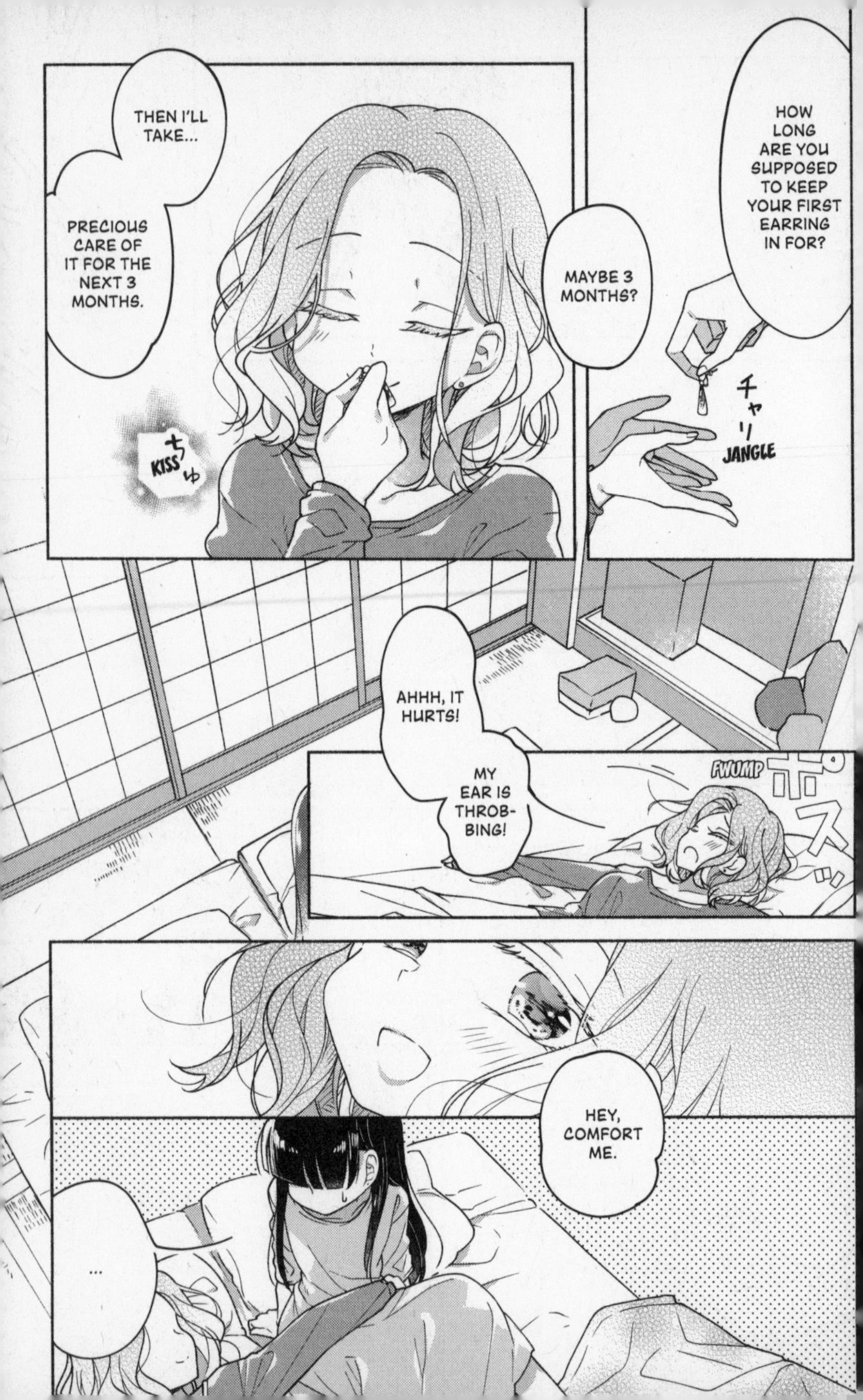

HOW LONG ARE YOU SUPPOSED TO KEEP YOUR FIRST EARRING IN FOR?
チャリ
JANGLE
MAYBE 3 MONTHS?
THEN I'LL TAKE...
PRECIOUS CARE OF IT FOR THE NEXT 3 MONTHS.
ちゅ
KISS
AHHH, IT HURTS!
MY EAR IS THROB-BING!
ポスッ
FWUMP
HEY, COMFORT ME.
...

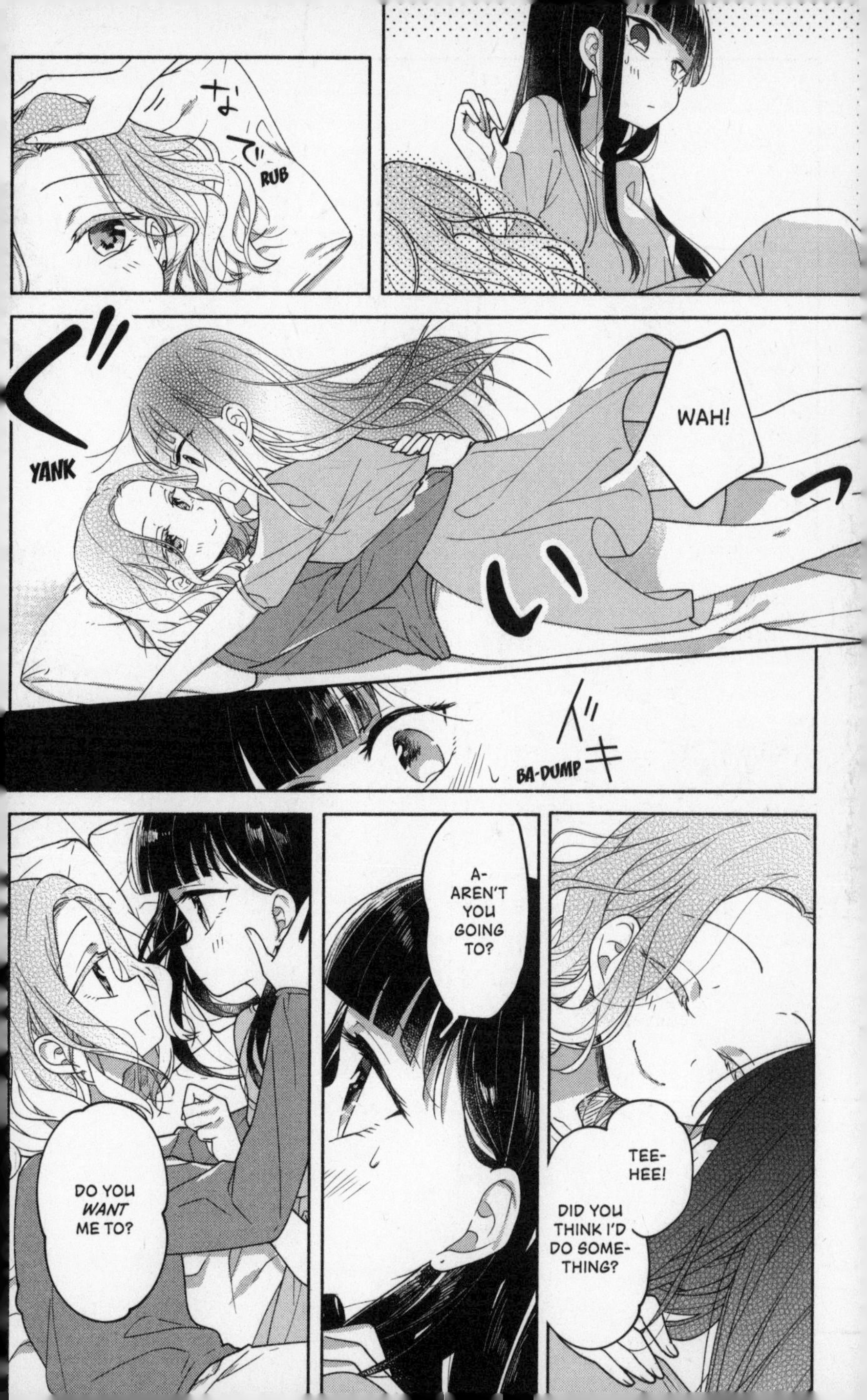
なで
RUB
WAH!
ぐい
YANK
ドキ
BA-DUMP
TEE-HEE!
DID YOU THINK I'D DO SOME-THING?
A- AREN'T YOU GOING TO?
DO YOU *WANT* ME TO?

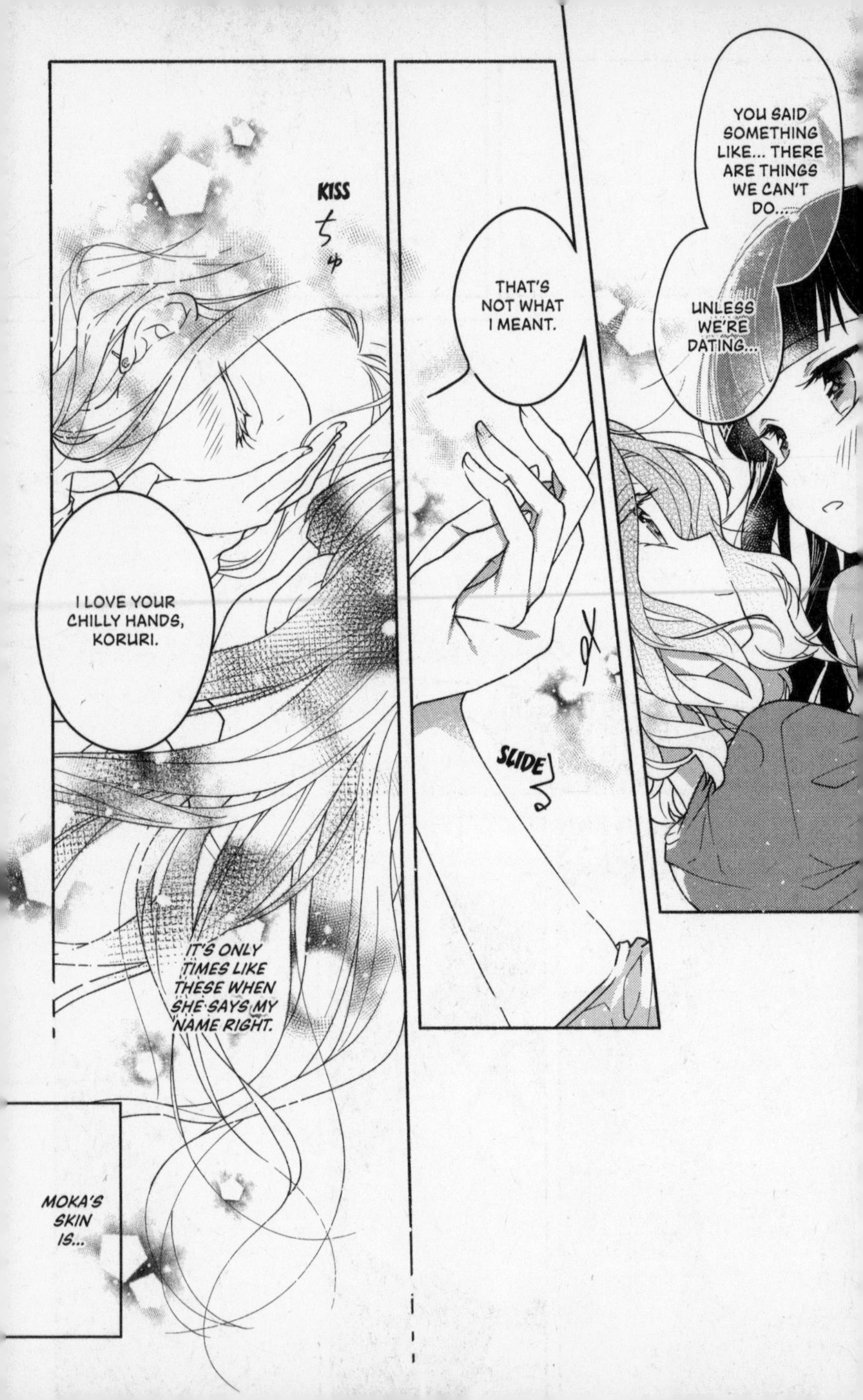
YOU SAID SOMETHING LIKE... THERE ARE THINGS WE CAN'T DO...
UNLESS WE'RE DATING...
THAT'S NOT WHAT I MEANT.
SLIDE
する
KISS
ちゅ
I LOVE YOUR CHILLY HANDS, KORURI.
IT'S ONLY TIMES LIKE THESE WHEN SHE SAYS MY NAME RIGHT.
MOKA'S SKIN IS...

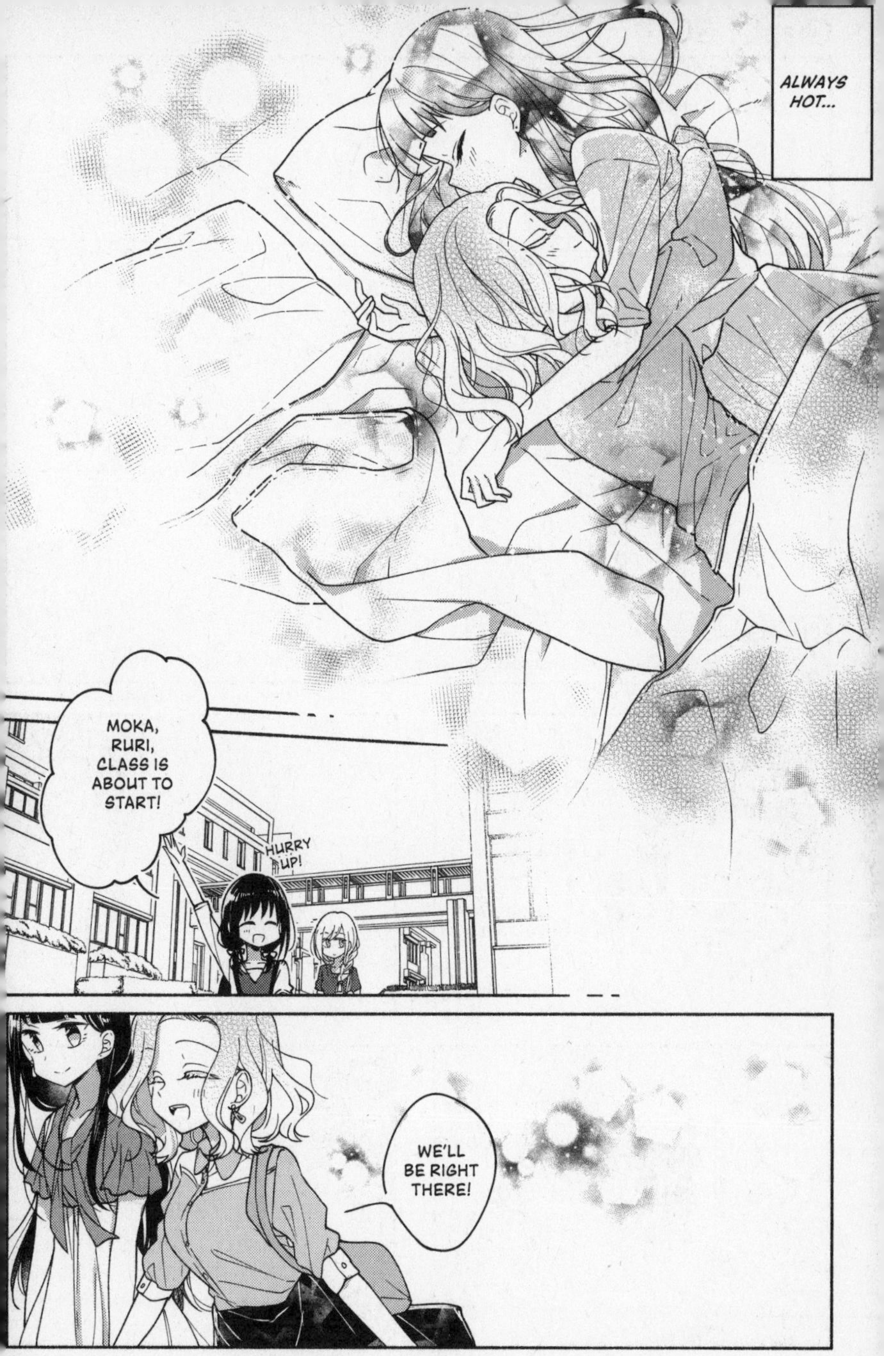
ALWAYS HOT...
MOKA, RURI, CLASS IS ABOUT TO START!
HURRY UP!
WE'LL BE RIGHT THERE!

Chapter 50

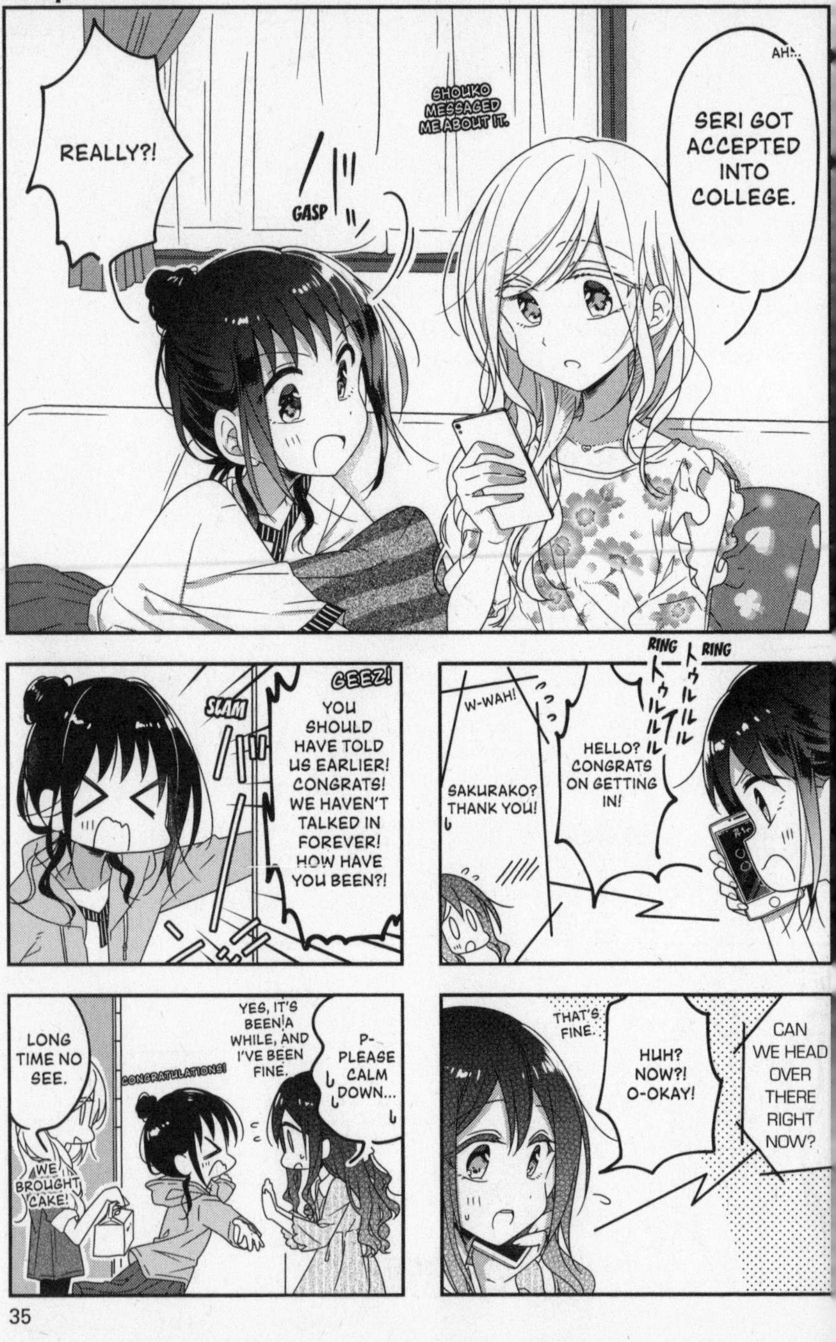
AH...
SERI GOT ACCEPTED INTO COLLEGE.
SHOUKO MESSAGED ME ABOUT IT.
GASP
REALLY?!
RING RING
HELLO? CONGRATS ON GETTING IN!
SAKURAKO? THANK YOU!
W-WAH!
GEEZ!
YOU SHOULD HAVE TOLD US EARLIER! CONGRATS! WE HAVEN'T TALKED IN FOREVER! HOW HAVE YOU BEEN?!
SLAM
CAN WE HEAD OVER THERE RIGHT NOW?
THAT'S FINE.
HUH? NOW?! O-OKAY!
P-PLEASE CALM DOWN...
YES, IT'S BEEN A WHILE, AND I'VE BEEN FINE.
CONGRATULATIONS!
LONG TIME NO SEE.
WE BROUGHT CAKE!

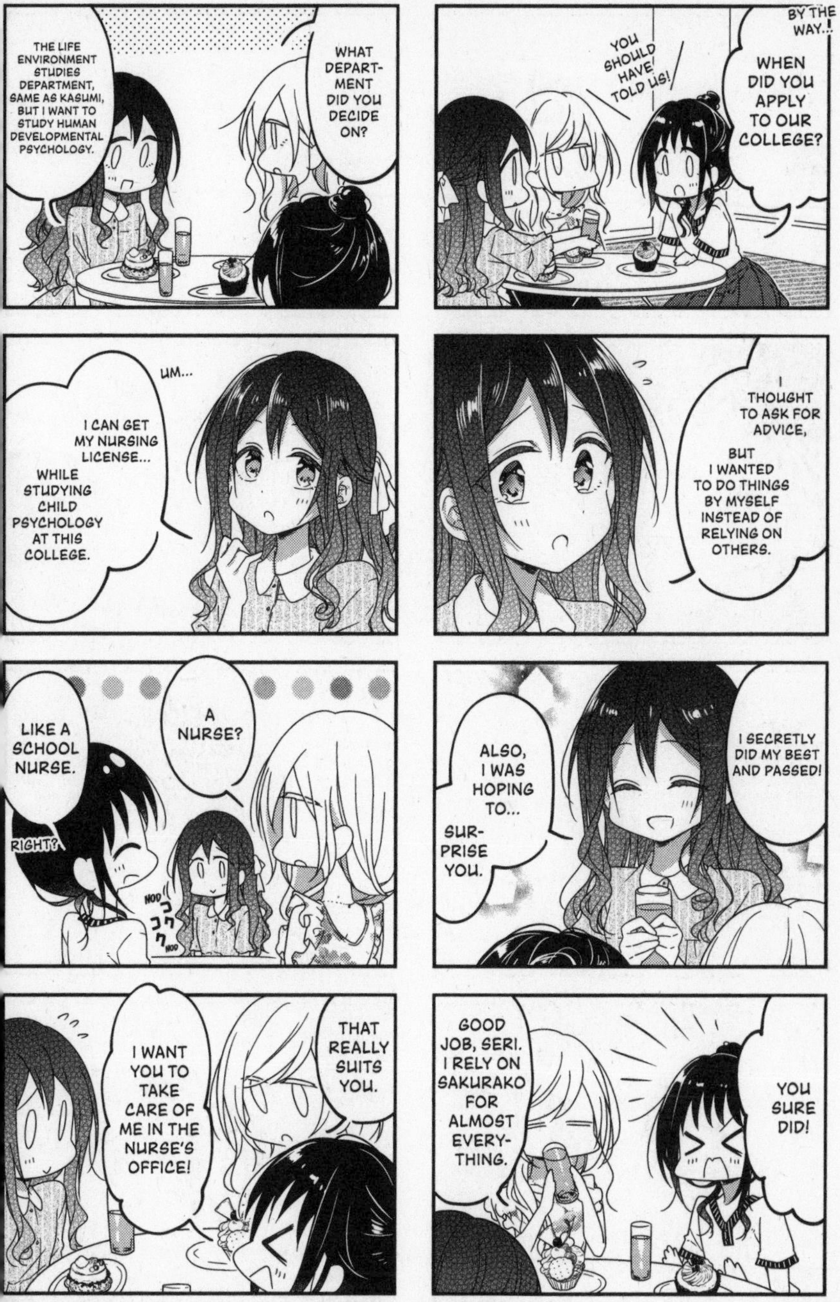
BY THE WAY..!
WHEN DID YOU APPLY TO OUR COLLEGE?
YOU SHOULD HAVE TOLD US!
I THOUGHT TO ASK FOR ADVICE,
BUT I WANTED TO DO THINGS BY MYSELF INSTEAD OF RELYING ON OTHERS.
I SECRETLY DID MY BEST AND PASSED!
ALSO, I WAS HOPING TO...
SUR-PRISE YOU.
YOU SURE DID!
GOOD JOB, SERI. I RELY ON SAKURAKO FOR ALMOST EVERY-THING.
WHAT DEPART-MENT DID YOU DECIDE ON?
THE LIFE ENVIRONMENT STUDIES DEPARTMENT, SAME AS KASUMI, BUT I WANT TO STUDY HUMAN DEVELOPMENTAL PSYCHOLOGY.
UM...
I CAN GET MY NURSING LICENSE...
WHILE STUDYING CHILD PSYCHOLOGY AT THIS COLLEGE.
A NURSE?
LIKE A SCHOOL NURSE.
RIGHT?
NOD
NOD
THAT REALLY SUITS YOU.
I WANT YOU TO TAKE CARE OF ME IN THE NURSE'S OFFICE!

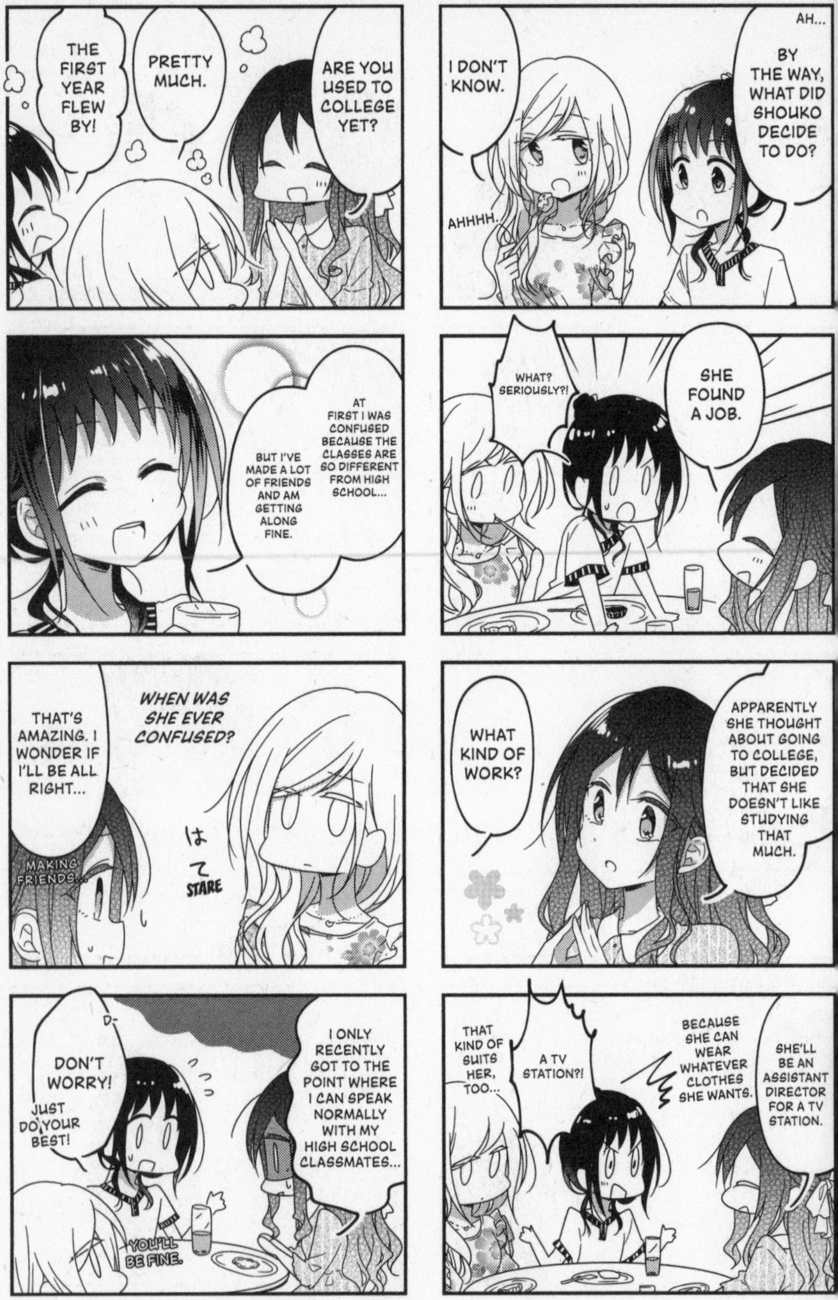
AH...
BY THE WAY, WHAT DID SHOUKO DECIDE TO DO?
I DON'T KNOW.
AHHHH.
SHE FOUND A JOB.
WHAT? SERIOUSLY?!
APPARENTLY SHE THOUGHT ABOUT GOING TO COLLEGE, BUT DECIDED THAT SHE DOESN'T LIKE STUDYING THAT MUCH.
WHAT KIND OF WORK?
SHE'LL BE AN ASSISTANT DIRECTOR FOR A TV STATION.
BECAUSE SHE CAN WEAR WHATEVER CLOTHES SHE WANTS.
A TV STATION?!
THAT KIND OF SUITS HER, TOO...
ARE YOU USED TO COLLEGE YET?
PRETTY MUCH.
THE FIRST YEAR FLEW BY!
AT FIRST I WAS CONFUSED BECAUSE THE CLASSES ARE SO DIFFERENT FROM HIGH SCHOOL...
BUT I'VE MADE A LOT OF FRIENDS AND AM GETTING ALONG FINE.
WHEN WAS SHE EVER CONFUSED?
THAT'S AMAZING. I WONDER IF I'LL BE ALL RIGHT...
はて
STARE
MAKING FRIENDS...
I ONLY RECENTLY GOT TO THE POINT WHERE I CAN SPEAK NORMALLY WITH MY HIGH SCHOOL CLASSMATES...
D- DON'T WORRY!
JUST DO YOUR BEST!
YOU'LL BE FINE.

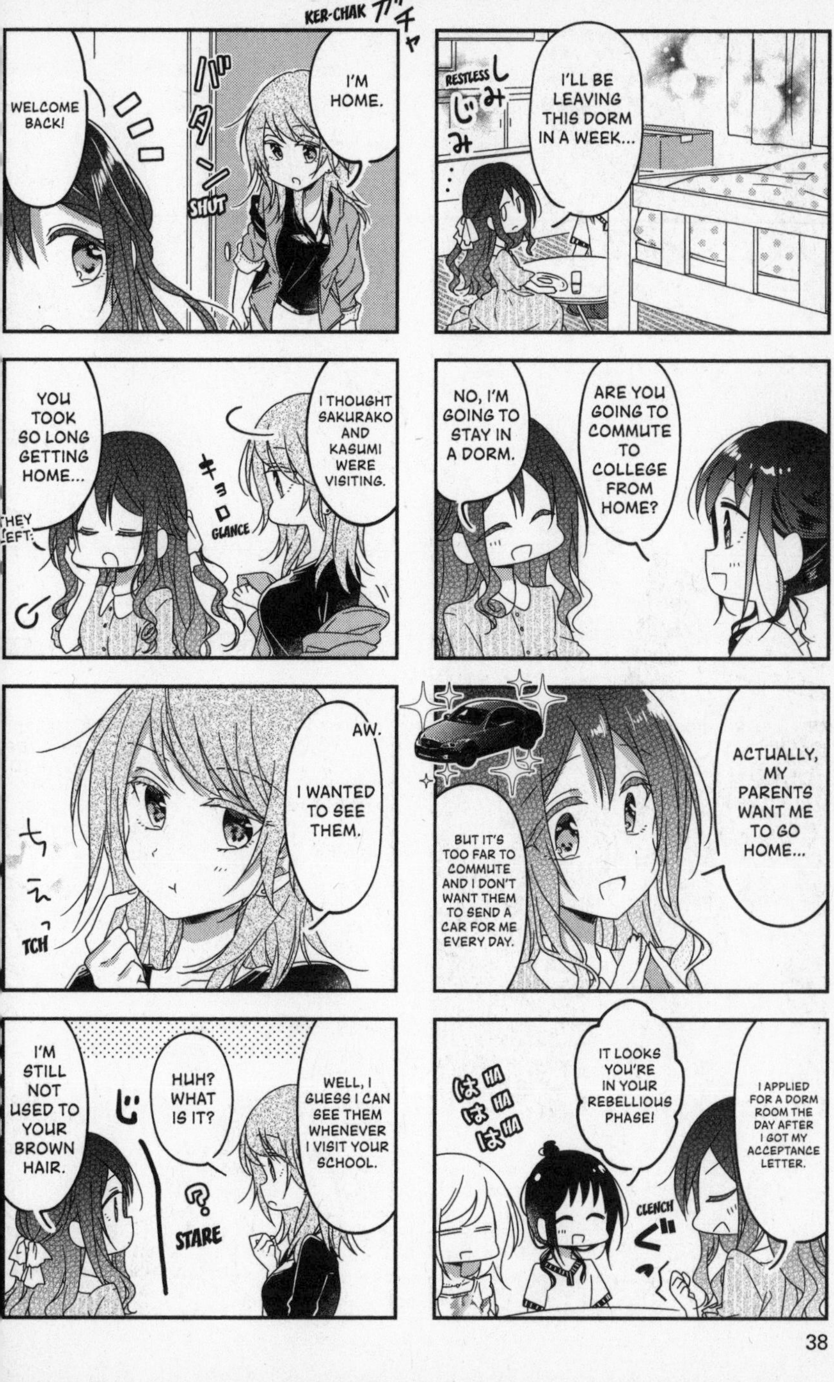
RESTLESS しみじみ
I'LL BE LEAVING THIS DORM IN A WEEK...
KER-CHAK ガチャ
I'M HOME.
バタン
SHUT
WELCOME BACK!
ARE YOU GOING TO COMMUTE TO COLLEGE FROM HOME?
NO, I'M GOING TO STAY IN A DORM.
I THOUGHT SAKURAKO AND KASUMI WERE VISITING.
キョロ
GLANCE
YOU TOOK SO LONG GETTING HOME...
ACTUALLY, MY PARENTS WANT ME TO GO HOME...
BUT IT'S TOO FAR TO COMMUTE AND I DON'T WANT THEM TO SEND A CAR FOR ME EVERY DAY.
AW.
I WANTED TO SEE THEM.
ちぇっ
TCH
I APPLIED FOR A DORM ROOM THE DAY AFTER I GOT MY ACCEPTANCE LETTER.
IT LOOKS YOU'RE IN YOUR REBELLIOUS PHASE!
ははは HA HA HA
CLENCH ぐっ
WELL, I GUESS I CAN SEE THEM WHENEVER I VISIT YOUR SCHOOL.
HUH? WHAT IS IT?
STARE じー
I'M STILL NOT USED TO YOUR BROWN HAIR.

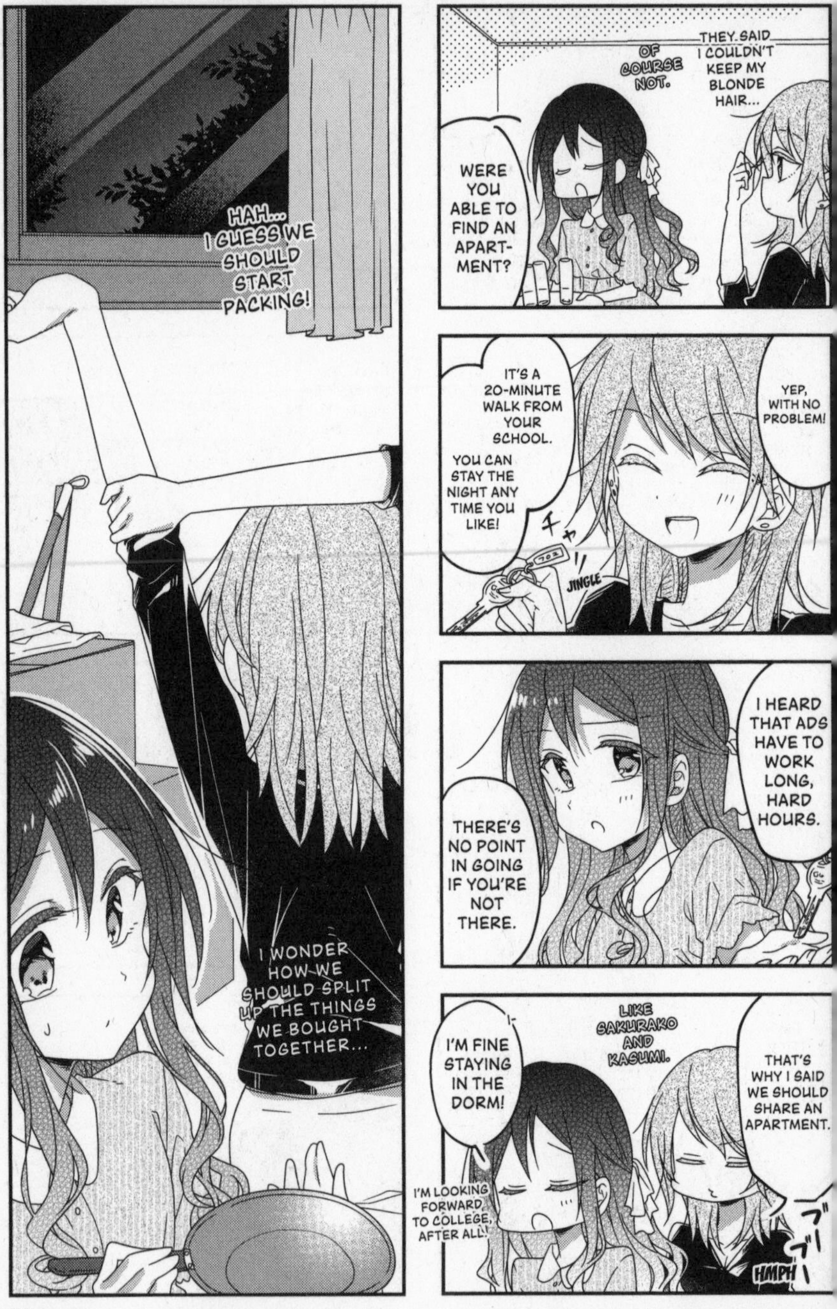
THEY SAID I COULDN'T KEEP MY BLONDE HAIR...
OF COURSE NOT.
WERE YOU ABLE TO FIND AN APART-MENT?
YEP, WITH NO PROBLEM!
IT'S A 20-MINUTE WALK FROM YOUR SCHOOL.
YOU CAN STAY THE NIGHT ANY TIME YOU LIKE!
チャ
JINGLE
I HEARD THAT ADS HAVE TO WORK LONG, HARD HOURS.
THERE'S NO POINT IN GOING IF YOU'RE NOT THERE.
THAT'S WHY I SAID WE SHOULD SHARE AN APARTMENT.
LIKE SAKURAKO AND KASUMI.
I'M FINE STAYING IN THE DORM!
I'M LOOKING FORWARD TO COLLEGE, AFTER ALL!
ブーブー
HMPH
HAH... I GUESS WE SHOULD START PACKING!
I WONDER HOW WE SHOULD SPLIT UP THE THINGS WE BOUGHT TOGETHER...

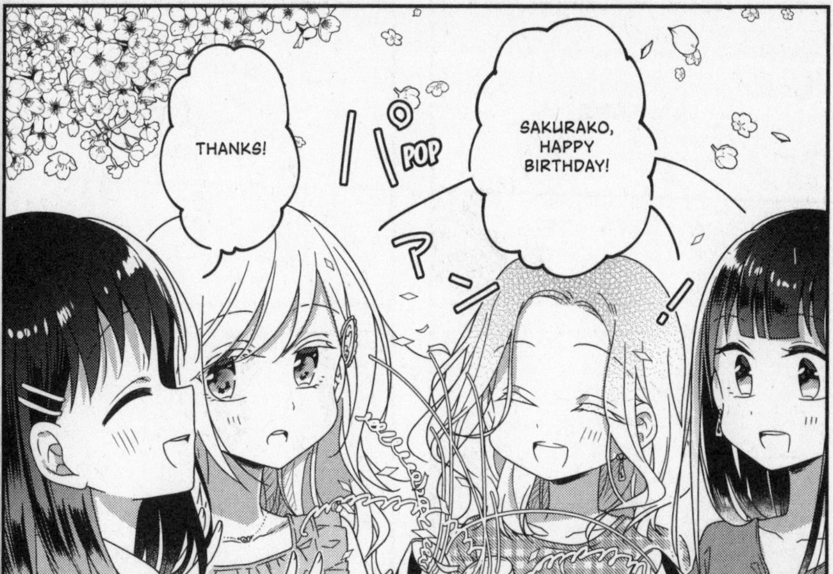
SAKURAKO, HAPPY BIRTHDAY!
POP
THANKS!
THE CHERRY BLOSSOMS ARE IN FULL BLOOM!
PERFECT FOR YOUR BIRTHDAY!
EVERYTHING ABOUT YOU SCREAMS "SPRING"!
HER HEAD IS FILLED WITH SPRING THROUGHOUT THE YEAR.
YOU CAN DRINK ALCOHOL NOW.*
YEP!

*IN JAPAN THE LEGAL DRINKING AGE IS 20, NOT 21.

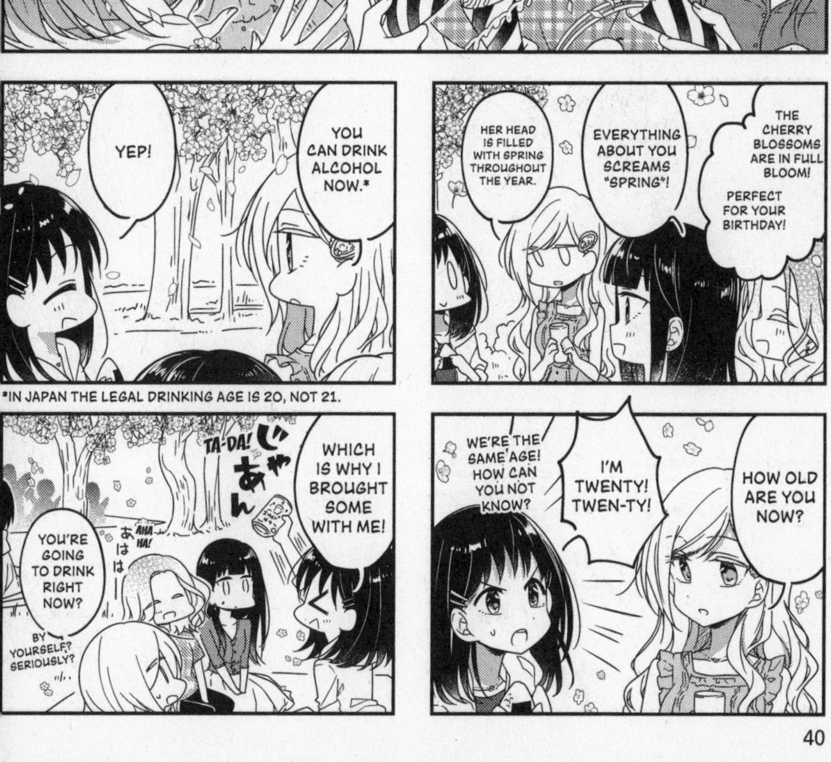
HOW OLD ARE YOU NOW?
I'M TWENTY! TWEN-TY!
WE'RE THE SAME AGE! HOW CAN YOU NOT KNOW?
WHICH IS WHY I BROUGHT SOME WITH ME!
TA-DA!
じゃあん
AHA HA!
あはは
YOU'RE GOING TO DRINK RIGHT NOW?
BY YOURSELF? SERIOUSLY?

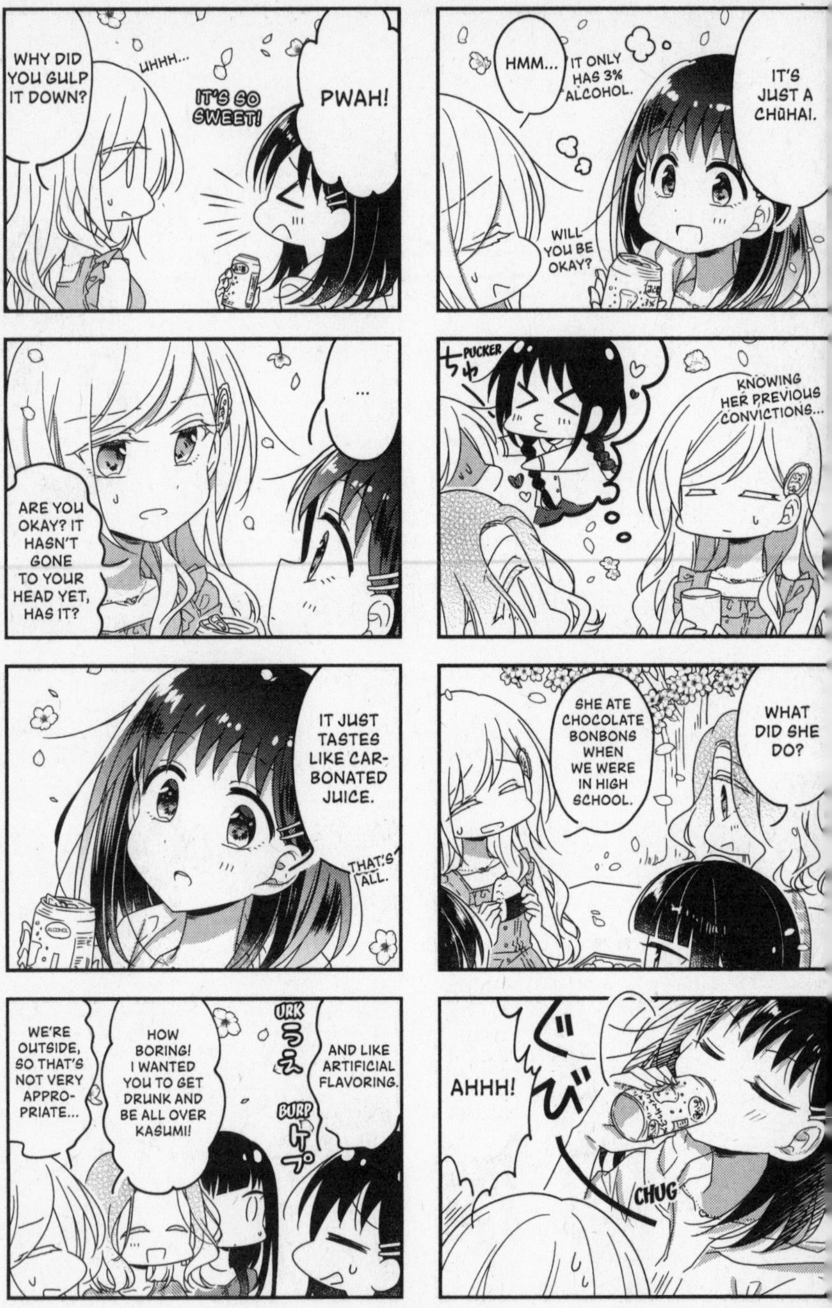
IT'S JUST A CHŪHAI.
IT ONLY HAS 3% ALCOHOL.
HMM...
WILL YOU BE OKAY?
KNOWING HER PREVIOUS CONVICTIONS...
PUCKER
ちゅ
WHAT DID SHE DO?
SHE ATE CHOCOLATE BONBONS WHEN WE WERE IN HIGH SCHOOL.
ぐび
AHHH!
CHUG
PWAH!
IT'S SO SWEET!
UHHH...
WHY DID YOU GULP IT DOWN?
...
ARE YOU OKAY? IT HASN'T GONE TO YOUR HEAD YET, HAS IT?
IT JUST TASTES LIKE CARBONATED JUICE.
THAT'S ALL.
AND LIKE ARTIFICIAL FLAVORING.
URK
うえ
BURP
ケプ
HOW BORING! I WANTED YOU TO GET DRUNK AND BE ALL OVER KASUMI!
WE'RE OUTSIDE, SO THAT'S NOT VERY APPROPRIATE...

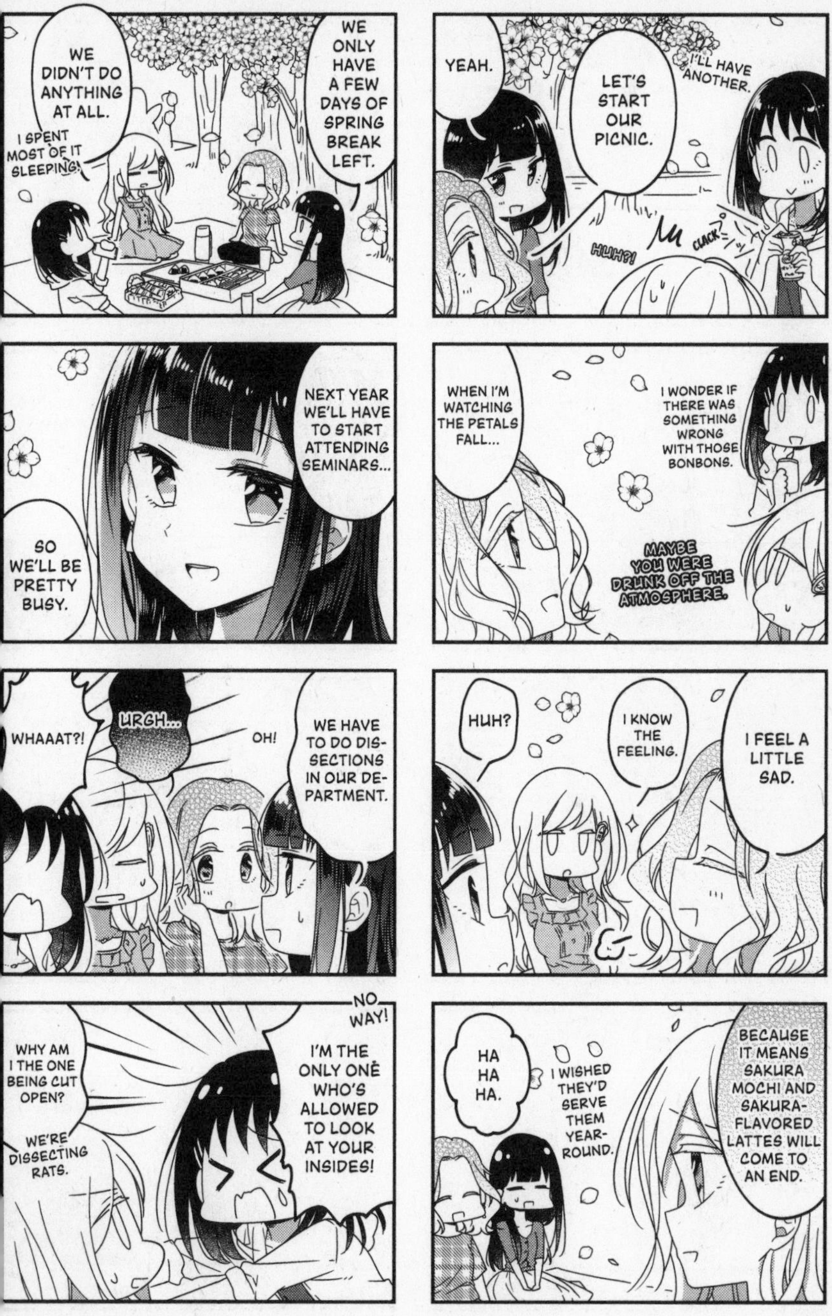
I'LL HAVE ANOTHER.
LET'S START OUR PICNIC.
YEAH.
CLACK
HUHH?!
I WONDER IF THERE WAS SOMETHING WRONG WITH THOSE BONBONS.
WHEN I'M WATCHING THE PETALS FALL...
MAYBE YOU WERE DRUNK OFF THE ATMOSPHERE.
I FEEL A LITTLE SAD.
I KNOW THE FEELING.
HUH?
BECAUSE IT MEANS SAKURA MOCHI AND SAKURA-FLAVORED LATTES WILL COME TO AN END.
I WISHED THEY'D SERVE THEM YEAR-ROUND.
HA HA HA.
WE ONLY HAVE A FEW DAYS OF SPRING BREAK LEFT.
WE DIDN'T DO ANYTHING AT ALL.
I SPENT MOST OF IT SLEEPING.
NEXT YEAR WE'LL HAVE TO START ATTENDING SEMINARS...
SO WE'LL BE PRETTY BUSY.
WE HAVE TO DO DISSECTIONS IN OUR DEPARTMENT.
OH!
URGH...
WHAAAT?!
NO WAY!
I'M THE ONLY ONE WHO'S ALLOWED TO LOOK AT YOUR INSIDES!
WHY AM I THE ONE BEING CUT OPEN?
WE'RE DISSECTING RATS.

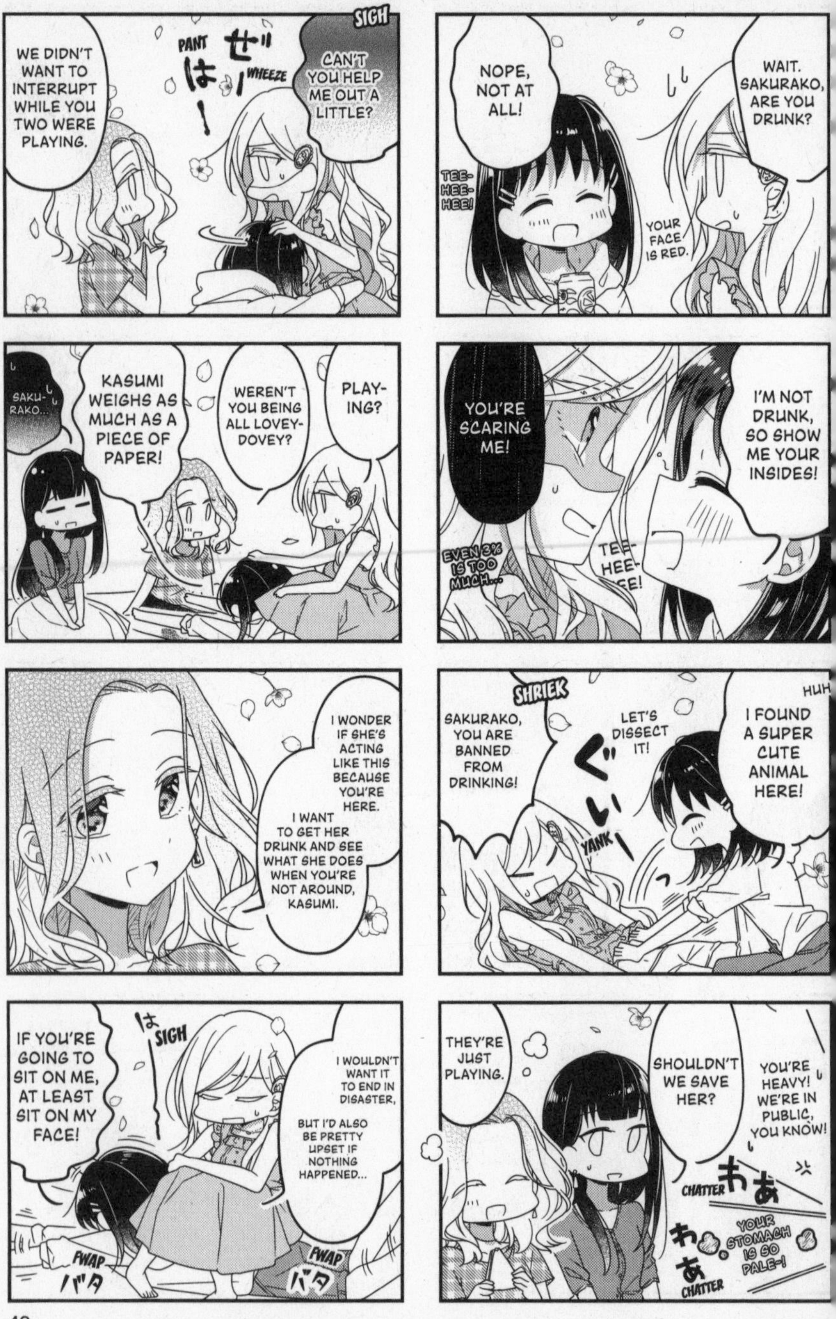
WAIT. SAKURAKO, ARE YOU DRUNK?
NOPE, NOT AT ALL!
YOUR FACE IS RED.
TEE-HEE-HEE!
I'M NOT DRUNK, SO SHOW ME YOUR INSIDES!
YOU'RE SCARING ME!
TEE-HEE-HEE!
EVEN 3% IS TOO MUCH...
HUH
I FOUND A SUPER CUTE ANIMAL HERE!
LET'S DISSECT IT!
SHRIEK
SAKURAKO, YOU ARE BANNED FROM DRINKING!
ぐい
YANK
YOU'RE HEAVY! WE'RE IN PUBLIC, YOU KNOW!
SHOULDN'T WE SAVE HER?
THEY'RE JUST PLAYING.
CHATTER わあ
YOUR STOMACH IS SO PALE-!
わあ CHATTER
SIGH
CAN'T YOU HELP ME OUT A LITTLE?
PANT ぜぃ
WHEEZE
は
WE DIDN'T WANT TO INTERRUPT WHILE YOU TWO WERE PLAYING.
PLAY-ING?
WEREN'T YOU BEING ALL LOVEY-DOVEY?
KASUMI WEIGHS AS MUCH AS A PIECE OF PAPER!
SAKU-RAKO...
I WONDER IF SHE'S ACTING LIKE THIS BECAUSE YOU'RE HERE.
I WANT TO GET HER DRUNK AND SEE WHAT SHE DOES WHEN YOU'RE NOT AROUND, KASUMI.
I WOULDN'T WANT IT TO END IN DISASTER,
BUT I'D ALSO BE PRETTY UPSET IF NOTHING HAPPENED...
は SIGH
IF YOU'RE GOING TO SIT ON ME, AT LEAST SIT ON MY FACE!
FWAP バタ
FWAP バタ

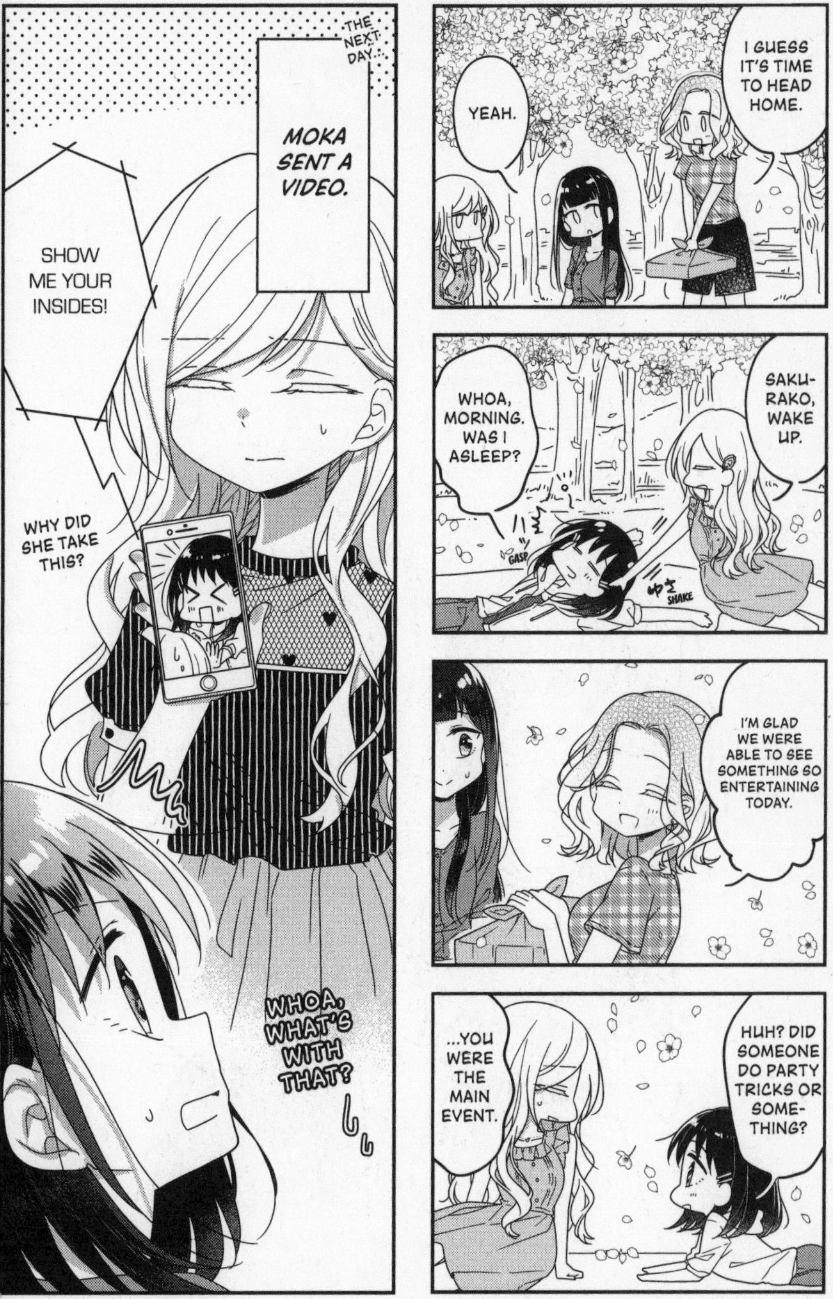
I GUESS IT'S TIME TO HEAD HOME.
YEAH.
SAKU-RAKO, WAKE UP.
WHOA, MORNING. WAS I ASLEEP?
GASP
SHAKE
I'M GLAD WE WERE ABLE TO SEE SOMETHING SO ENTERTAINING TODAY.
HUH? DID SOMEONE DO PARTY TRICKS OR SOME-THING?
...YOU WERE THE MAIN EVENT.
THE NEXT DAY...
MOKA SENT A VIDEO.
SHOW ME YOUR INSIDES!
WHY DID SHE TAKE THIS?
WHOA, WHAT'S WITH THAT?

Illustration gallery of Yukiko

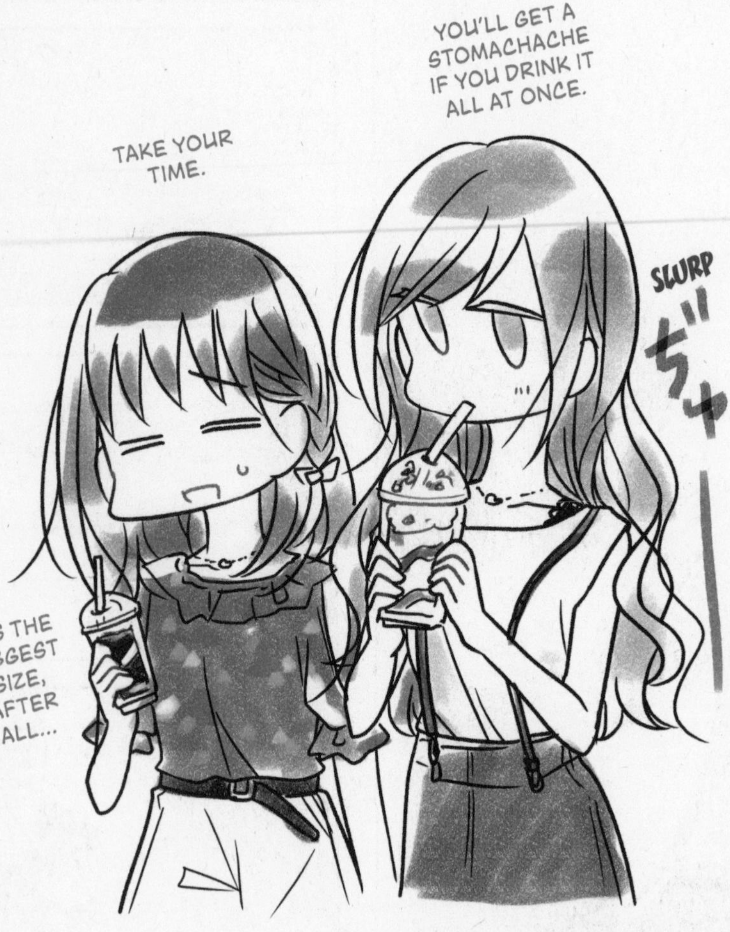
YOU'LL GET A STOMACHACHE IF YOU DRINK IT ALL AT ONCE.
SLURP
TAKE YOUR TIME.
IT'S THE BIGGEST SIZE, AFTER ALL...

Futaribeya
A ROOM FOR TWO

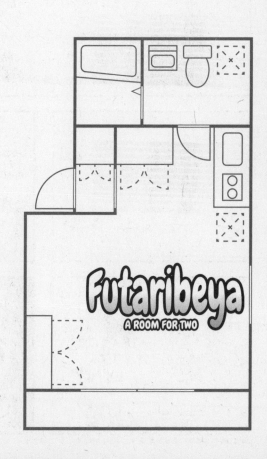

Chapter 51

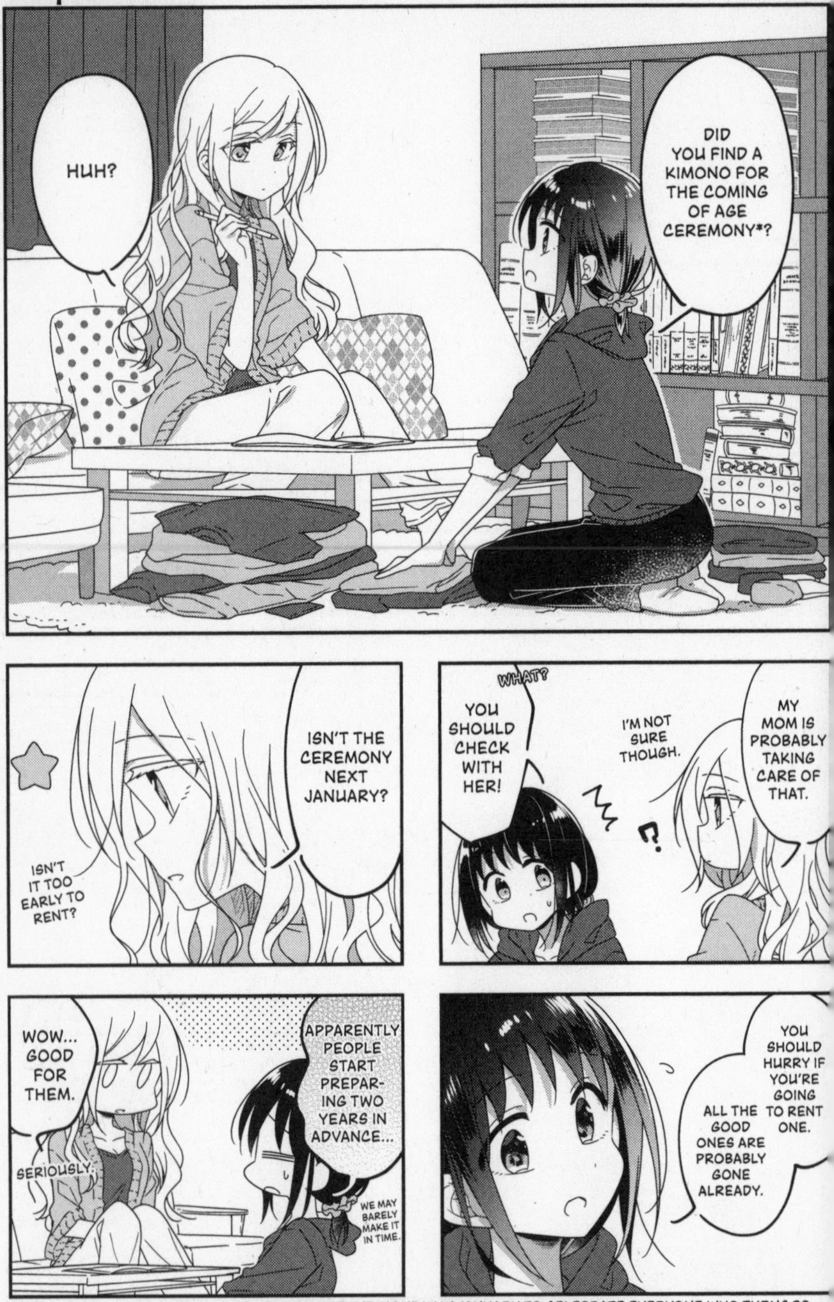
DID YOU FIND A KIMONO FOR THE COMING OF AGE CEREMONY*?
HUH?
MY MOM IS PROBABLY TAKING CARE OF THAT.
I'M NOT SURE THOUGH.
WHAT?
YOU SHOULD CHECK WITH HER!
ISN'T THE CEREMONY NEXT JANUARY?
ISN'T IT TOO EARLY TO RENT?
YOU SHOULD HURRY IF YOU'RE GOING TO RENT ONE.
ALL THE GOOD ONES ARE PROBABLY GONE ALREADY.
APPARENTLY PEOPLE START PREPARING TWO YEARS IN ADVANCE...
WE MAY BARELY MAKE IT IN TIME.
WOW... GOOD FOR THEM.
SERIOUSLY.

*THE COMING OF AGE CEREMONY IS HELD ON THE 2ND MONDAY IN JANUARY TO CELEBRATE EVERYONE WHO TURNS 20 (THE LEGAL AGE OF ADULTHOOD) BETWEEN APRIL 2ND OF THE PREVIOUS YEAR AND APRIL 1ST OF THE CURRENT YEAR.

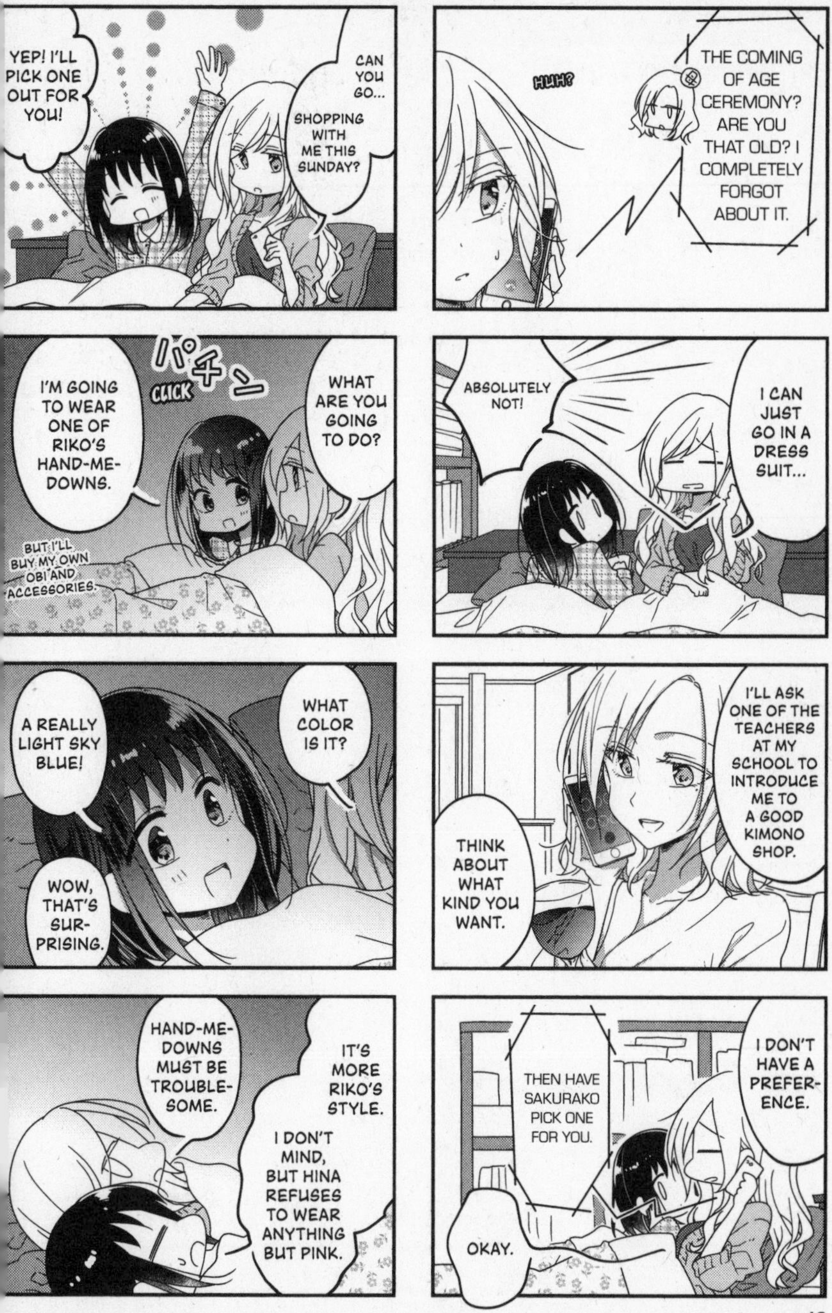
THE COMING OF AGE CEREMONY? ARE YOU THAT OLD? I COMPLETELY FORGOT ABOUT IT.
HUH?
I CAN JUST GO IN A DRESS SUIT...
ABSOLUTELY NOT!
I'LL ASK ONE OF THE TEACHERS AT MY SCHOOL TO INTRODUCE ME TO A GOOD KIMONO SHOP.
THINK ABOUT WHAT KIND YOU WANT.
I DON'T HAVE A PREFERENCE.
THEN HAVE SAKURAKO PICK ONE FOR YOU.
OKAY.
CAN YOU GO...
SHOPPING WITH ME THIS SUNDAY?
YEP! I'LL PICK ONE OUT FOR YOU!
WHAT ARE YOU GOING TO DO?
パチン
CLICK
I'M GOING TO WEAR ONE OF RIKO'S HAND-ME-DOWNS.
BUT I'LL BUY MY OWN OBI AND ACCESSORIES.
WHAT COLOR IS IT?
A REALLY LIGHT SKY BLUE!
WOW, THAT'S SURPRISING.
IT'S MORE RIKO'S STYLE.
HAND-ME-DOWNS MUST BE TROUBLESOME.
I DON'T MIND, BUT HINA REFUSES TO WEAR ANYTHING BUT PINK.

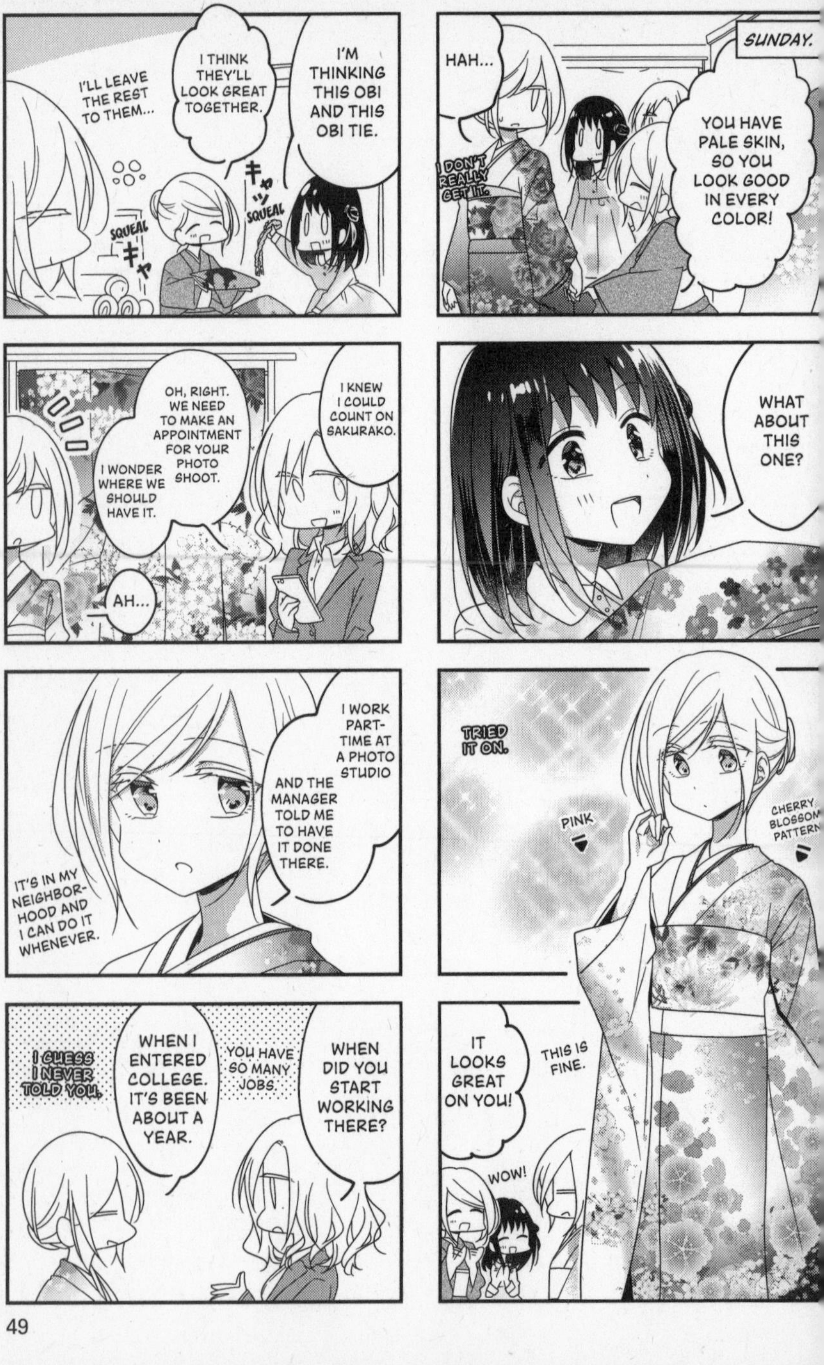
SUNDAY.
YOU HAVE PALE SKIN, SO YOU LOOK GOOD IN EVERY COLOR!
HAH...
I DON'T REALLY GET IT.
WHAT ABOUT THIS ONE?
TRIED IT ON.
CHERRY BLOSSOM PATTERN
PINK
THIS IS FINE.
IT LOOKS GREAT ON YOU!
WOW!
I'M THINKING THIS OBI AND THIS OBI TIE.
I THINK THEY'LL LOOK GREAT TOGETHER.
キャッ
SQUEAL
I'LL LEAVE THE REST TO THEM...
SQUEAL
キャ
I KNEW I COULD COUNT ON SAKURAKO.
OH, RIGHT. WE NEED TO MAKE AN APPOINTMENT FOR YOUR PHOTO SHOOT.
I WONDER WHERE WE SHOULD HAVE IT.
AH...
I WORK PART-TIME AT A PHOTO STUDIO
AND THE MANAGER TOLD ME TO HAVE IT DONE THERE.
IT'S IN MY NEIGHBORHOOD AND I CAN DO IT WHENEVER.
WHEN DID YOU START WORKING THERE?
YOU HAVE SO MANY JOBS.
WHEN I ENTERED COLLEGE. IT'S BEEN ABOUT A YEAR.
I GUESS I NEVER TOLD YOU.

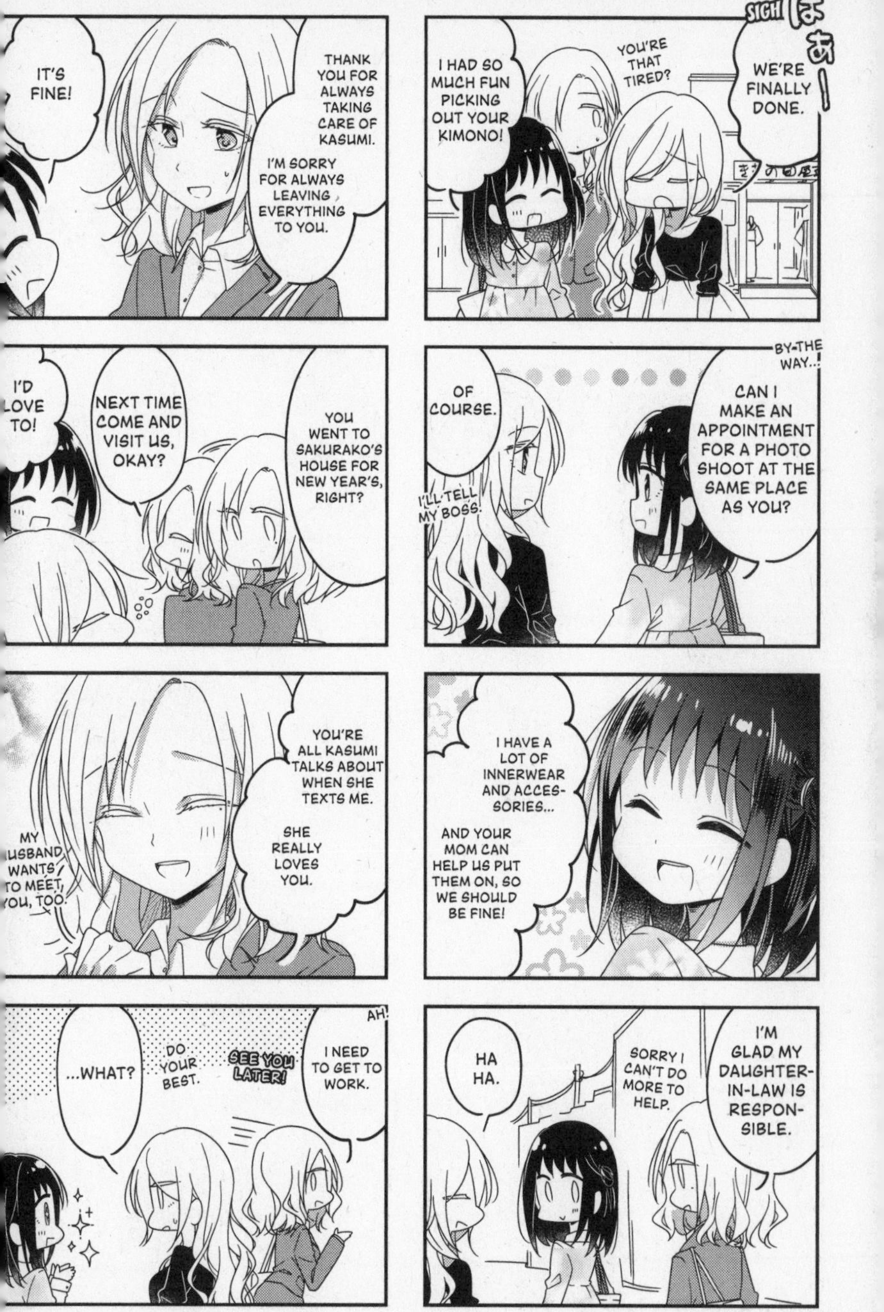
SIGH はぁー
WE'RE FINALLY DONE.
YOU'RE THAT TIRED?
I HAD SO MUCH FUN PICKING OUT YOUR KIMONO!
BY THE WAY...!
CAN I MAKE AN APPOINTMENT FOR A PHOTO SHOOT AT THE SAME PLACE AS YOU?
OF COURSE.
I'LL TELL MY BOSS.
I HAVE A LOT OF INNERWEAR AND ACCES-SORIES...
AND YOUR MOM CAN HELP US PUT THEM ON, SO WE SHOULD BE FINE!
I'M GLAD MY DAUGHTER-IN-LAW IS RESPON-SIBLE.
SORRY I CAN'T DO MORE TO HELP.
HA HA.
THANK YOU FOR ALWAYS TAKING CARE OF KASUMI.
I'M SORRY FOR ALWAYS LEAVING EVERYTHING TO YOU.
IT'S FINE!
YOU WENT TO SAKURAKO'S HOUSE FOR NEW YEAR'S, RIGHT?
NEXT TIME COME AND VISIT US, OKAY?
I'D LOVE TO!
YOU'RE ALL KASUMI TALKS ABOUT WHEN SHE TEXTS ME.
SHE REALLY LOVES YOU.
MY HUSBAND WANTS TO MEET YOU, TOO.
AH!
I NEED TO GET TO WORK.
SEE YOU LATER!
DO YOUR BEST.
...WHAT?

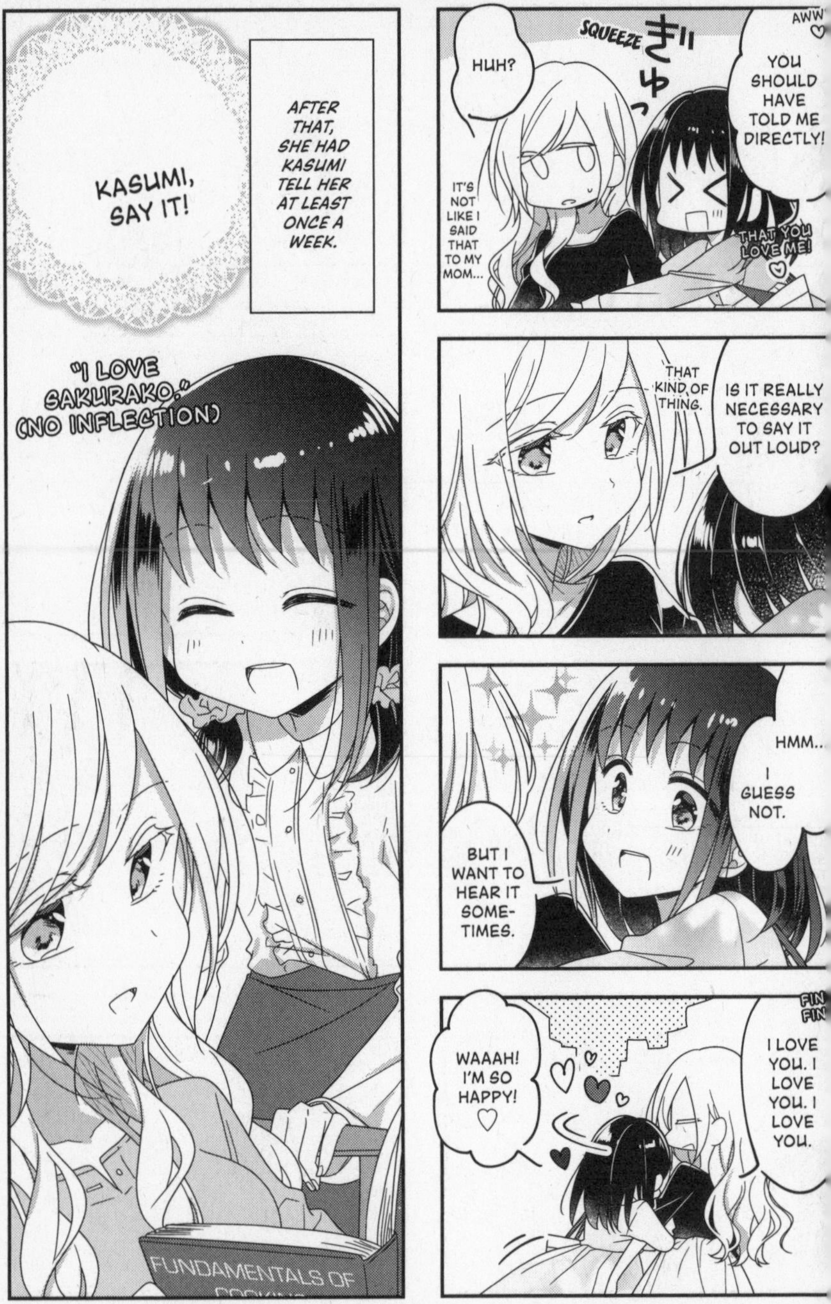
AWW ♡
YOU SHOULD HAVE TOLD ME DIRECTLY!
THAT YOU LOVE ME! ♡
SQUEEZE
ぎゅっ
HUH?
IT'S NOT LIKE I SAID THAT TO MY MOM...
IS IT REALLY NECESSARY TO SAY IT OUT LOUD?
THAT KIND OF THING.
HMM... I GUESS NOT.
BUT I WANT TO HEAR IT SOMETIMES.
FIN FIN
I LOVE YOU. I LOVE YOU. I LOVE YOU.
WAAAH! I'M SO HAPPY! ♡
AFTER THAT, SHE HAD KASUMI TELL HER AT LEAST ONCE A WEEK.
KASUMI, SAY IT!
"I LOVE SAKURAKO." (NO INFLECTION)
FUNDAMENTALS OF

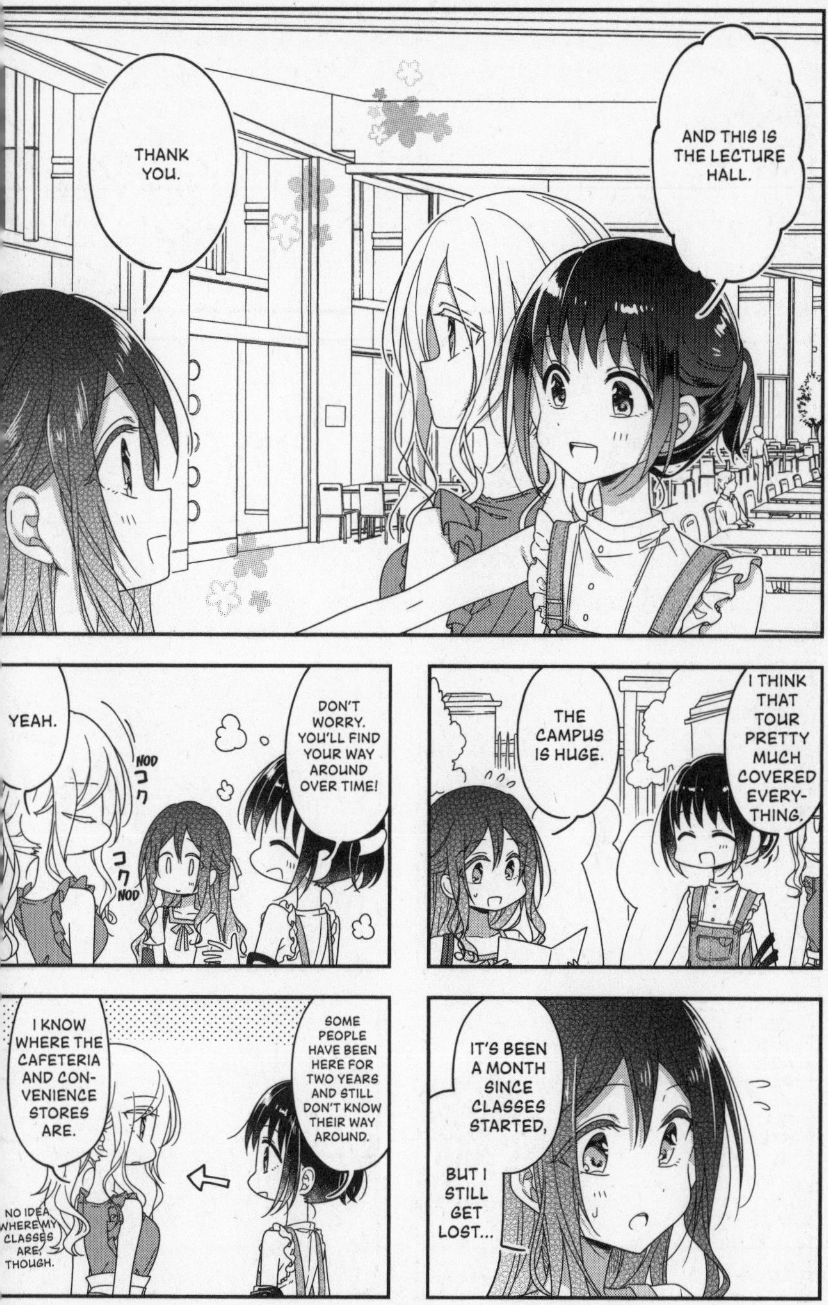
AND THIS IS THE LECTURE HALL.
THANK YOU.
I THINK THAT TOUR PRETTY MUCH COVERED EVERYTHING.
THE CAMPUS IS HUGE.
DON'T WORRY. YOU'LL FIND YOUR WAY AROUND OVER TIME!
コク NOD
コク NOD
YEAH.
IT'S BEEN A MONTH SINCE CLASSES STARTED,
BUT I STILL GET LOST...
SOME PEOPLE HAVE BEEN HERE FOR TWO YEARS AND STILL DON'T KNOW THEIR WAY AROUND.
I KNOW WHERE THE CAFETERIA AND CONVENIENCE STORES ARE.
NO IDEA WHERE MY CLASSES ARE, THOUGH.

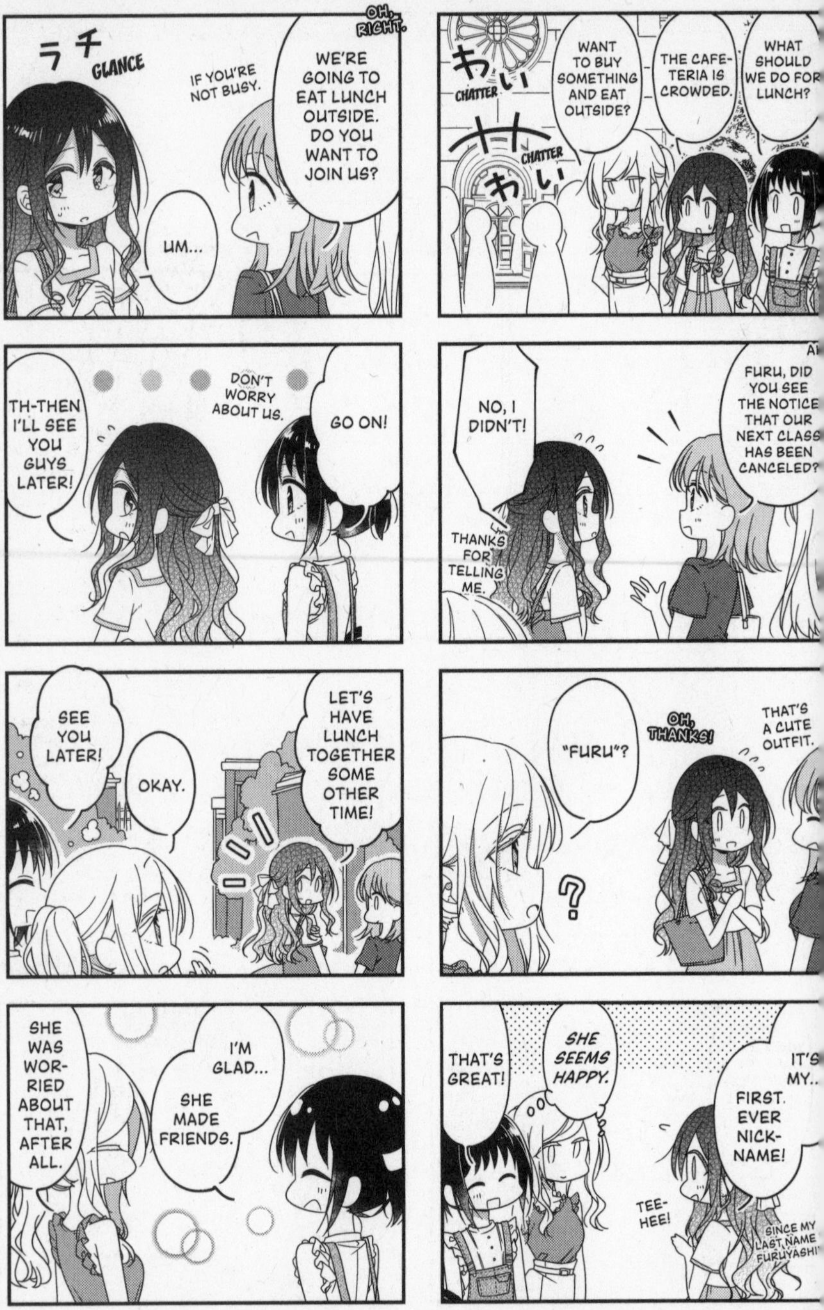
WHAT SHOULD WE DO FOR LUNCH?
THE CAFETERIA IS CROWDED.
WANT TO BUY SOMETHING AND EAT OUTSIDE?
CHATTER
CHATTER
FURU, DID YOU SEE THE NOTICE THAT OUR NEXT CLASS HAS BEEN CANCELED?
NO, I DIDN'T!
THANKS FOR TELLING ME.
THAT'S A CUTE OUTFIT.
OH, THANKS!
"FURU"?
IT'S MY..
FIRST EVER NICKNAME!
SINCE MY LAST NAME FURUYASHI
TEE-HEE!
SHE SEEMS HAPPY.
THAT'S GREAT!
OH, RIGHT.
WE'RE GOING TO EAT LUNCH OUTSIDE. DO YOU WANT TO JOIN US?
IF YOU'RE NOT BUSY.
GLANCE
UM...
GO ON!
DON'T WORRY ABOUT US.
TH-THEN I'LL SEE YOU GUYS LATER!
LET'S HAVE LUNCH TOGETHER SOME OTHER TIME!
OKAY.
SEE YOU LATER!
I'M GLAD...
SHE MADE FRIENDS.
SHE WAS WORRIED ABOUT THAT, AFTER ALL.

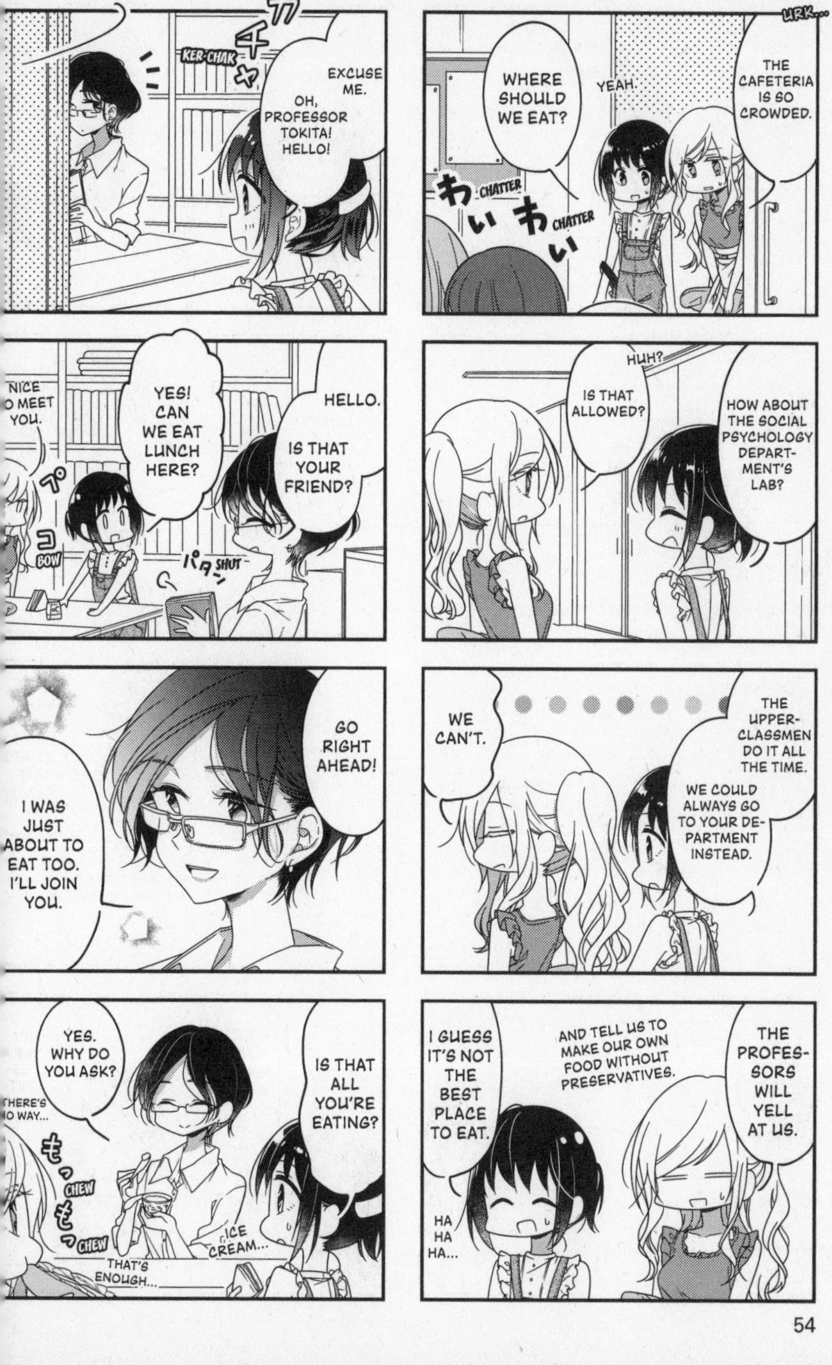
URK...
THE CAFETERIA IS SO CROWDED.
YEAH.
WHERE SHOULD WE EAT?
CHATTER
CHATTER
HOW ABOUT THE SOCIAL PSYCHOLOGY DEPART-MENT'S LAB?
HUH?
IS THAT ALLOWED?
THE UPPER-CLASSMEN DO IT ALL THE TIME.
WE COULD ALWAYS GO TO YOUR DE-PARTMENT INSTEAD.
WE CAN'T.
THE PROFES-SORS WILL YELL AT US.
AND TELL US TO MAKE OUR OWN FOOD WITHOUT PRESERVATIVES.
I GUESS IT'S NOT THE BEST PLACE TO EAT.
HA HA HA...
KER-CHAK
EXCUSE ME.
OH, PROFESSOR TOKITA! HELLO!
HELLO.
IS THAT YOUR FRIEND?
YES! CAN WE EAT LUNCH HERE?
SHUT
BOW
NICE O MEET YOU.
GO RIGHT AHEAD!
I WAS JUST ABOUT TO EAT TOO. I'LL JOIN YOU.
IS THAT ALL YOU'RE EATING?
YES. WHY DO YOU ASK?
THERE'S O WAY...
CHEW
CHEW
ICE CREAM...
THAT'S ENOUGH...

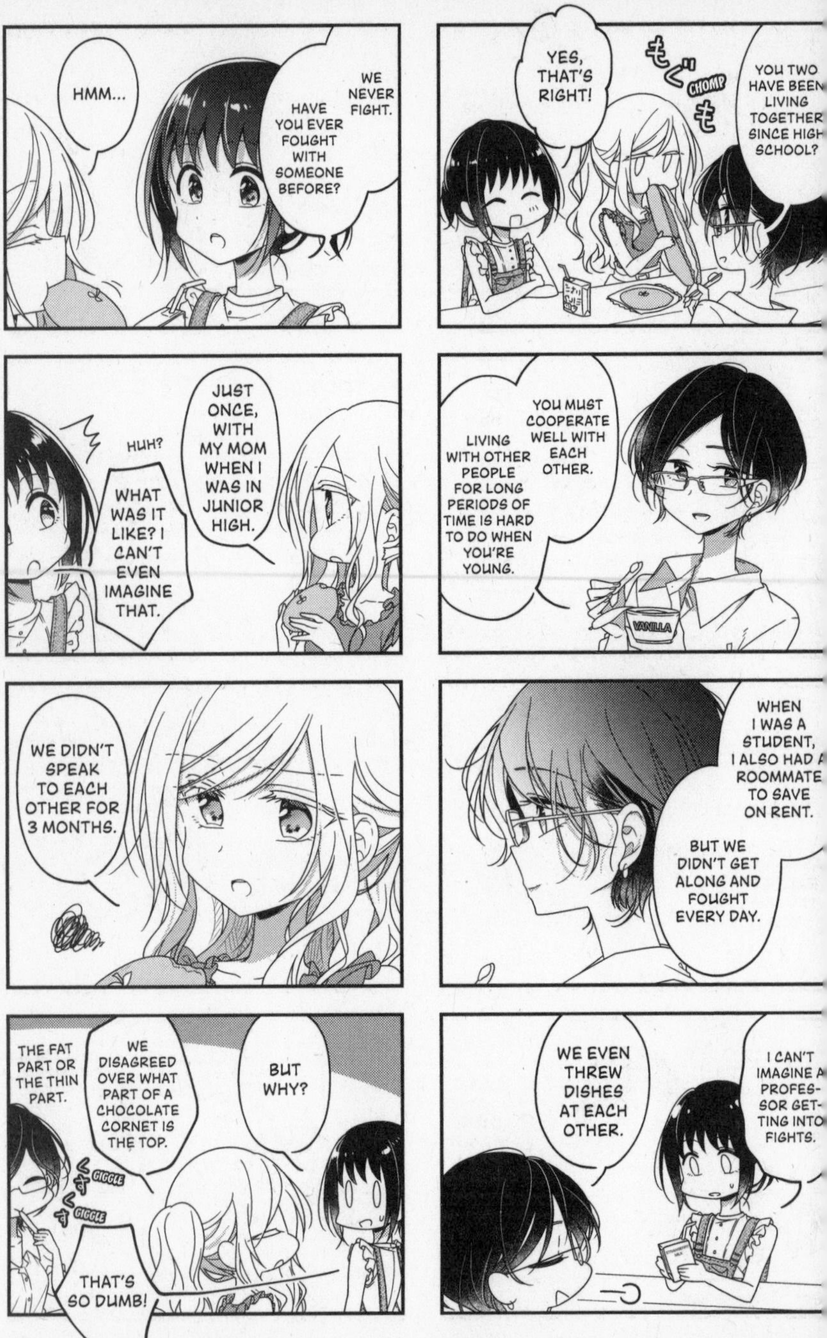
YOU TWO HAVE BEEN LIVING TOGETHER SINCE HIGH SCHOOL?
もぐ CHOMP も
YES, THAT'S RIGHT!
YOU MUST COOPERATE WELL WITH EACH OTHER.
LIVING WITH OTHER PEOPLE FOR LONG PERIODS OF TIME IS HARD TO DO WHEN YOU'RE YOUNG.
VANILLA
WHEN I WAS A STUDENT, I ALSO HAD A ROOMMATE TO SAVE ON RENT.
BUT WE DIDN'T GET ALONG AND FOUGHT EVERY DAY.
I CAN'T IMAGINE A PROFES-SOR GET-TING INTO FIGHTS.
WE EVEN THREW DISHES AT EACH OTHER.
WE NEVER FIGHT.
HAVE YOU EVER FOUGHT WITH SOMEONE BEFORE?
HMM...
JUST ONCE, WITH MY MOM WHEN I WAS IN JUNIOR HIGH.
HUH?
WHAT WAS IT LIKE? I CAN'T EVEN IMAGINE THAT.
WE DIDN'T SPEAK TO EACH OTHER FOR 3 MONTHS.
BUT WHY?
WE DISAGREED OVER WHAT PART OF A CHOCOLATE CORNET IS THE TOP.
THE FAT PART OR THE THIN PART.
くす GIGGLE くす GIGGLE
THAT'S SO DUMB!

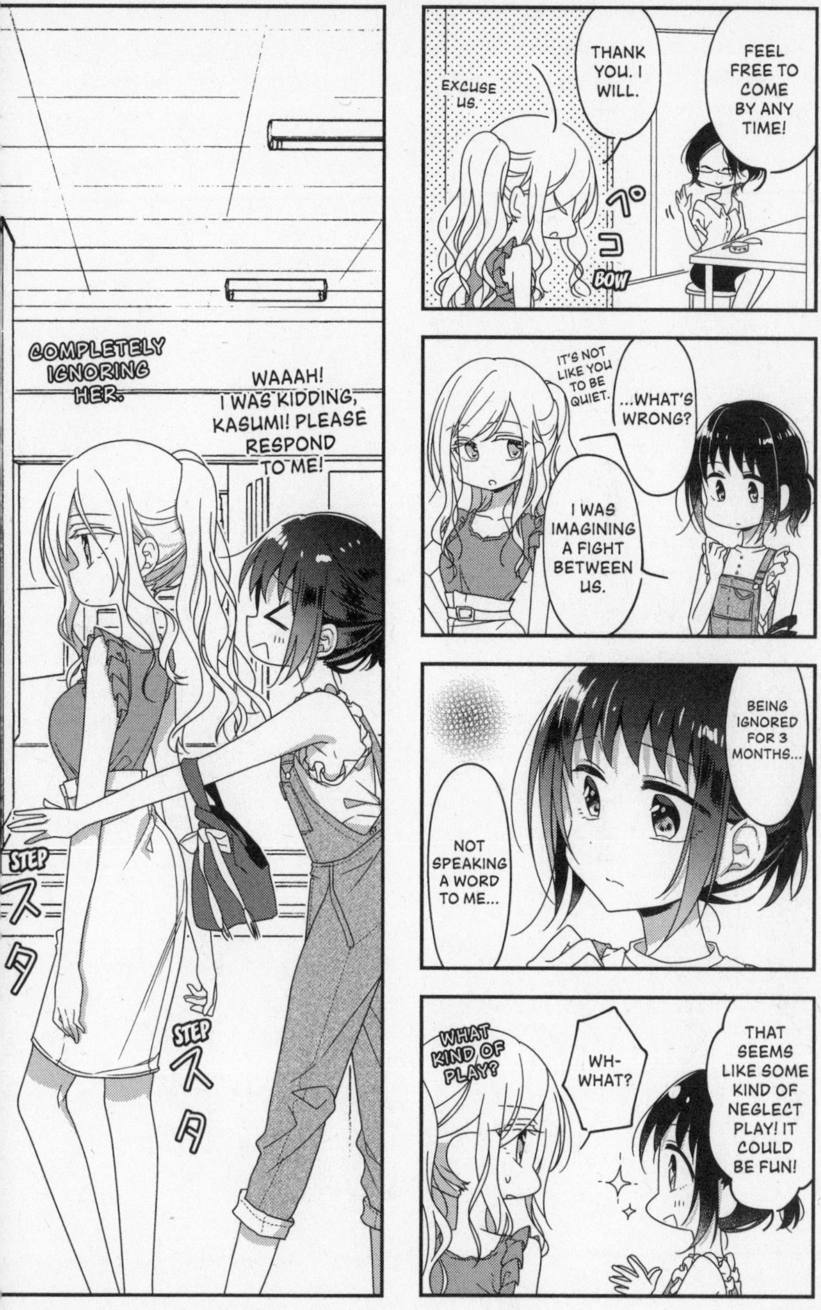
FEEL FREE TO COME BY ANY TIME!
THANK YOU. I WILL.
EXCUSE US.
ペコ
BOW
...WHAT'S WRONG?
IT'S NOT LIKE YOU TO BE QUIET.
I WAS IMAGINING A FIGHT BETWEEN US.
BEING IGNORED FOR 3 MONTHS...
NOT SPEAKING A WORD TO ME...
THAT SEEMS LIKE SOME KIND OF NEGLECT PLAY! IT COULD BE FUN!
WH-WHAT?
WHAT KIND OF PLAY?
WAAAH! I WAS KIDDING, KASUMI! PLEASE RESPOND TO ME!
COMPLETELY IGNORING HER.
STEP
スタ
STEP
スタ

Illustration gallery of Yukiko

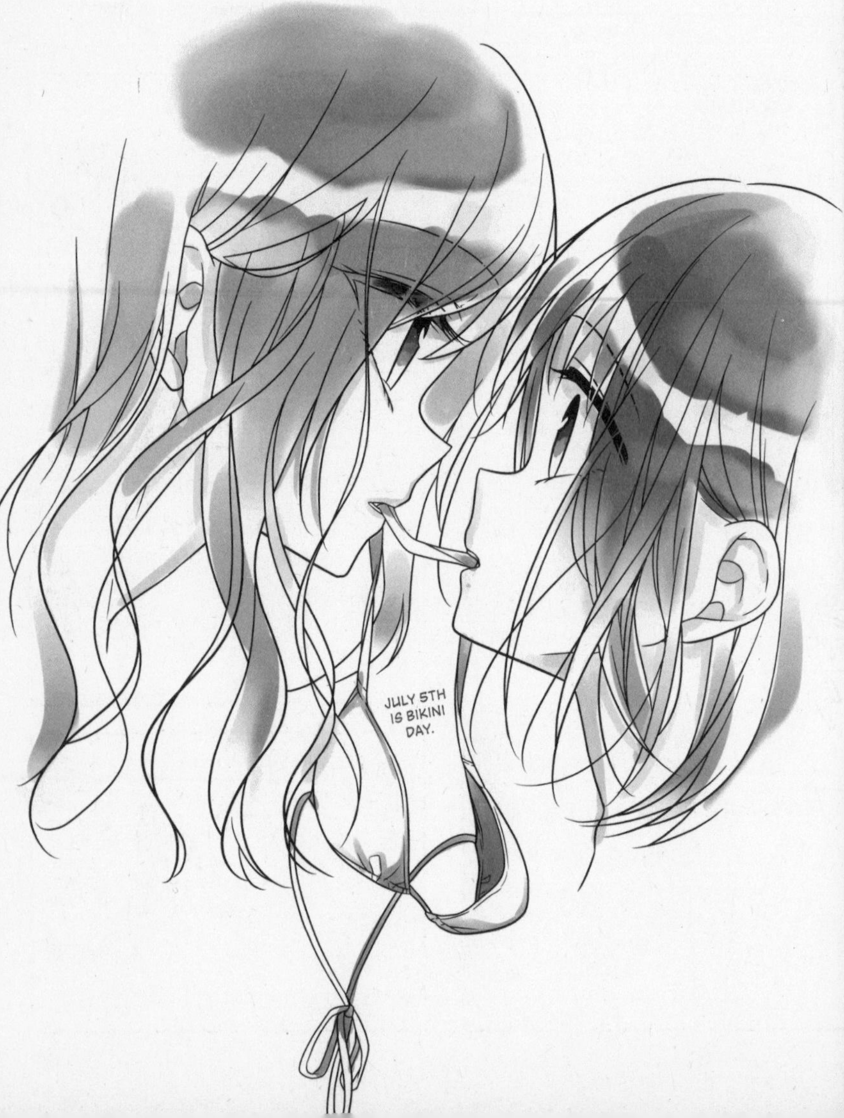
JULY 5TH IS BIKINI DAY.

Futaribeya
A ROOM FOR TWO

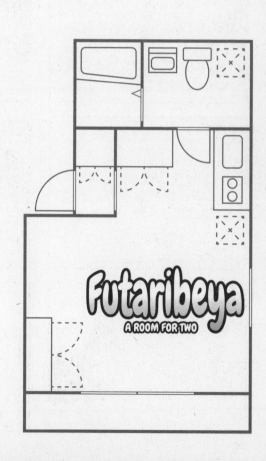

Chapter 51.5

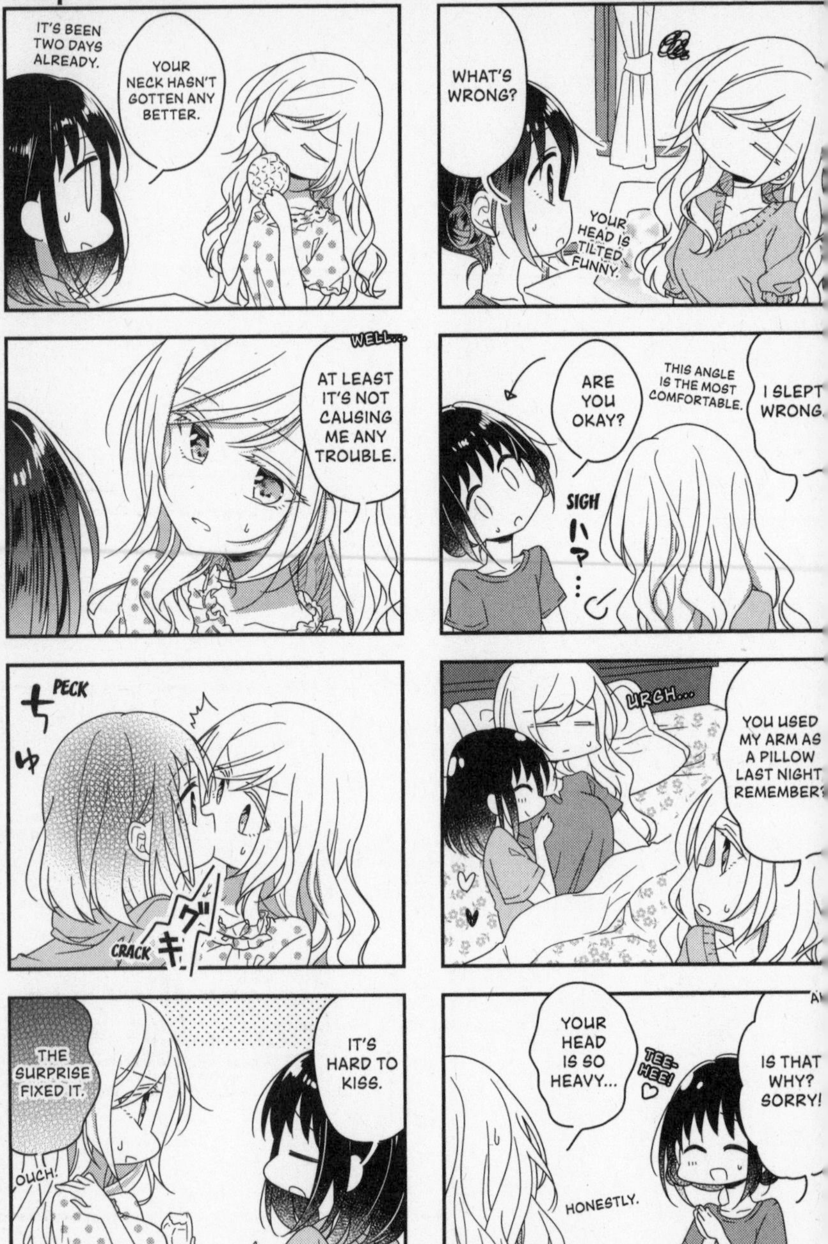
WHAT'S WRONG?
YOUR HEAD IS TILTED FUNNY.
I SLEPT WRONG.
THIS ANGLE IS THE MOST COMFORTABLE.
ARE YOU OKAY?
SIGH
ハァ…
URGH...
YOU USED MY ARM AS A PILLOW LAST NIGHT, REMEMBER?
IS THAT WHY? SORRY!
TEE-HEE!
YOUR HEAD IS SO HEAVY...
HONESTLY.
IT'S BEEN TWO DAYS ALREADY.
YOUR NECK HASN'T GOTTEN ANY BETTER.
WELL...
AT LEAST IT'S NOT CAUSING ME ANY TROUBLE.
PECK
ちゅ
グキ
CRACK
IT'S HARD TO KISS.
THE SURPRISE FIXED IT.
OUCH!

Futaribeya
A ROOM FOR TWO

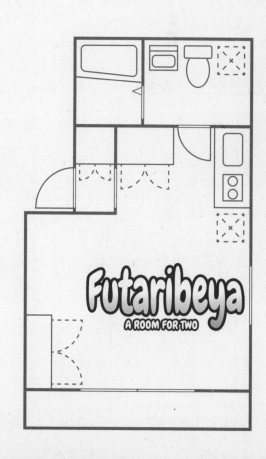

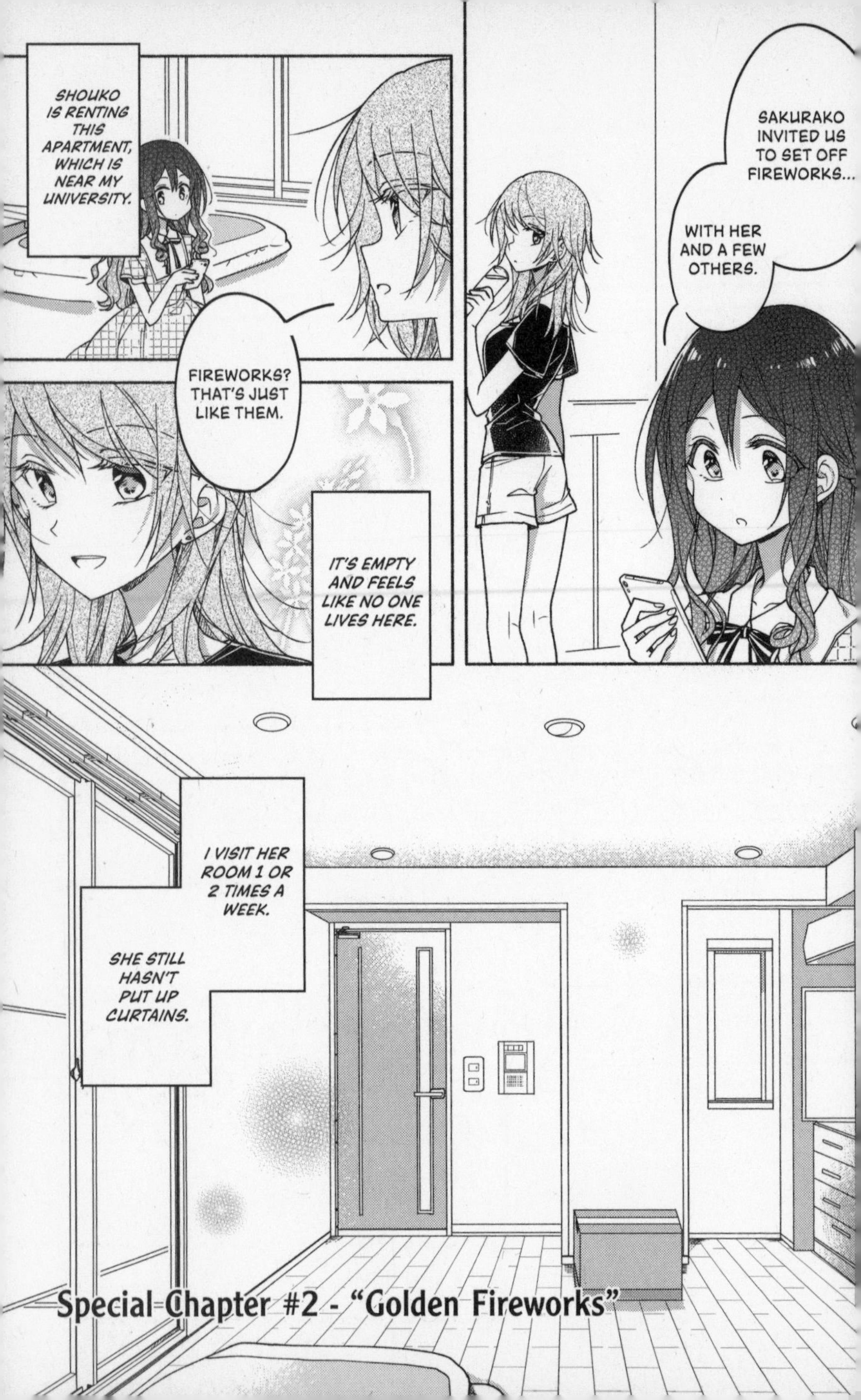
SAKURAKO INVITED US TO SET OFF FIREWORKS...
WITH HER AND A FEW OTHERS.
SHOUKO IS RENTING THIS APARTMENT, WHICH IS NEAR MY UNIVERSITY.
FIREWORKS? THAT'S JUST LIKE THEM.
IT'S EMPTY AND FEELS LIKE NO ONE LIVES HERE.
I VISIT HER ROOM 1 OR 2 TIMES A WEEK.
SHE STILL HASN'T PUT UP CURTAINS.
Special Chapter #2 - "Golden Fireworks"

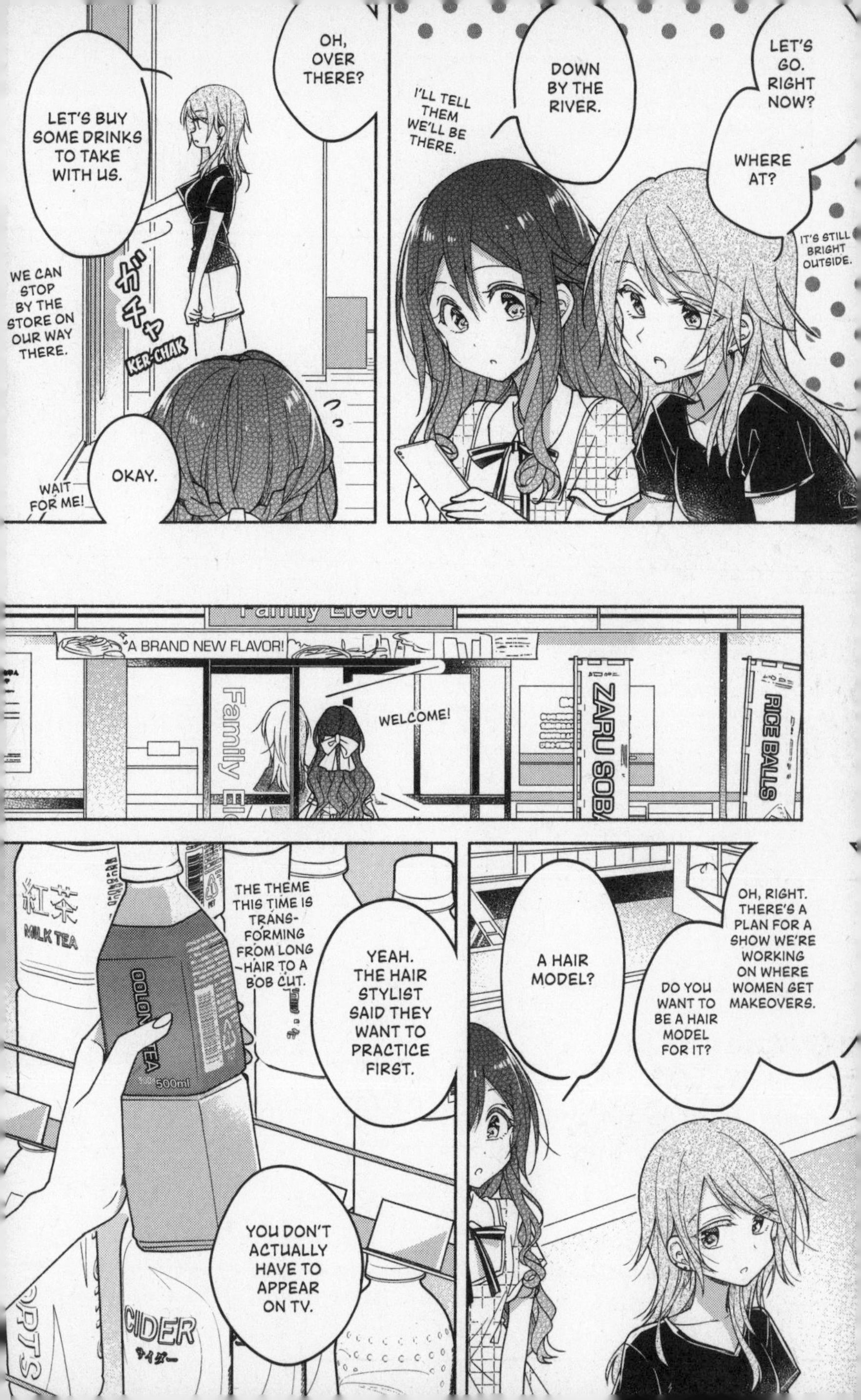
LET'S GO. RIGHT NOW?
WHERE AT?
IT'S STILL BRIGHT OUTSIDE.
DOWN BY THE RIVER.
I'LL TELL THEM WE'LL BE THERE.
OH, OVER THERE?
LET'S BUY SOME DRINKS TO TAKE WITH US.
WE CAN STOP BY THE STORE ON OUR WAY THERE.
ガチャ
KER-CHAK
OKAY.
WAIT FOR ME!
Family Eleven
A BRAND NEW FLAVOR!
RICE BALLS
ZARU SOBA
WELCOME!
OH, RIGHT. THERE'S A PLAN FOR A SHOW WE'RE WORKING ON WHERE WOMEN GET MAKEOVERS.
DO YOU WANT TO BE A HAIR MODEL FOR IT?
A HAIR MODEL?
YEAH. THE HAIR STYLIST SAID THEY WANT TO PRACTICE FIRST.
THE THEME THIS TIME IS TRANS-FORMING FROM LONG HAIR TO A BOB CUT.
YOU DON'T ACTUALLY HAVE TO APPEAR ON TV.
紅茶
MILK TEA
500ml
CIDER

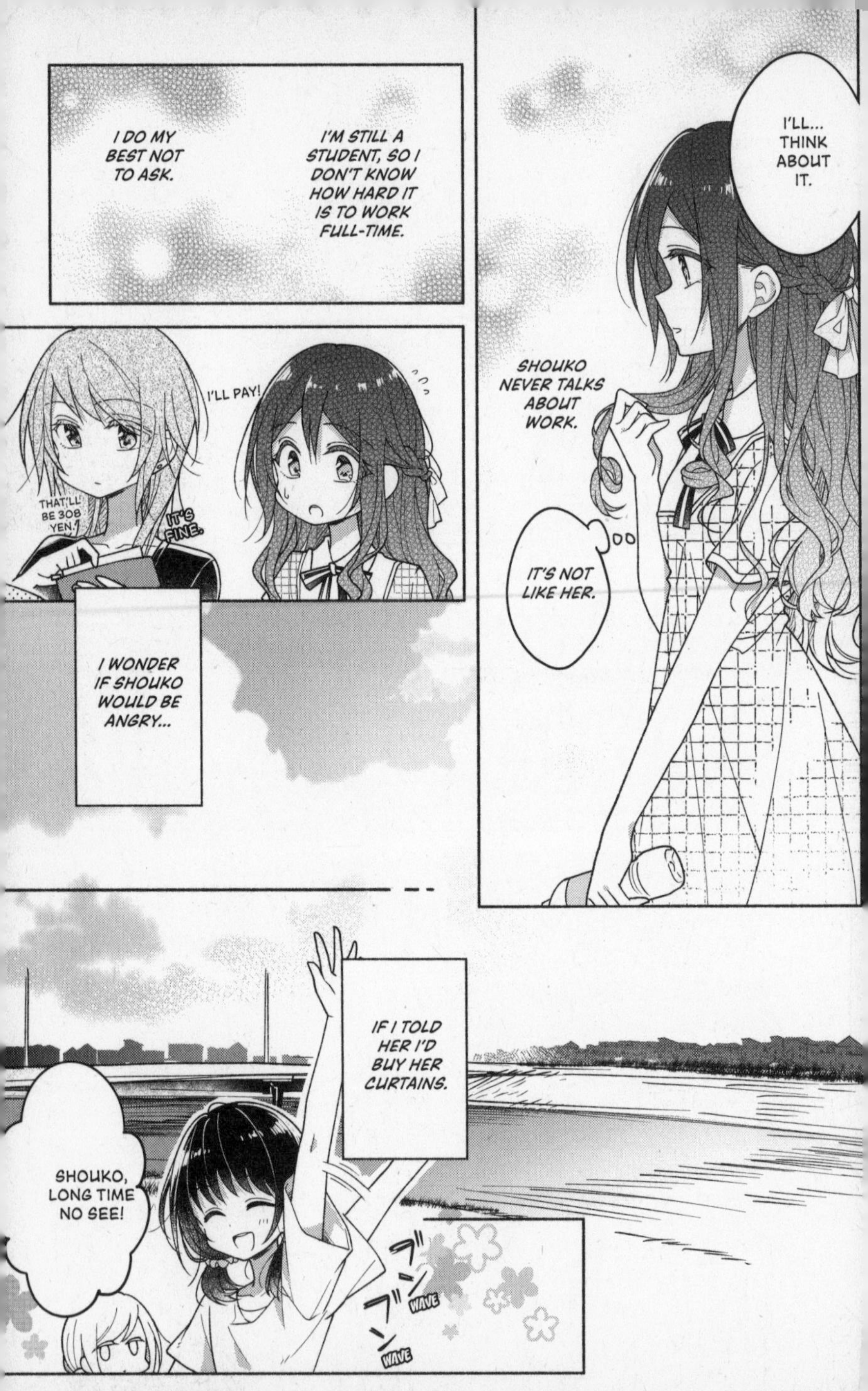
I'LL... THINK ABOUT IT.
SHOUKO NEVER TALKS ABOUT WORK.
IT'S NOT LIKE HER.
I'M STILL A STUDENT, SO I DON'T KNOW HOW HARD IT IS TO WORK FULL-TIME.
I DO MY BEST NOT TO ASK.
I'LL PAY!
IT'S FINE.
THAT'LL BE 308 YEN.
I WONDER IF SHOUKO WOULD BE ANGRY...
IF I TOLD HER I'D BUY HER CURTAINS.
WAVE
WAVE
SHOUKO, LONG TIME NO SEE!

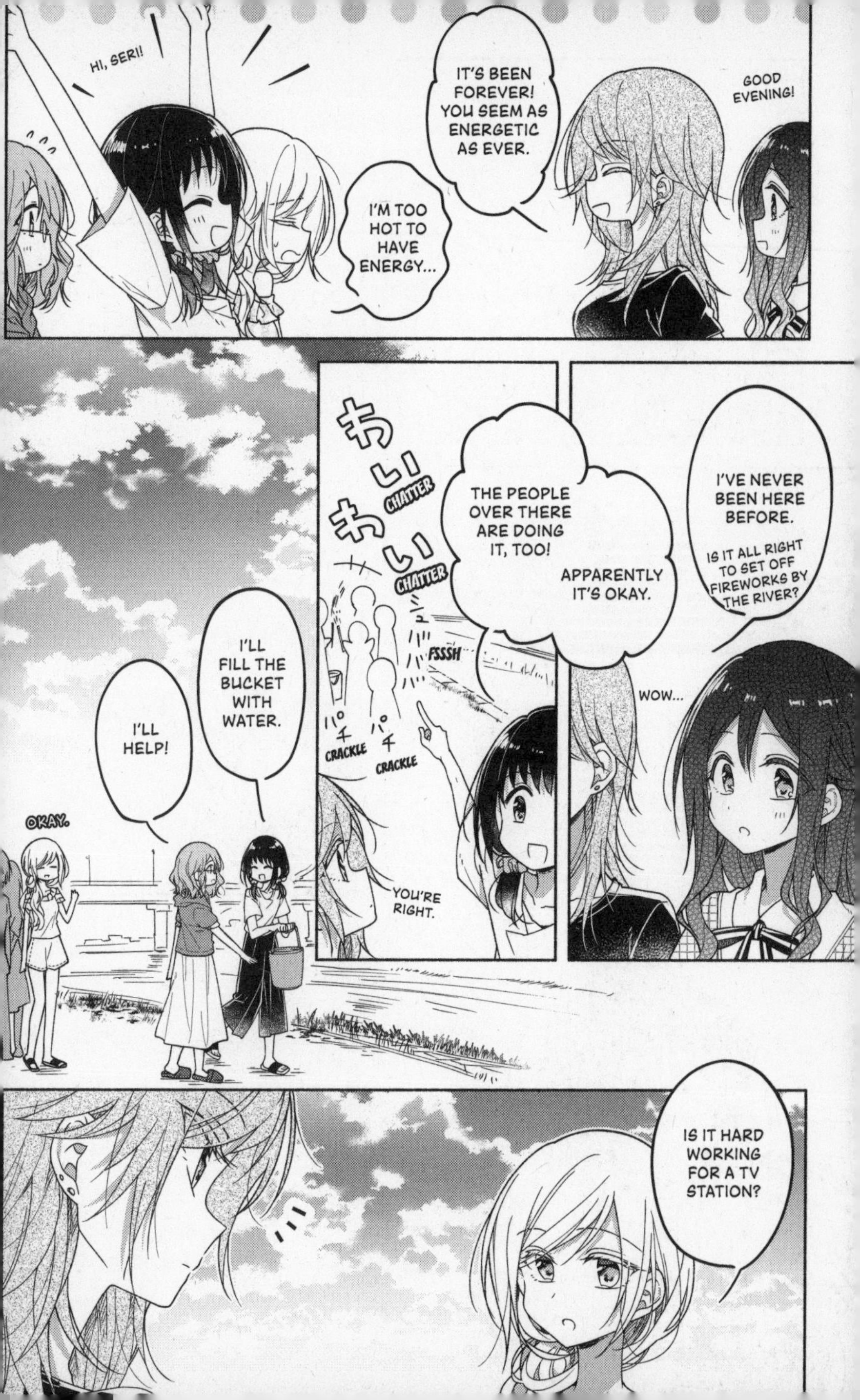
GOOD EVENING!
IT'S BEEN FOREVER! YOU SEEM AS ENERGETIC AS EVER.
I'M TOO HOT TO HAVE ENERGY...
HI, SERI!
I'VE NEVER BEEN HERE BEFORE.
IS IT ALL RIGHT TO SET OFF FIREWORKS BY THE RIVER?
WOW...
APPARENTLY IT'S OKAY.
THE PEOPLE OVER THERE ARE DOING IT, TOO!
わい CHATTER
わい CHATTER
FSSSH
パチ CRACKLE
パチ CRACKLE
YOU'RE RIGHT.
I'LL FILL THE BUCKET WITH WATER.
I'LL HELP!
OKAY.
IS IT HARD WORKING FOR A TV STATION?

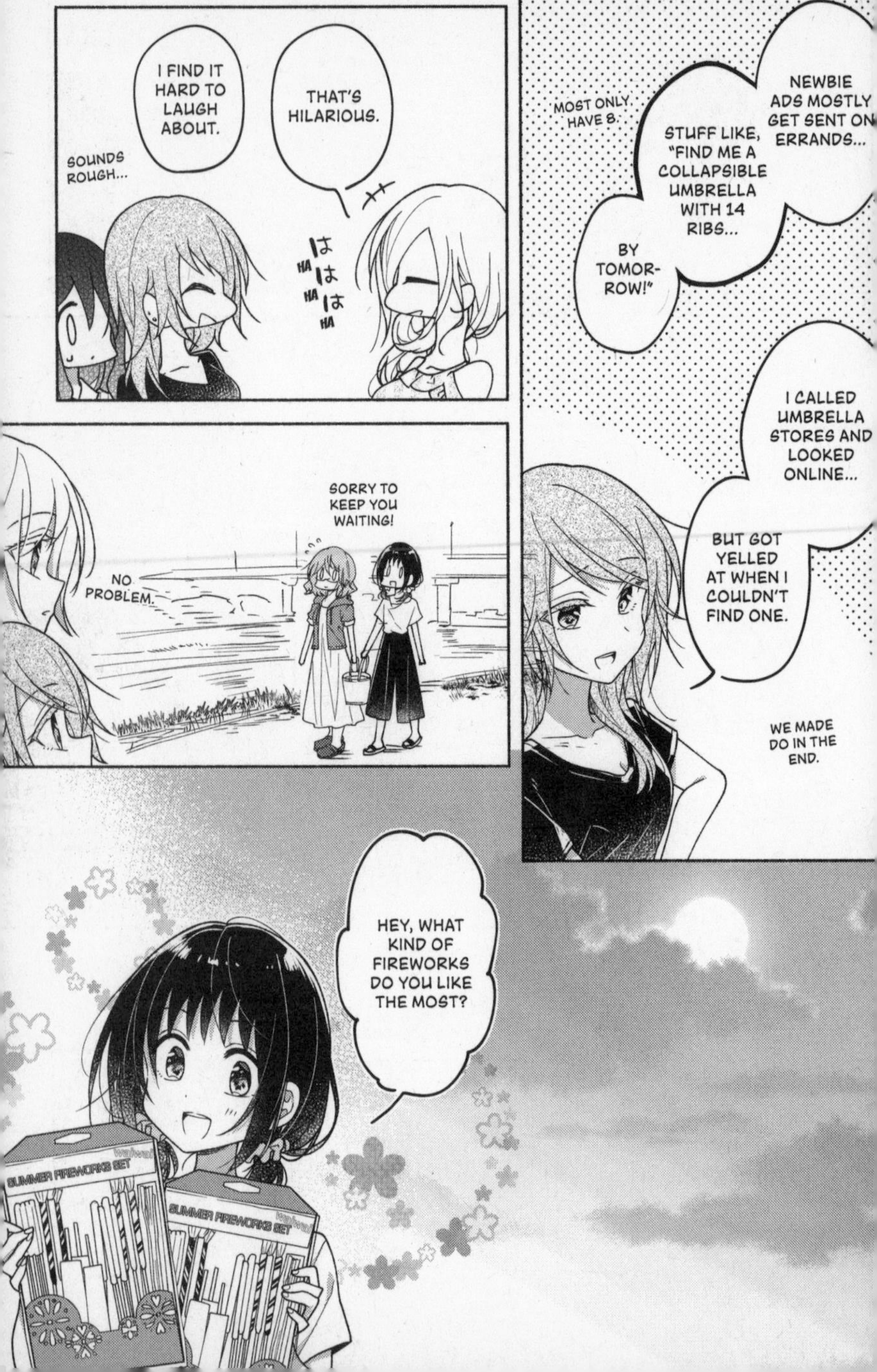
NEWBIE ADS MOSTLY GET SENT ON ERRANDS...
STUFF LIKE, "FIND ME A COLLAPSIBLE UMBRELLA WITH 14 RIBS...
BY TOMOR-ROW!"
MOST ONLY HAVE 8.
I CALLED UMBRELLA STORES AND LOOKED ONLINE...
BUT GOT YELLED AT WHEN I COULDN'T FIND ONE.
WE MADE DO IN THE END.
THAT'S HILARIOUS.
ははは HA HA HA
I FIND IT HARD TO LAUGH ABOUT.
SOUNDS ROUGH...
SORRY TO KEEP YOU WAITING!
NO PROBLEM.
HEY, WHAT KIND OF FIREWORKS DO YOU LIKE THE MOST?
SUMMER FIREWORKS SET
SUMMER FIREWORKS SET

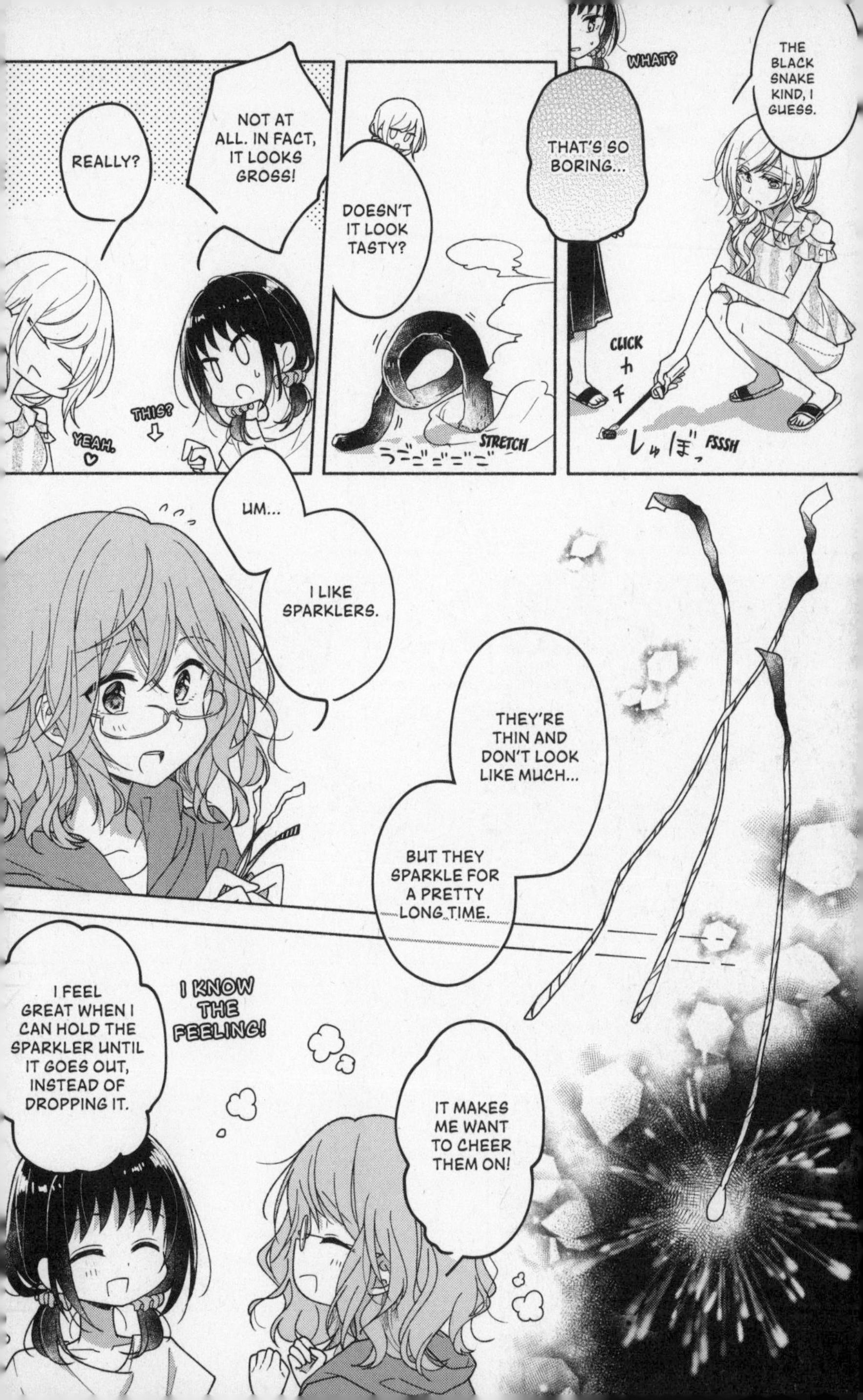
THE BLACK SNAKE KIND, I GUESS.
WHAT?
THAT'S SO BORING...
CLICK
カチ
しゅぼっ
FSSSH
DOESN'T IT LOOK TASTY?
STRETCH
うごごごご
NOT AT ALL. IN FACT, IT LOOKS GROSS!
REALLY?
THIS?
YEAH. ♥
UM...
I LIKE SPARKLERS.
THEY'RE THIN AND DON'T LOOK LIKE MUCH...
BUT THEY SPARKLE FOR A PRETTY LONG TIME.
I FEEL GREAT WHEN I CAN HOLD THE SPARKLER UNTIL IT GOES OUT, INSTEAD OF DROPPING IT.
I KNOW THE FEELING!
IT MAKES ME WANT TO CHEER THEM ON!

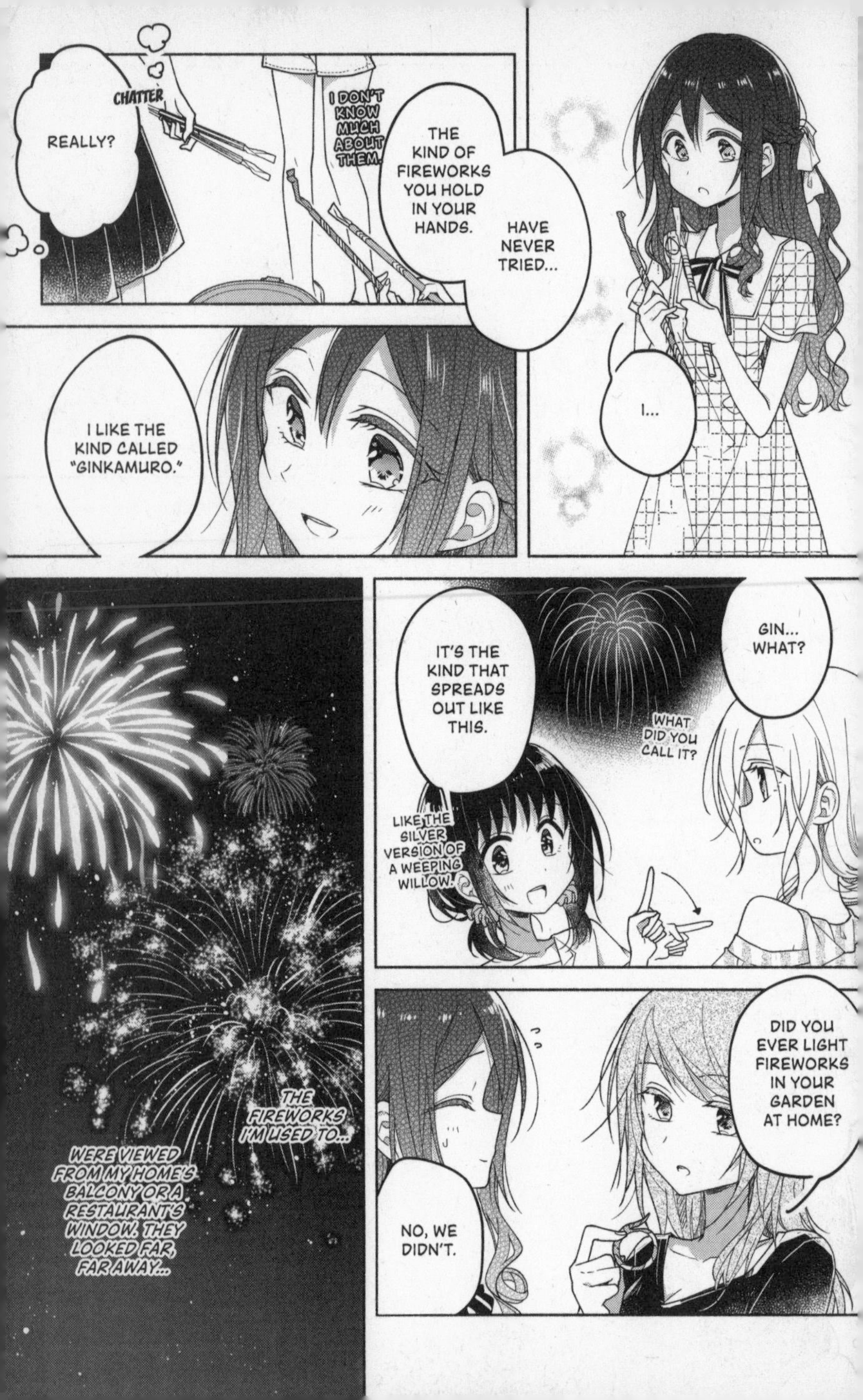
I...
HAVE NEVER TRIED...
THE KIND OF FIREWORKS YOU HOLD IN YOUR HANDS.
I DON'T KNOW MUCH ABOUT THEM.
CHATTER
REALLY?
I LIKE THE KIND CALLED "GINKAMURO."
GIN... WHAT?
WHAT DID YOU CALL IT?
IT'S THE KIND THAT SPREADS OUT LIKE THIS.
LIKE THE SILVER VERSION OF A WEEPING WILLOW.
DID YOU EVER LIGHT FIREWORKS IN YOUR GARDEN AT HOME?
NO, WE DIDN'T.
THE FIREWORKS I'M USED TO...
WERE VIEWED FROM MY HOME'S BALCONY OR A RESTAURANT'S WINDOW. THEY LOOKED FAR, FAR AWAY...

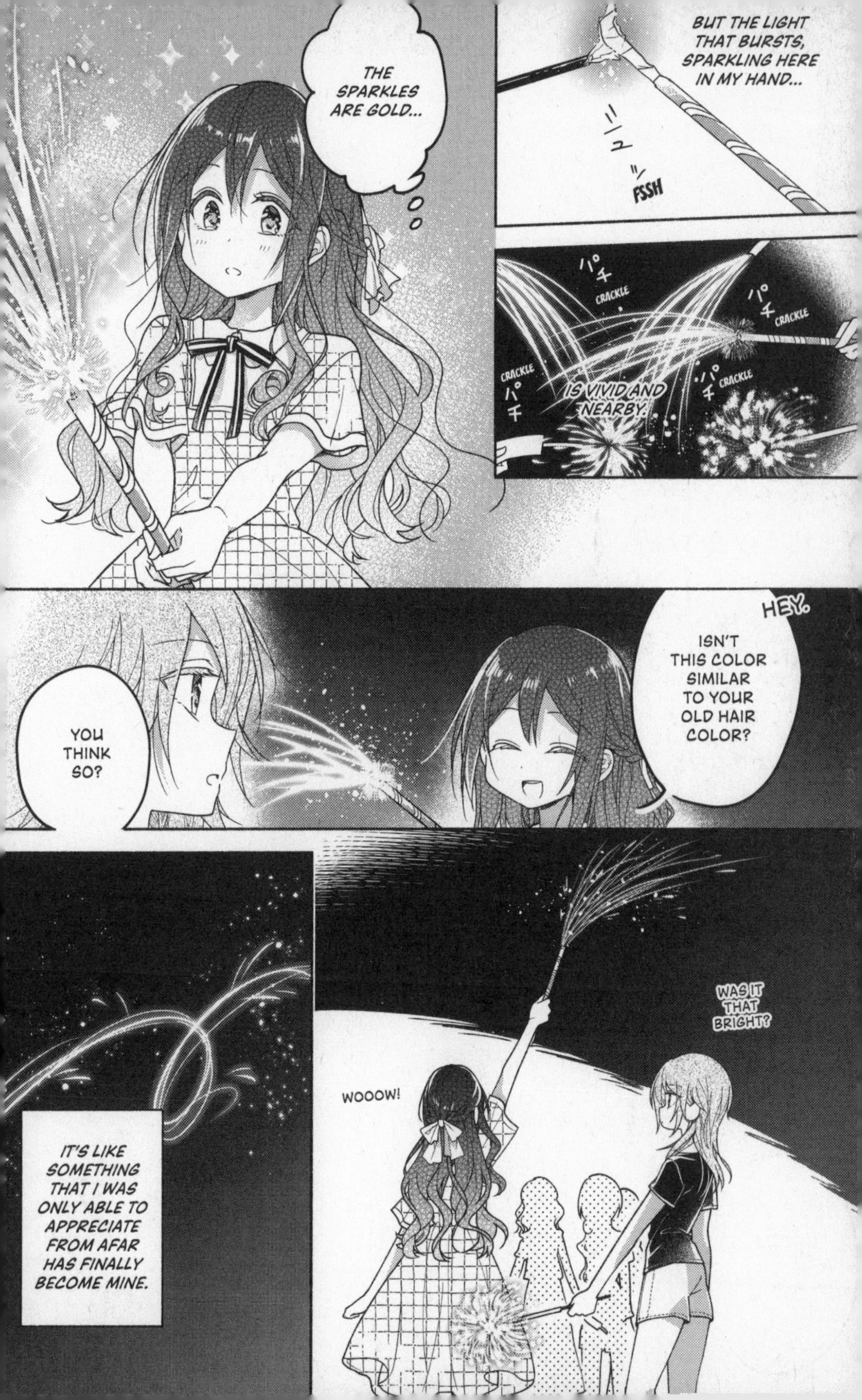
BUT THE LIGHT THAT BURSTS, SPARKLING HERE IN MY HAND...
シュ
FSSH
パチ
CRACKLE
パチ
CRACKLE
CRACKLE
パチ
パチ
CRACKLE
IS VIVID AND NEARBY.
THE SPARKLES ARE GOLD...
HEY.
ISN'T THIS COLOR SIMILAR TO YOUR OLD HAIR COLOR?
YOU THINK SO?
WAS IT THAT BRIGHT?
WOOOW!
IT'S LIKE SOMETHING THAT I WAS ONLY ABLE TO APPRECIATE FROM AFAR HAS FINALLY BECOME MINE.

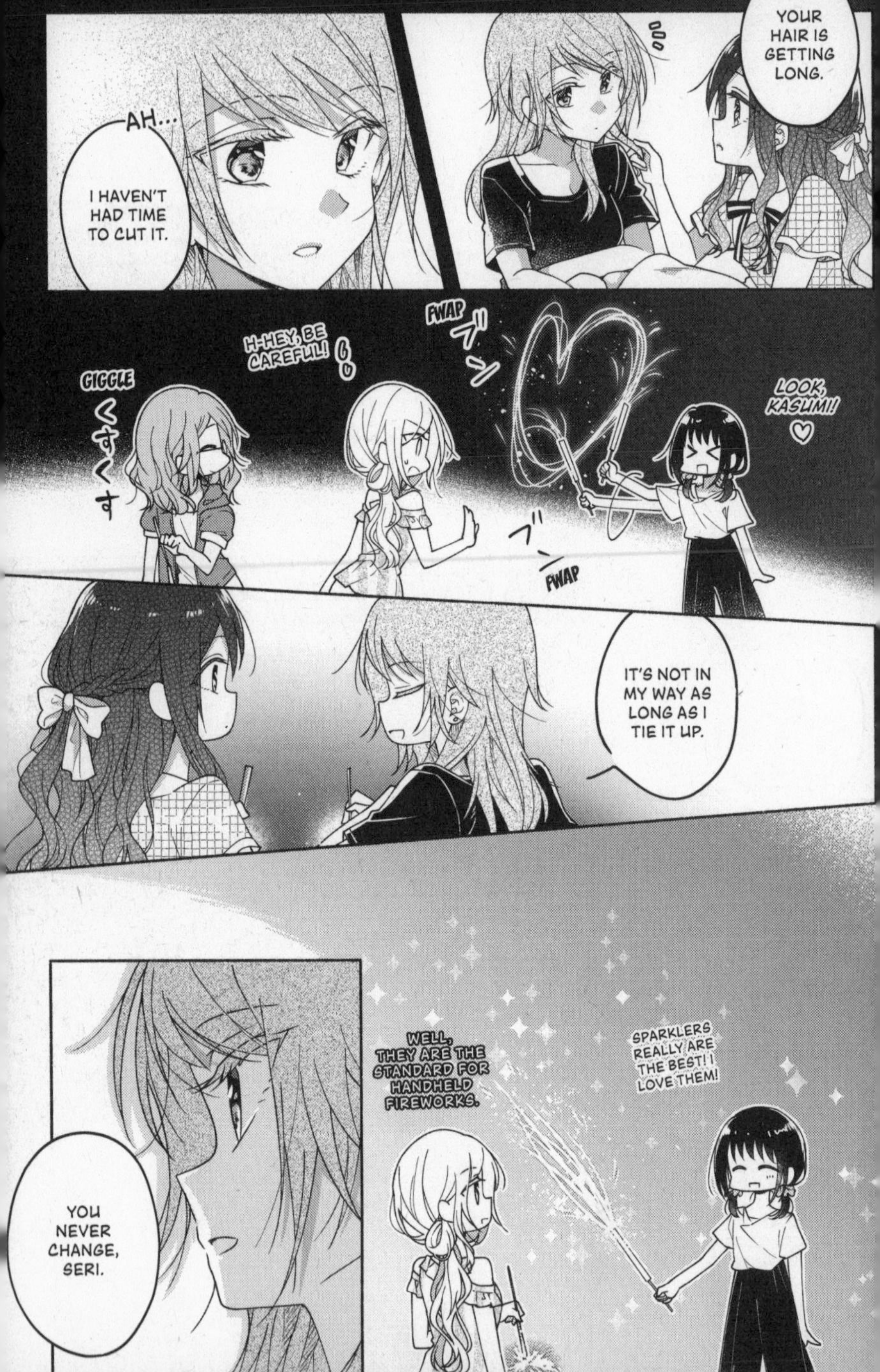
YOUR HAIR IS GETTING LONG.
AH...
I HAVEN'T HAD TIME TO CUT IT.
LOOK, KASUMI! ♥
FWAP
ブン
H-HEY, BE CAREFUL!
GIGGLE
くすくす
ブン
FWAP
IT'S NOT IN MY WAY AS LONG AS I TIE IT UP.
SPARKLERS REALLY ARE THE BEST! I LOVE THEM!
WELL, THEY ARE THE STANDARD FOR HANDHELD FIREWORKS.
YOU NEVER CHANGE, SERI.

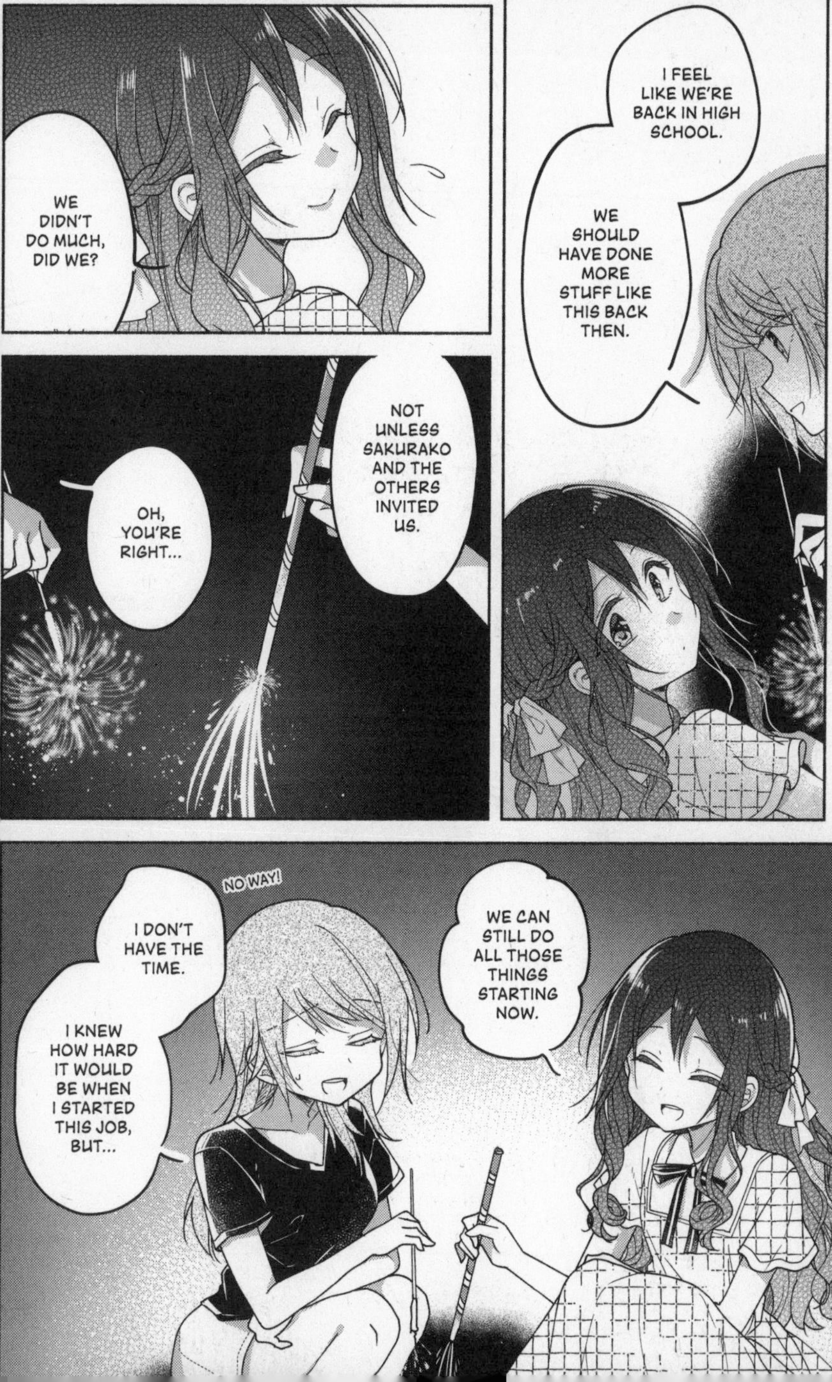
I FEEL LIKE WE'RE BACK IN HIGH SCHOOL.
WE SHOULD HAVE DONE MORE STUFF LIKE THIS BACK THEN.
WE DIDN'T DO MUCH, DID WE?
NOT UNLESS SAKURAKO AND THE OTHERS INVITED US.
OH, YOU'RE RIGHT...
WE CAN STILL DO ALL THOSE THINGS STARTING NOW.
NO WAY!
I DON'T HAVE THE TIME.
I KNEW HOW HARD IT WOULD BE WHEN I STARTED THIS JOB, BUT...

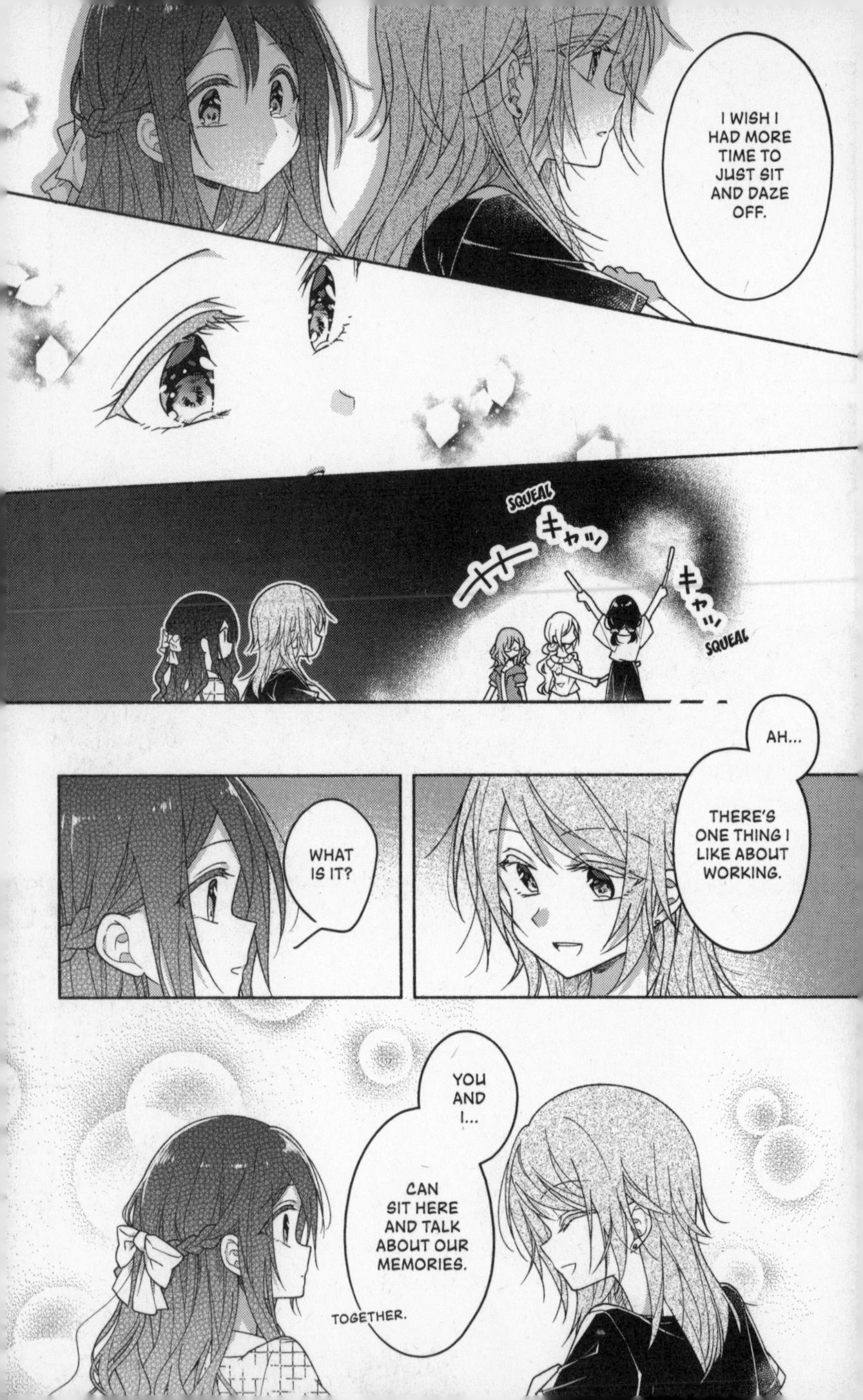
I WISH I HAD MORE TIME TO JUST SIT AND DAZE OFF.
キャッ
SQUEAL
SQUEAL
キャッ
キャー
AH...
THERE'S ONE THING I LIKE ABOUT WORKING.
WHAT IS IT?
YOU AND I...
CAN SIT HERE AND TALK ABOUT OUR MEMORIES.
TOGETHER.

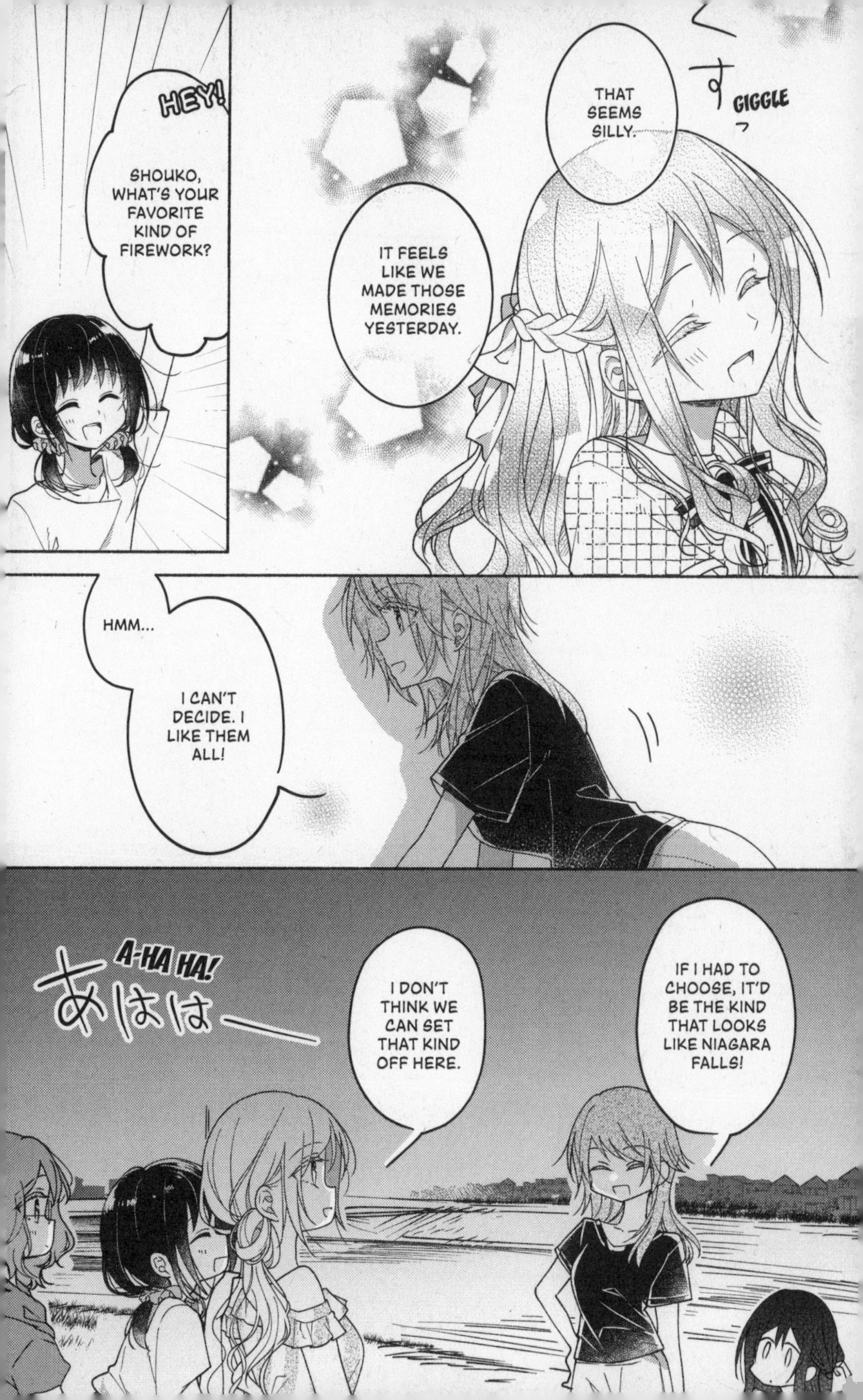
くすっ
GIGGLE
THAT SEEMS SILLY.
IT FEELS LIKE WE MADE THOSE MEMORIES YESTERDAY.
HEY!
SHOUKO, WHAT'S YOUR FAVORITE KIND OF FIREWORK?
HMM...
I CAN'T DECIDE. I LIKE THEM ALL!
IF I HAD TO CHOOSE, IT'D BE THE KIND THAT LOOKS LIKE NIAGARA FALLS!
I DON'T THINK WE CAN SET THAT KIND OFF HERE.
あはは—
A-HA HA!

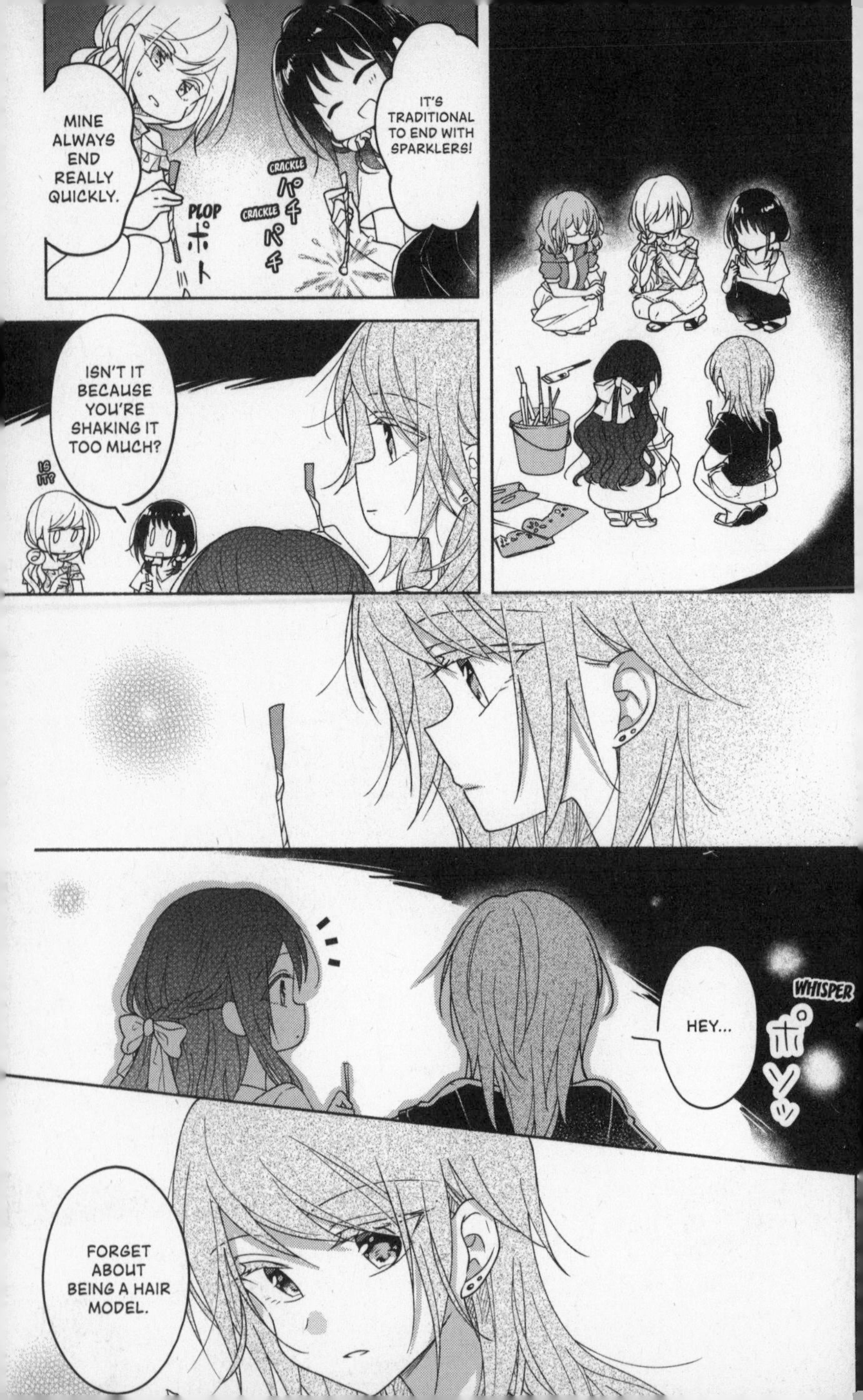
IT'S TRADITIONAL TO END WITH SPARKLERS!
CRACKLE パチ
CRACKLE パチ
MINE ALWAYS END REALLY QUICKLY.
PLOP ポト
ISN'T IT BECAUSE YOU'RE SHAKING IT TOO MUCH?
IS IT?
WHISPER ポッ
HEY...
FORGET ABOUT BEING A HAIR MODEL.

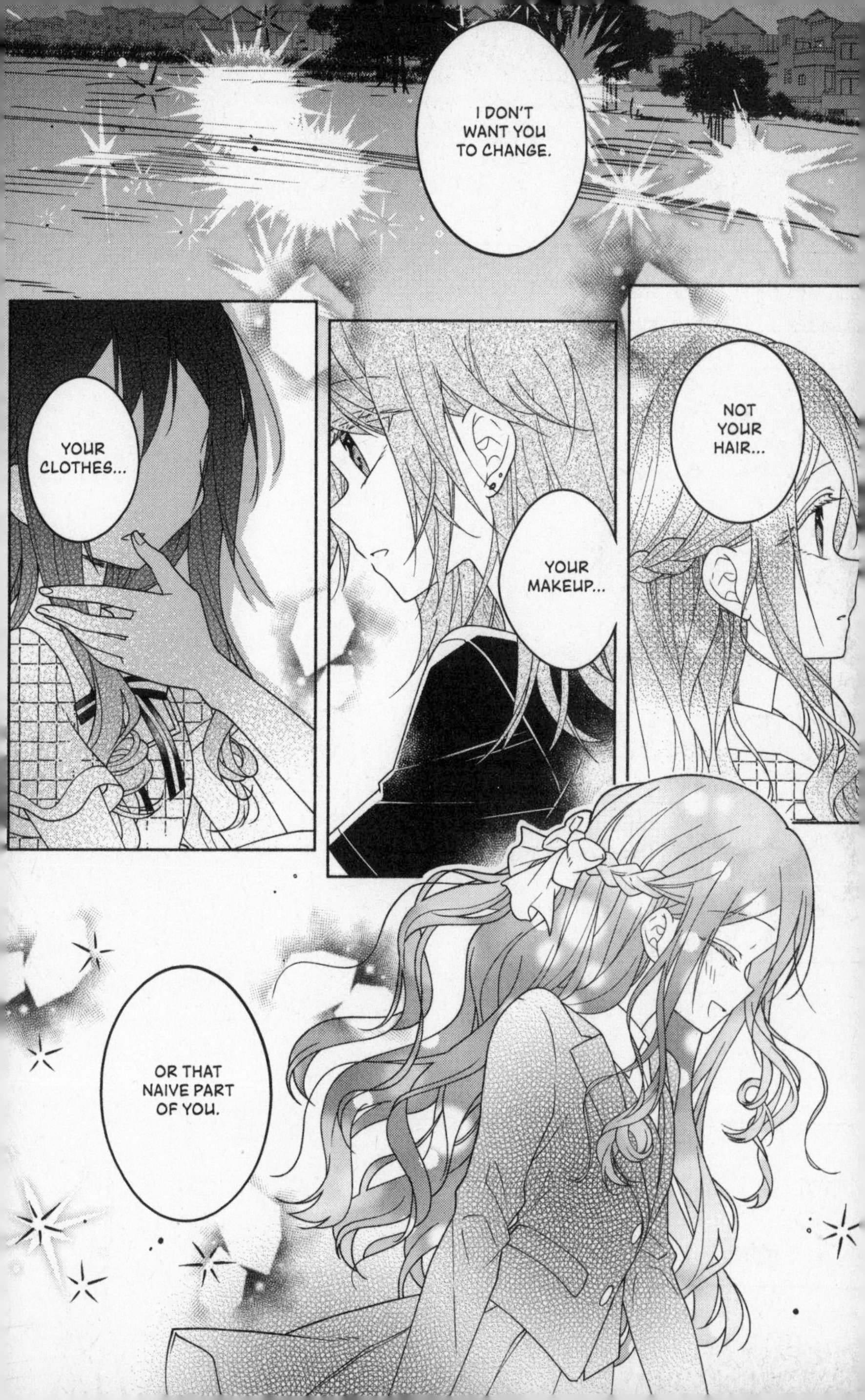
I DON'T WANT YOU TO CHANGE.
NOT YOUR HAIR...
YOUR MAKEUP...
YOUR CLOTHES...
OR THAT NAIVE PART OF YOU.

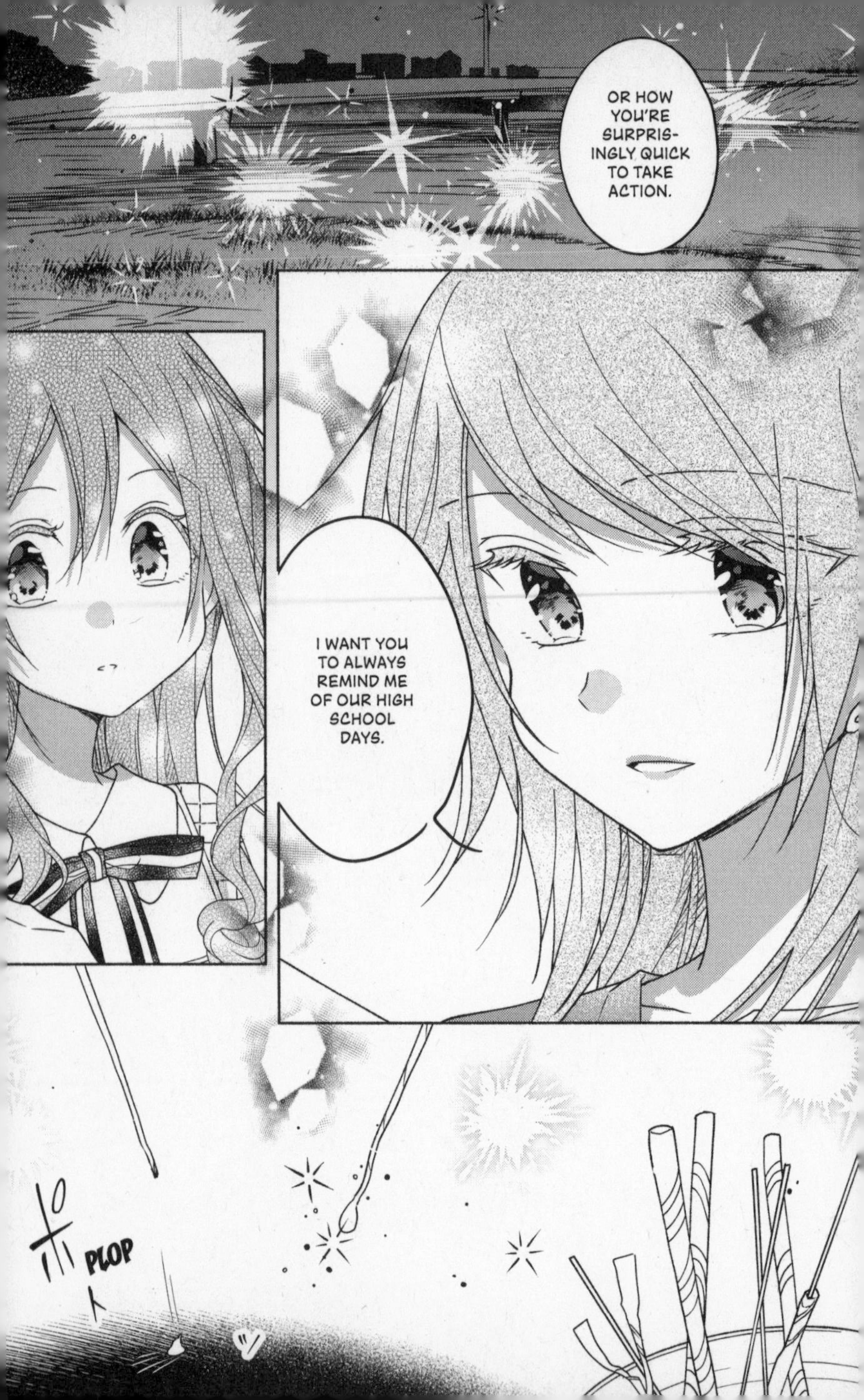
OR HOW YOU'RE SURPRIS-INGLY QUICK TO TAKE ACTION.
I WANT YOU TO ALWAYS REMIND ME OF OUR HIGH SCHOOL DAYS.
PLOP

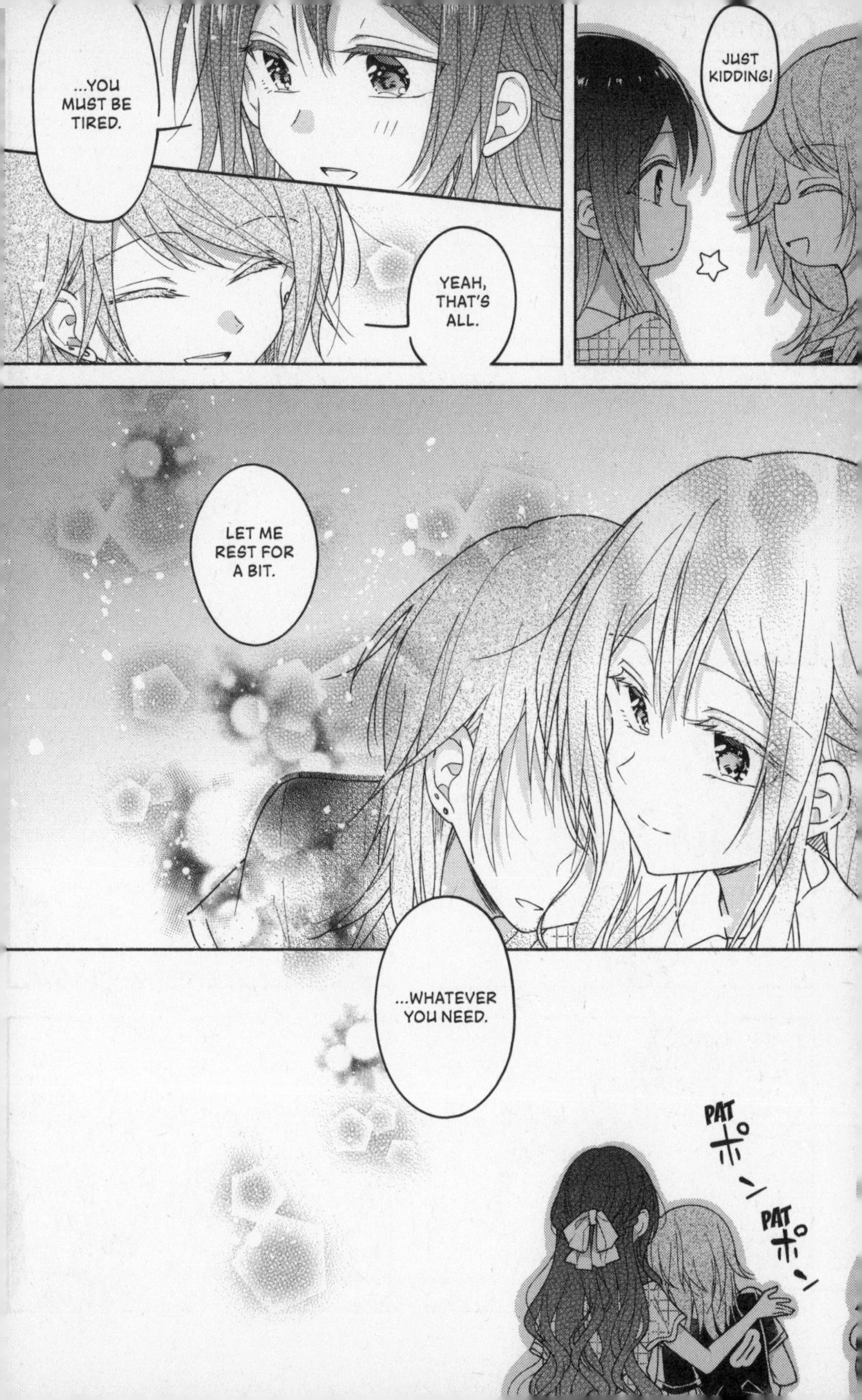
JUST KIDDING!
...YOU MUST BE TIRED.
YEAH, THAT'S ALL.
LET ME REST FOR A BIT.
...WHATEVER YOU NEED.
PAT
PAT

Chapter 52

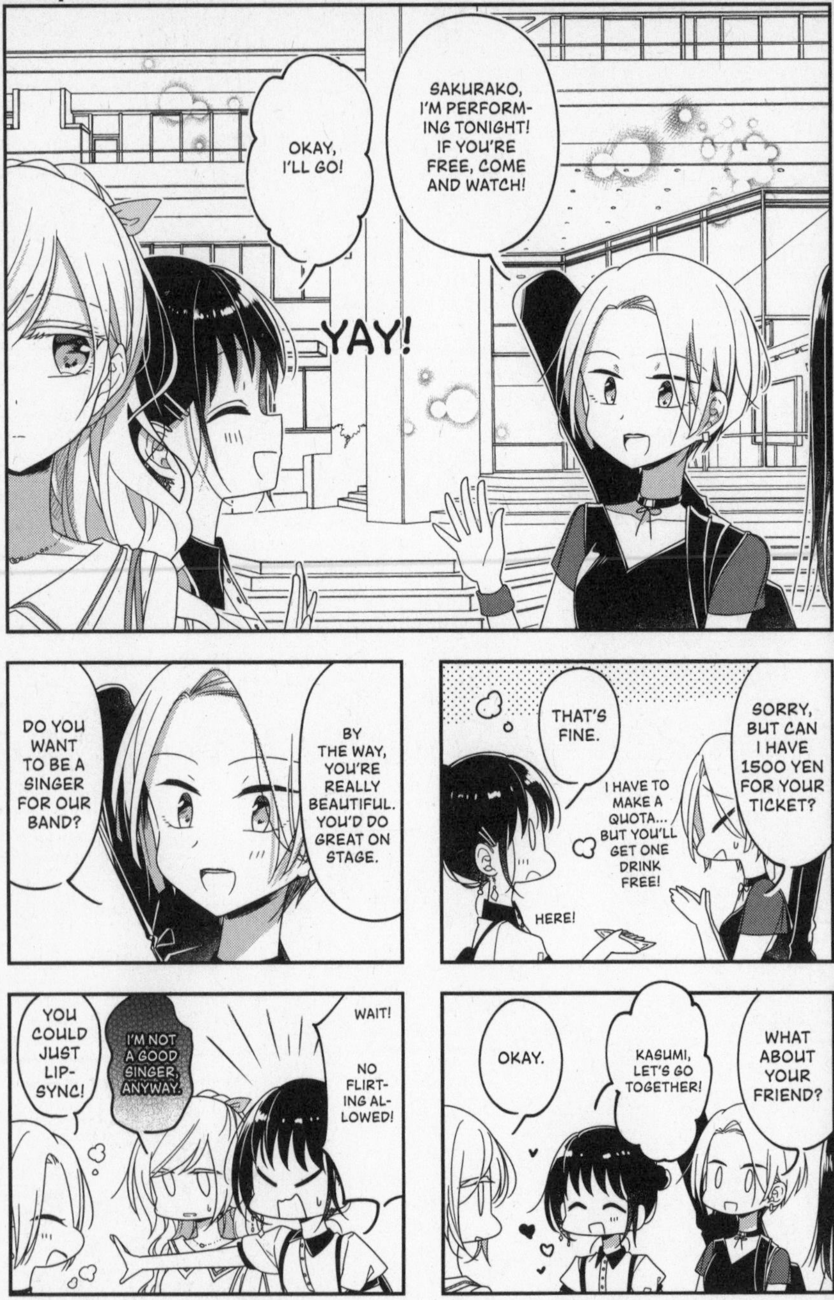

SAKURAKO, I'M PERFORMING TONIGHT! IF YOU'RE FREE, COME AND WATCH!
OKAY, I'LL GO!
YAY!
SORRY, BUT CAN I HAVE 1500 YEN FOR YOUR TICKET?
I HAVE TO MAKE A QUOTA... BUT YOU'LL GET ONE DRINK FREE!
THAT'S FINE.
HERE!
BY THE WAY, YOU'RE REALLY BEAUTIFUL. YOU'D DO GREAT ON STAGE.
DO YOU WANT TO BE A SINGER FOR OUR BAND?
WHAT ABOUT YOUR FRIEND?
KASUMI, LET'S GO TOGETHER!
OKAY.
WAIT!
NO FLIRTING ALLOWED!
I'M NOT A GOOD SINGER, ANYWAY.
YOU COULD JUST LIP-SYNC!

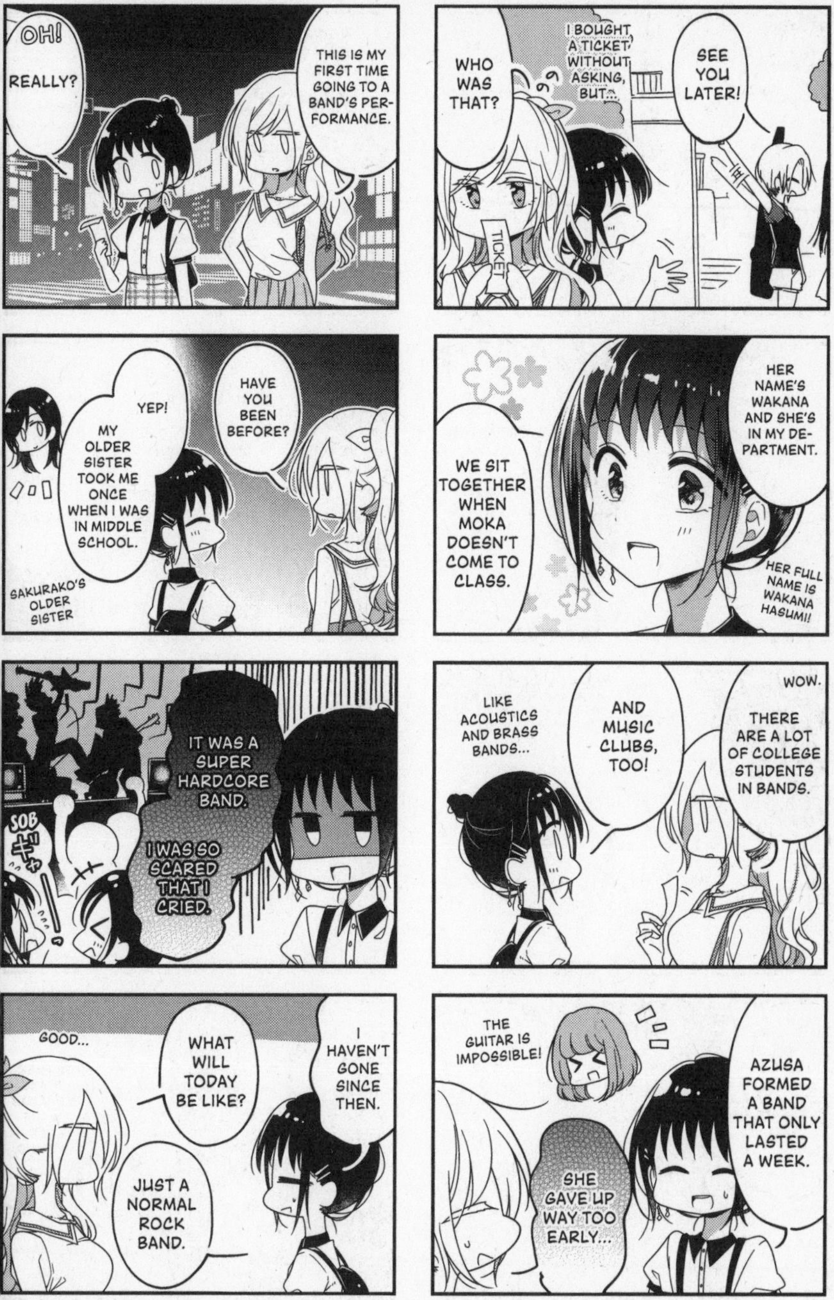
SEE YOU LATER!
I BOUGHT A TICKET WITHOUT ASKING, BUT...
WHO WAS THAT?
TICKET
HER NAME'S WAKANA AND SHE'S IN MY DEPARTMENT.
WE SIT TOGETHER WHEN MOKA DOESN'T COME TO CLASS.
HER FULL NAME IS WAKANA HASUMI!
WOW.
THERE ARE A LOT OF COLLEGE STUDENTS IN BANDS.
AND MUSIC CLUBS, TOO!
LIKE ACOUSTICS AND BRASS BANDS...
AZUSA FORMED A BAND THAT ONLY LASTED A WEEK.
THE GUITAR IS IMPOSSIBLE!
SHE GAVE UP WAY TOO EARLY...
THIS IS MY FIRST TIME GOING TO A BAND'S PERFORMANCE.
OH!
REALLY?
HAVE YOU BEEN BEFORE?
YEP!
MY OLDER SISTER TOOK ME ONCE WHEN I WAS IN MIDDLE SCHOOL.
SAKURAKO'S OLDER SISTER
IT WAS A SUPER HARDCORE BAND.
I WAS SO SCARED THAT I CRIED.
SOB
ギャ
I HAVEN'T GONE SINCE THEN.
WHAT WILL TODAY BE LIKE?
JUST A NORMAL ROCK BAND.
GOOD...

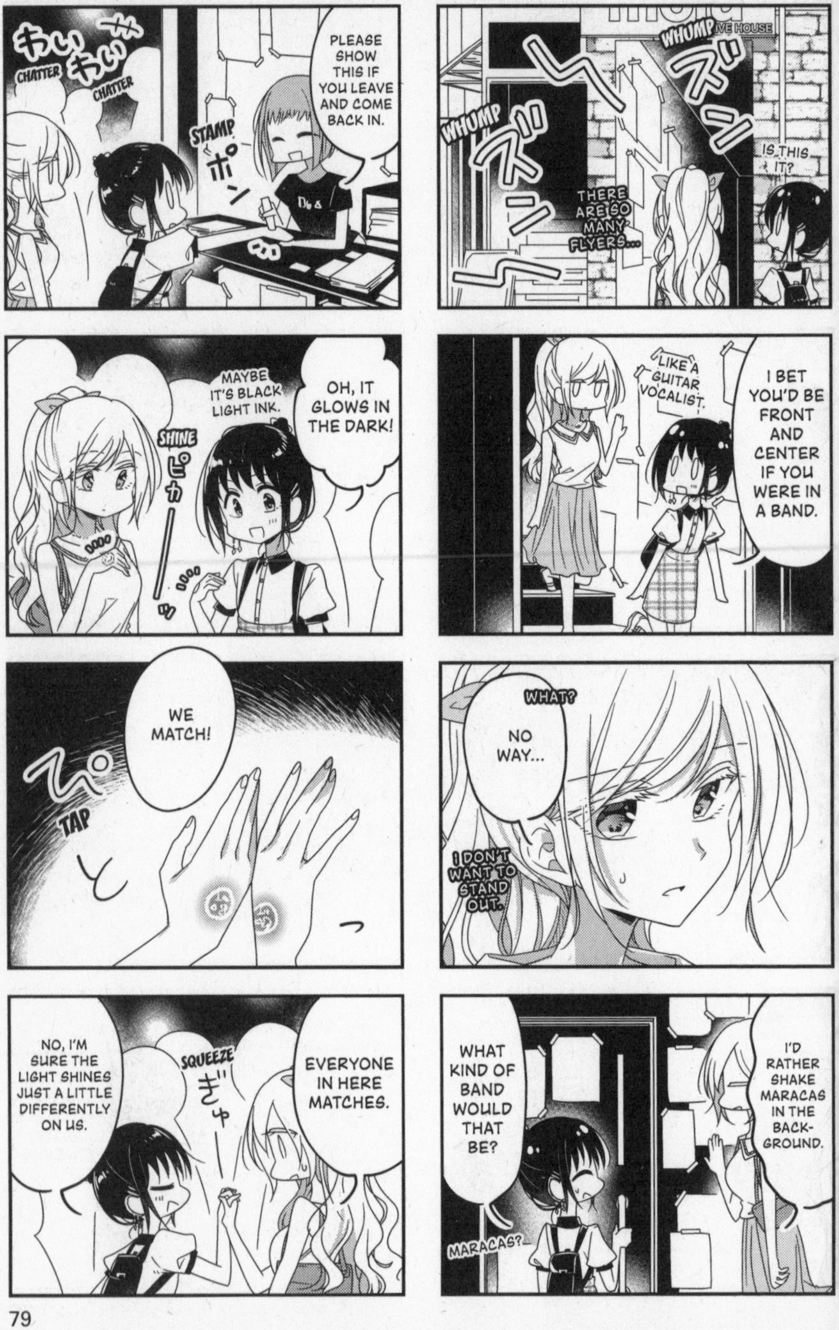

IVE HOUSE
WHUMP
WHUMP
IS THIS IT?
THERE ARE SO MANY FLYERS...
CHATTER
CHATTER
PLEASE SHOW THIS IF YOU LEAVE AND COME BACK IN.
STAMP
ポン
I BET YOU'D BE FRONT AND CENTER IF YOU WERE IN A BAND.
LIKE A GUITAR VOCALIST.
OH, IT GLOWS IN THE DARK!
MAYBE IT'S BLACK LIGHT INK.
SHINE
ピカー
WHAT?
NO WAY...
I DON'T WANT TO STAND OUT.
WE MATCH!
TAP
I'D RATHER SHAKE MARACAS IN THE BACK-GROUND.
WHAT KIND OF BAND WOULD THAT BE?
MARACAS?
EVERYONE IN HERE MATCHES.
SQUEEZE
ぎゅ
NO, I'M SURE THE LIGHT SHINES JUST A LITTLE DIFFERENTLY ON US.

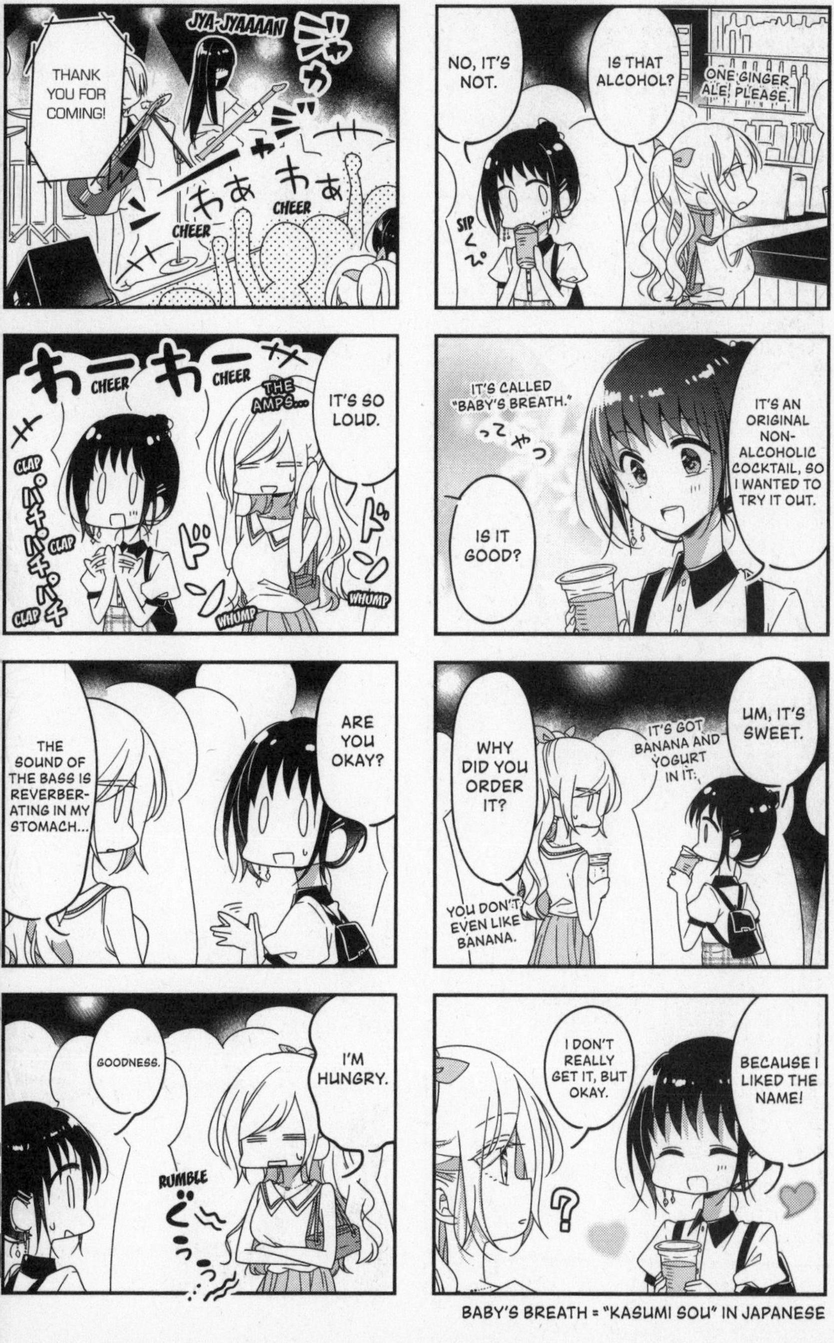
ONE GINGER ALE, PLEASE.
IS THAT ALCOHOL?
NO, IT'S NOT.
SIP
IT'S AN ORIGINAL NON-ALCOHOLIC COCKTAIL, SO I WANTED TO TRY IT OUT.
IT'S CALLED "BABY'S BREATH."
IS IT GOOD?
UM, IT'S SWEET.
IT'S GOT BANANA AND YOGURT IN IT.
WHY DID YOU ORDER IT?
YOU DON'T EVEN LIKE BANANA.
BECAUSE I LIKED THE NAME!
I DON'T REALLY GET IT, BUT OKAY.
JYA-JYAAAAN
THANK YOU FOR COMING!
CHEER
CHEER
IT'S SO LOUD.
THE AMPS...
CHEER
CHEER
CLAP
CLAP
CLAP
WHUMP
WHUMP
ARE YOU OKAY?
THE SOUND OF THE BASS IS REVERBERATING IN MY STOMACH...
I'M HUNGRY.
GOODNESS.
RUMBLE

BABY'S BREATH = "KASUMI SOU" IN JAPANESE

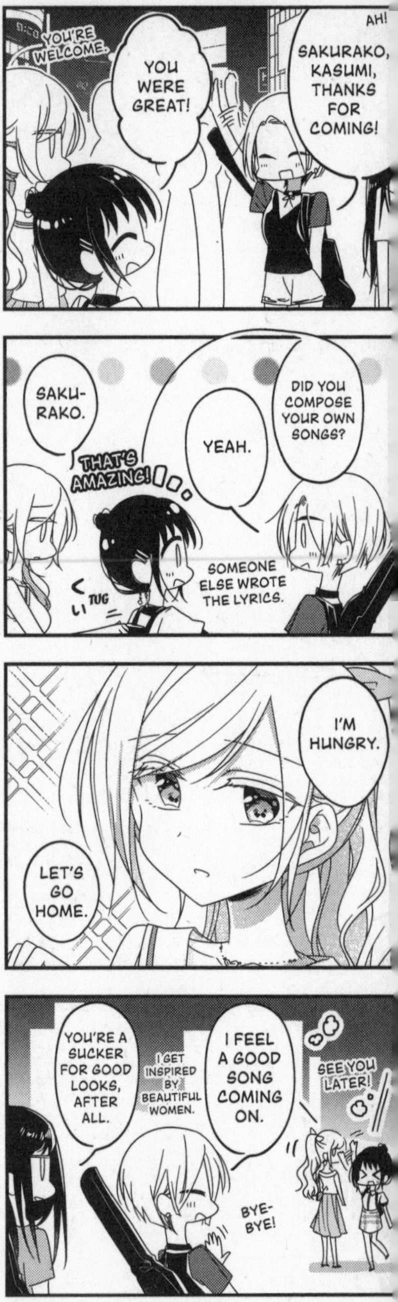
AH!
SAKURAKO, KASUMI, THANKS FOR COMING!
YOU WERE GREAT!
YOU'RE WELCOME.
DID YOU COMPOSE YOUR OWN SONGS?
YEAH.
SOMEONE ELSE WROTE THE LYRICS.
SAKU-RAKO.
THAT'S AMAZING!
TUG
I'M HUNGRY.
LET'S GO HOME.
SEE YOU LATER!
I FEEL A GOOD SONG COMING ON.
I GET INSPIRED BY BEAUTIFUL WOMEN.
YOU'RE A SUCKER FOR GOOD LOOKS, AFTER ALL.
BYE-BYE!

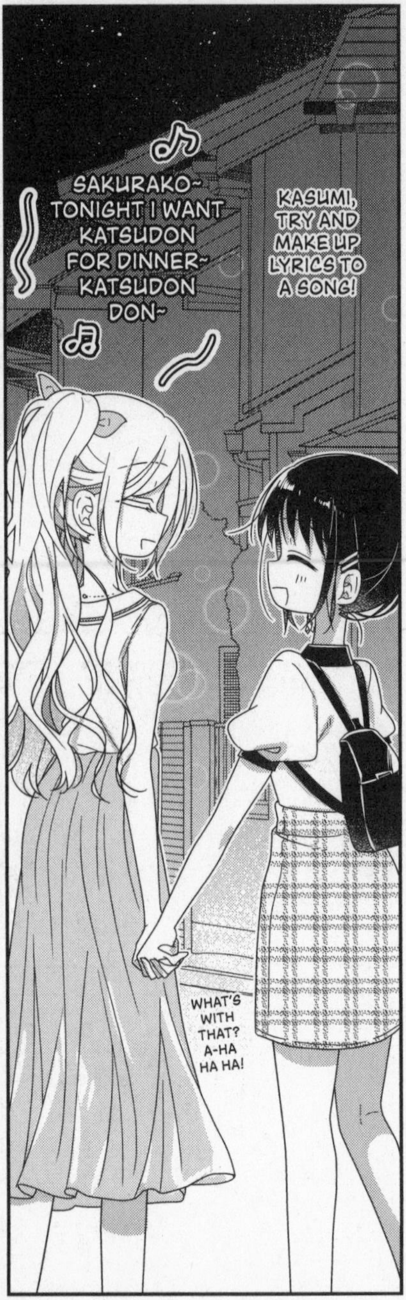
KASUMI, TRY AND MAKE UP LYRICS TO A SONG!
SAKURAKO~ TONIGHT I WANT KATSUDON FOR DINNER~ KATSUDON DON~
WHAT'S WITH THAT? A-HA HA HA!

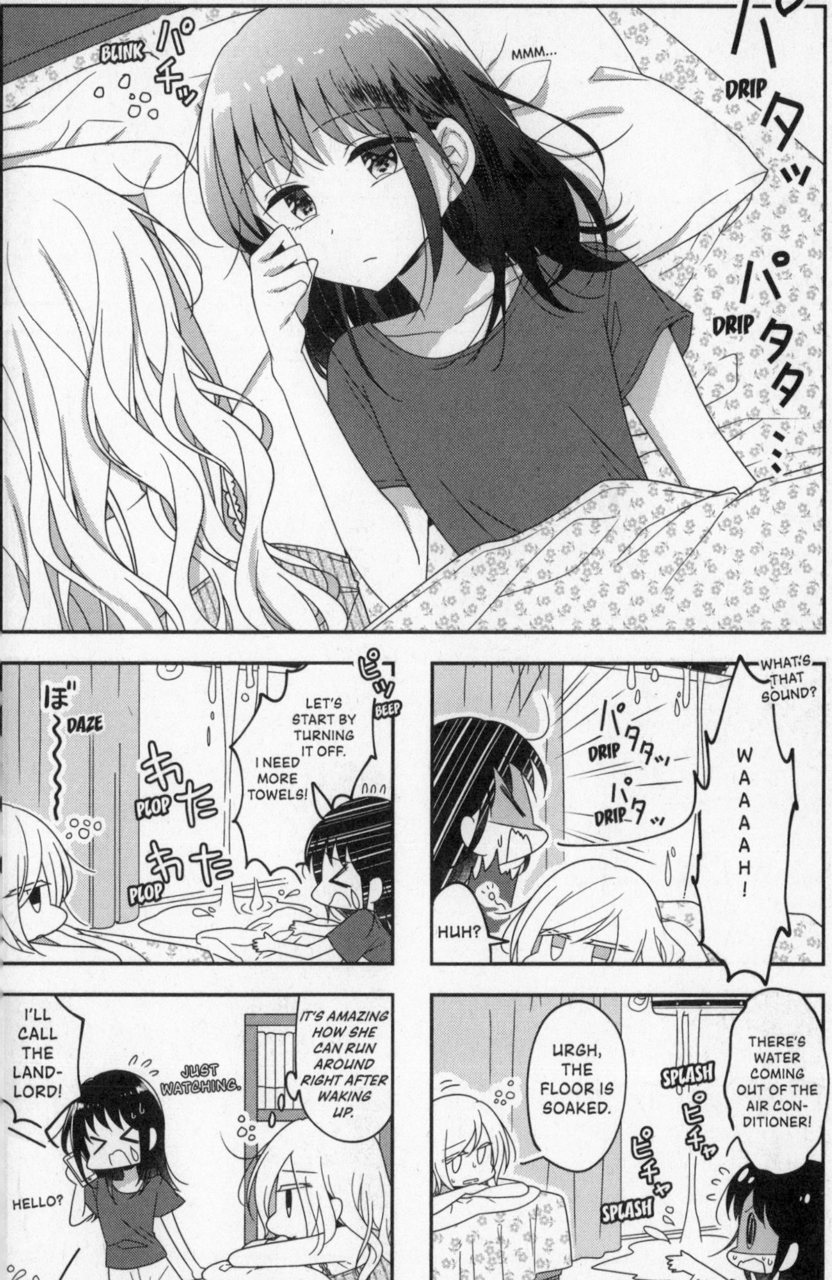

パタッ
DRIP
パタタ…
DRIP
MMM...
パチッ
BLINK
WHAT'S THAT SOUND?
WAAAAAH!
パタタッ
DRIP
パタッ
DRIP
HUH?
ピッ
BEEP
LET'S START BY TURNING IT OFF.
I NEED MORE TOWELS!
わた
PLOP
わた
PLOP
ぼ〜〜〜
DAZE
THERE'S WATER COMING OUT OF THE AIR CONDITIONER!
ピチャ
SPLASH
ピチャ
SPLASH
URGH, THE FLOOR IS SOAKED.
IT'S AMAZING HOW SHE CAN RUN AROUND RIGHT AFTER WAKING UP.
JUST WATCHING.
I'LL CALL THE LAND-LORD!
HELLO?

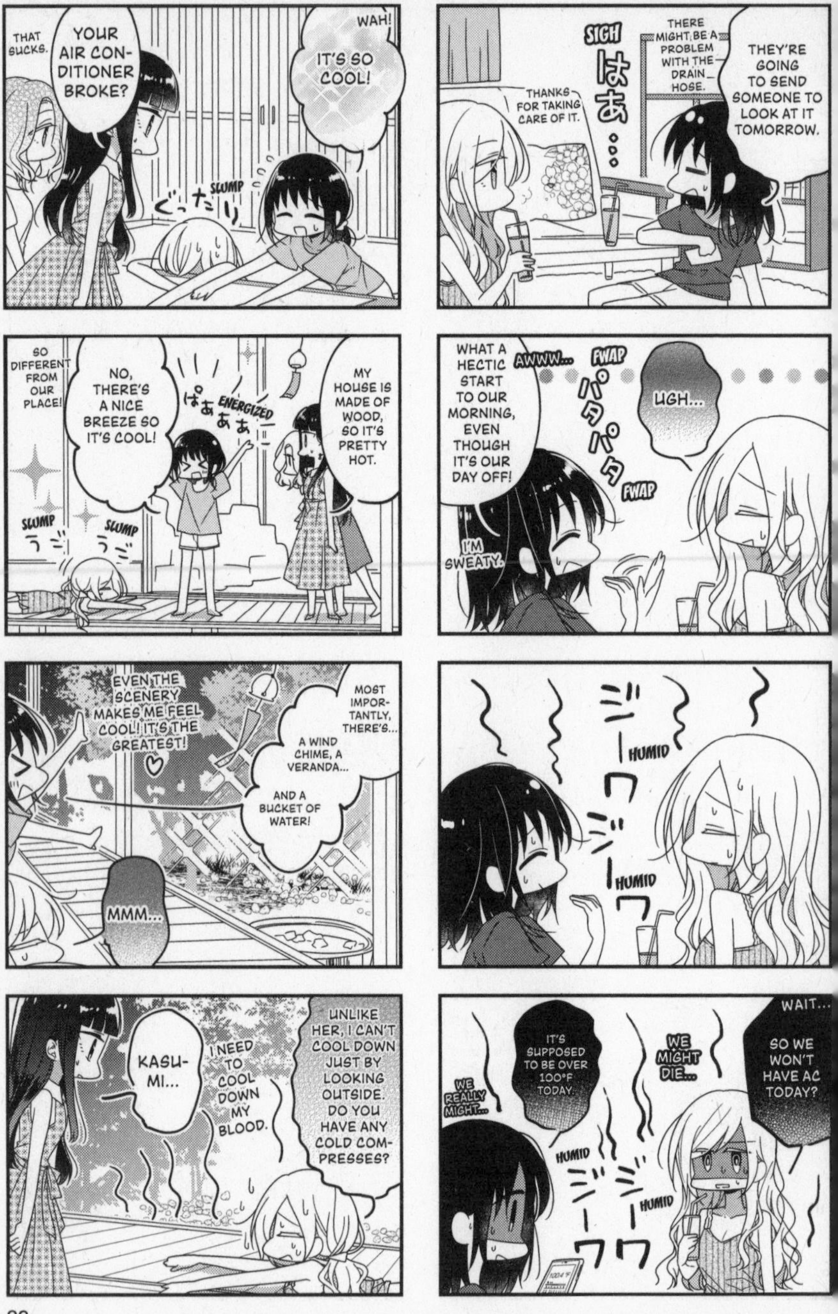
THEY'RE GOING TO SEND SOMEONE TO LOOK AT IT TOMORROW.
THERE MIGHT BE A PROBLEM WITH THE DRAIN HOSE.
SIGH
はあ…
THANKS FOR TAKING CARE OF IT.
UGH...
FWAP
パタパタ
FWAP
AWWW...
WHAT A HECTIC START TO OUR MORNING, EVEN THOUGH IT'S OUR DAY OFF!
I'M SWEATY.
ジーワ
HUMID
ジーワ
HUMID
WAIT...
SO WE WON'T HAVE AC TODAY?
WE MIGHT DIE...
IT'S SUPPOSED TO BE OVER 100°F TODAY.
WE REALLY MIGHT...
HUMID
ジージーワワ
HUMID
WAH!
IT'S SO COOL!
YOUR AIR CONDITIONER BROKE?
THAT SUCKS.
SLUMP
ぐったり
MY HOUSE IS MADE OF WOOD, SO IT'S PRETTY HOT.
ENERGIZED
ぱあぁ
NO, THERE'S A NICE BREEZE SO IT'S COOL!
SO DIFFERENT FROM OUR PLACE!
SLUMP
SLUMP
MOST IMPORTANTLY, THERE'S...
A WIND CHIME, A VERANDA...
AND A BUCKET OF WATER!
EVEN THE SCENERY MAKES ME FEEL COOL! IT'S THE GREATEST!
MMM...
UNLIKE HER, I CAN'T COOL DOWN JUST BY LOOKING OUTSIDE. DO YOU HAVE ANY COLD COMPRESSES?
I NEED TO COOL DOWN MY BLOOD.
KASUMI...

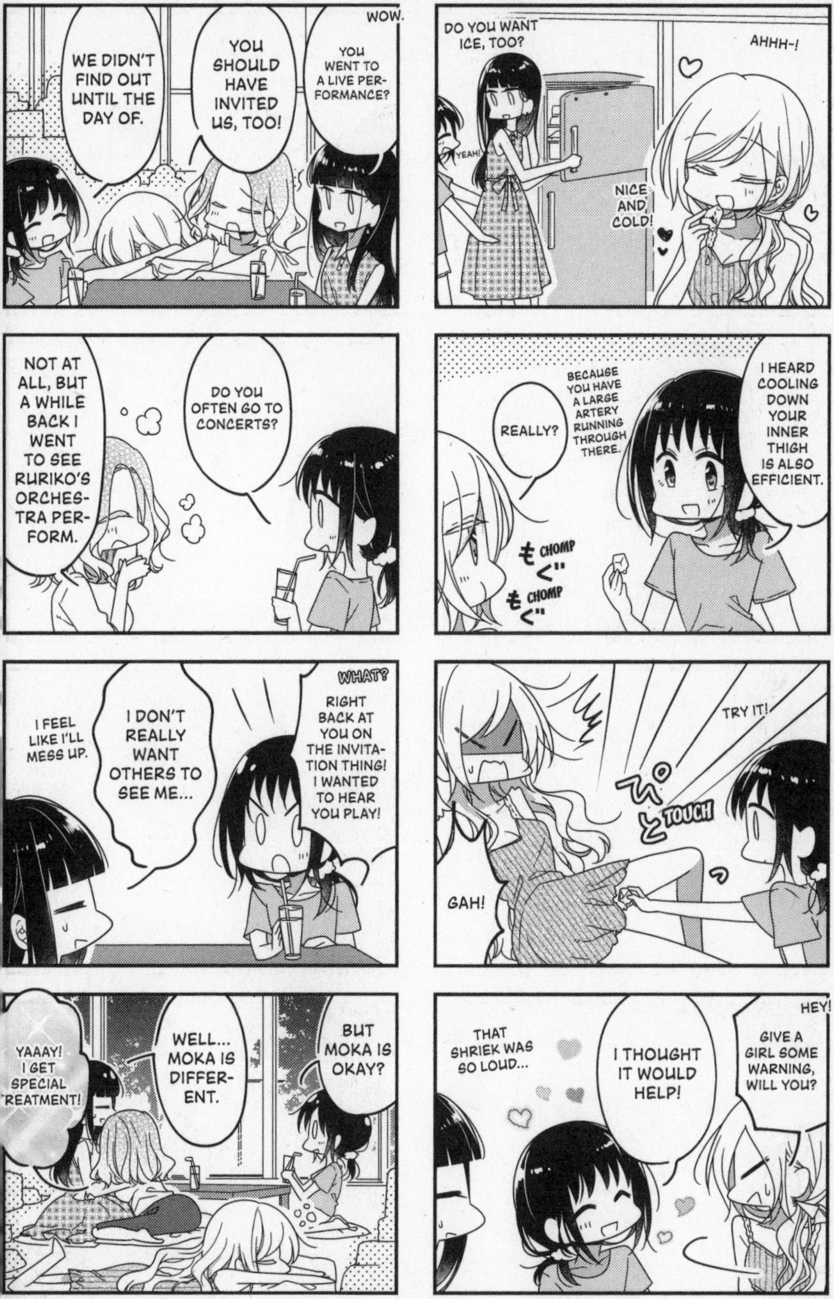
DO YOU WANT ICE, TOO?
YEAH!
AHHH~!
NICE AND COLD!
I HEARD COOLING DOWN YOUR INNER THIGH IS ALSO EFFICIENT.
BECAUSE YOU HAVE A LARGE ARTERY RUNNING THROUGH THERE.
REALLY?
もぐ CHOMP
もぐ CHOMP
TRY IT!
ぴと TOUCH
GAH!
HEY!
GIVE A GIRL SOME WARNING, WILL YOU?
I THOUGHT IT WOULD HELP!
THAT SHRIEK WAS SO LOUD...
WOW.
YOU WENT TO A LIVE PERFORMANCE?
YOU SHOULD HAVE INVITED US, TOO!
WE DIDN'T FIND OUT UNTIL THE DAY OF.
DO YOU OFTEN GO TO CONCERTS?
NOT AT ALL, BUT A WHILE BACK I WENT TO SEE RURIKO'S ORCHESTRA PERFORM.
WHAT?
RIGHT BACK AT YOU ON THE INVITATION THING! I WANTED TO HEAR YOU PLAY!
I DON'T REALLY WANT OTHERS TO SEE ME...
I FEEL LIKE I'LL MESS UP.
BUT MOKA IS OKAY?
WELL... MOKA IS DIFFERENT.
YAAAY! I GET SPECIAL TREATMENT!

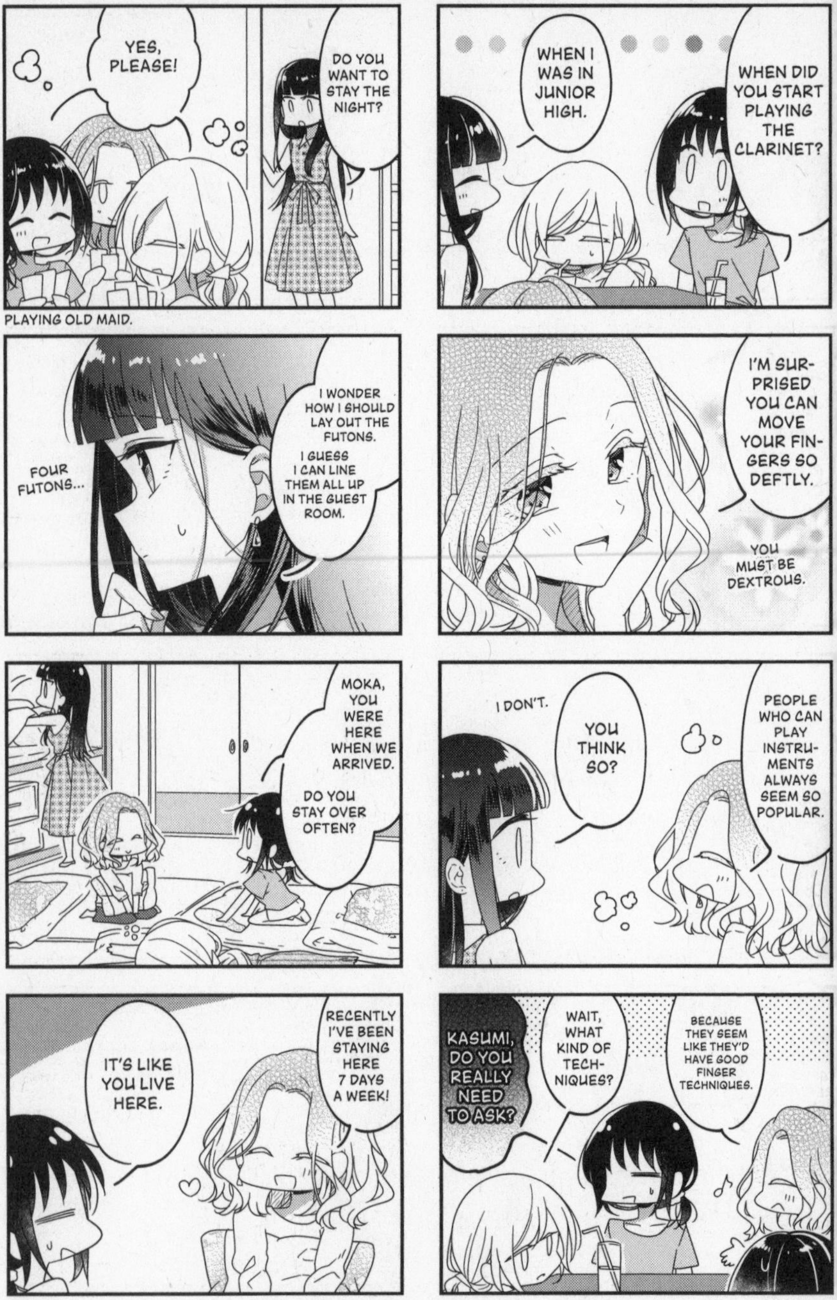
WHEN DID YOU START PLAYING THE CLARINET?
WHEN I WAS IN JUNIOR HIGH.
I'M SURPRISED YOU CAN MOVE YOUR FINGERS SO DEFTLY.
YOU MUST BE DEXTROUS.
PEOPLE WHO CAN PLAY INSTRUMENTS ALWAYS SEEM SO POPULAR.
YOU THINK SO?
I DON'T.
BECAUSE THEY SEEM LIKE THEY'D HAVE GOOD FINGER TECHNIQUES.
WAIT, WHAT KIND OF TECHNIQUES?
KASUMI, DO YOU REALLY NEED TO ASK?
DO YOU WANT TO STAY THE NIGHT?
YES, PLEASE!
PLAYING OLD MAID.
I WONDER HOW I SHOULD LAY OUT THE FUTONS.
I GUESS I CAN LINE THEM ALL UP IN THE GUEST ROOM.
FOUR FUTONS...
MOKA, YOU WERE HERE WHEN WE ARRIVED.
DO YOU STAY OVER OFTEN?
RECENTLY I'VE BEEN STAYING HERE 7 DAYS A WEEK!
IT'S LIKE YOU LIVE HERE.

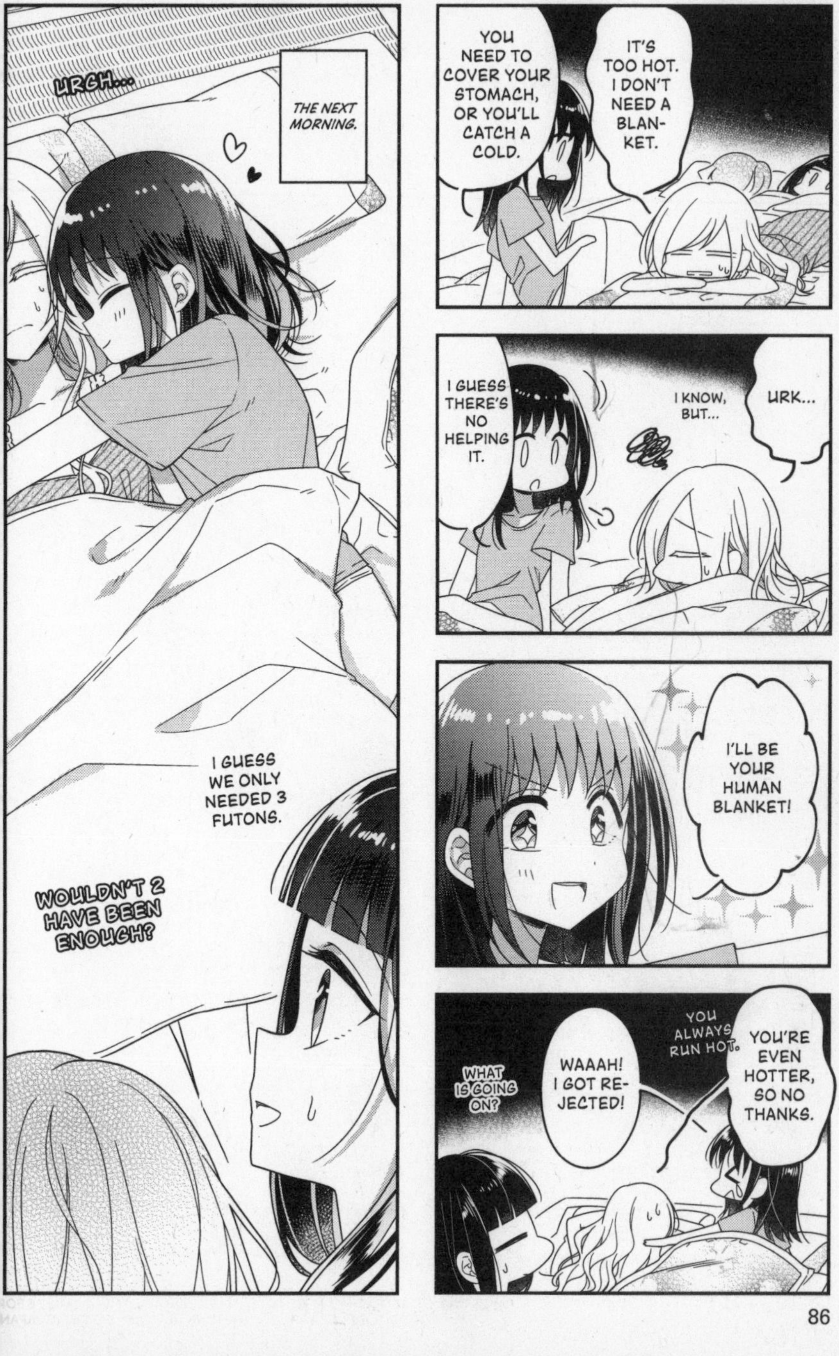
IT'S TOO HOT. I DON'T NEED A BLAN-KET.
YOU NEED TO COVER YOUR STOMACH, OR YOU'LL CATCH A COLD.
URK...
I KNOW, BUT...
I GUESS THERE'S NO HELPING IT.
I'LL BE YOUR HUMAN BLANKET!
YOU'RE EVEN HOTTER, SO NO THANKS.
YOU ALWAYS RUN HOT.
WAAAH! I GOT RE-JECTED!
WHAT IS GOING ON?
THE NEXT MORNING.
URGH...
I GUESS WE ONLY NEEDED 3 FUTONS.
WOULDN'T 2 HAVE BEEN ENOUGH?

Illustration gallery of Yukiko

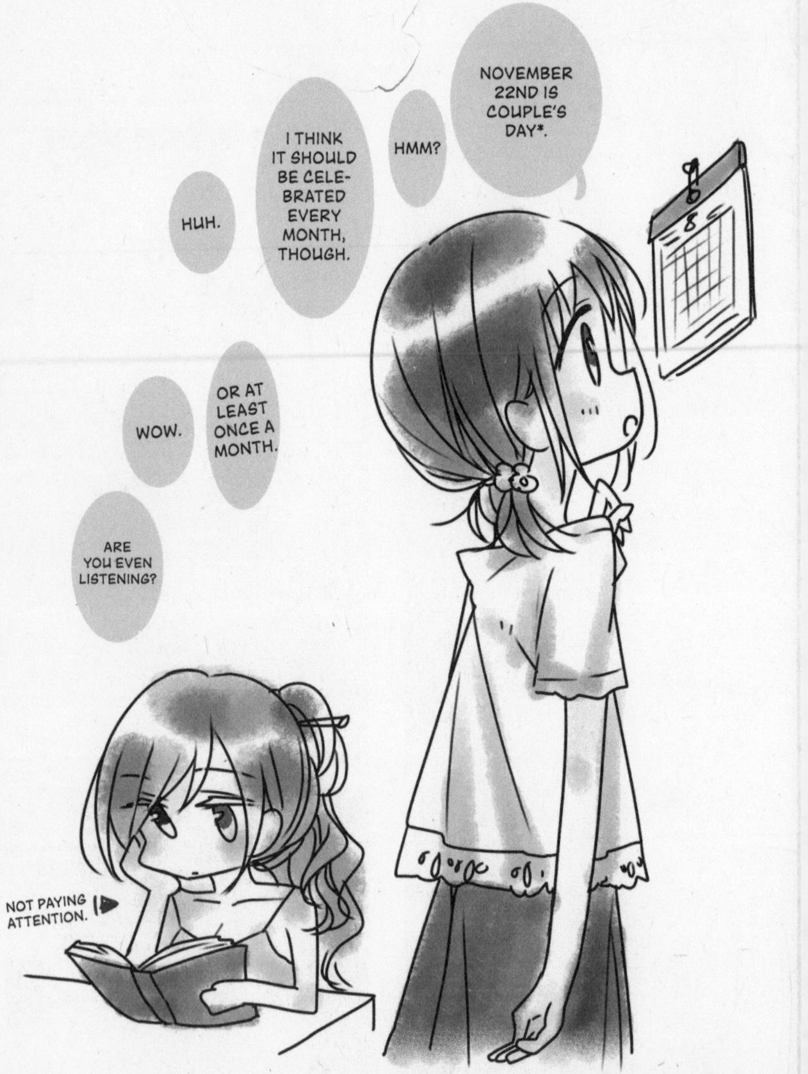
NOVEMBER 22ND IS COUPLE'S DAY*.
HMM?
I THINK IT SHOULD BE CELE-BRATED EVERY MONTH, THOUGH.
HUH.
OR AT LEAST ONCE A MONTH.
WOW.
ARE YOU EVEN LISTENING?
NOT PAYING ATTENTION.

*SOUNDING OUT EACH NUMBER IN 11/22 SOUNDS LIKE THE JAPANESE FOR "GOOD COUPLE," SO 11/22 IS KNOWN AS COUPLE'S DAY IN JAPAN.

Futaribeya
A ROOM FOR TWO

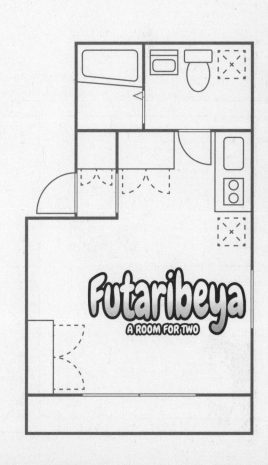

Chapter 53

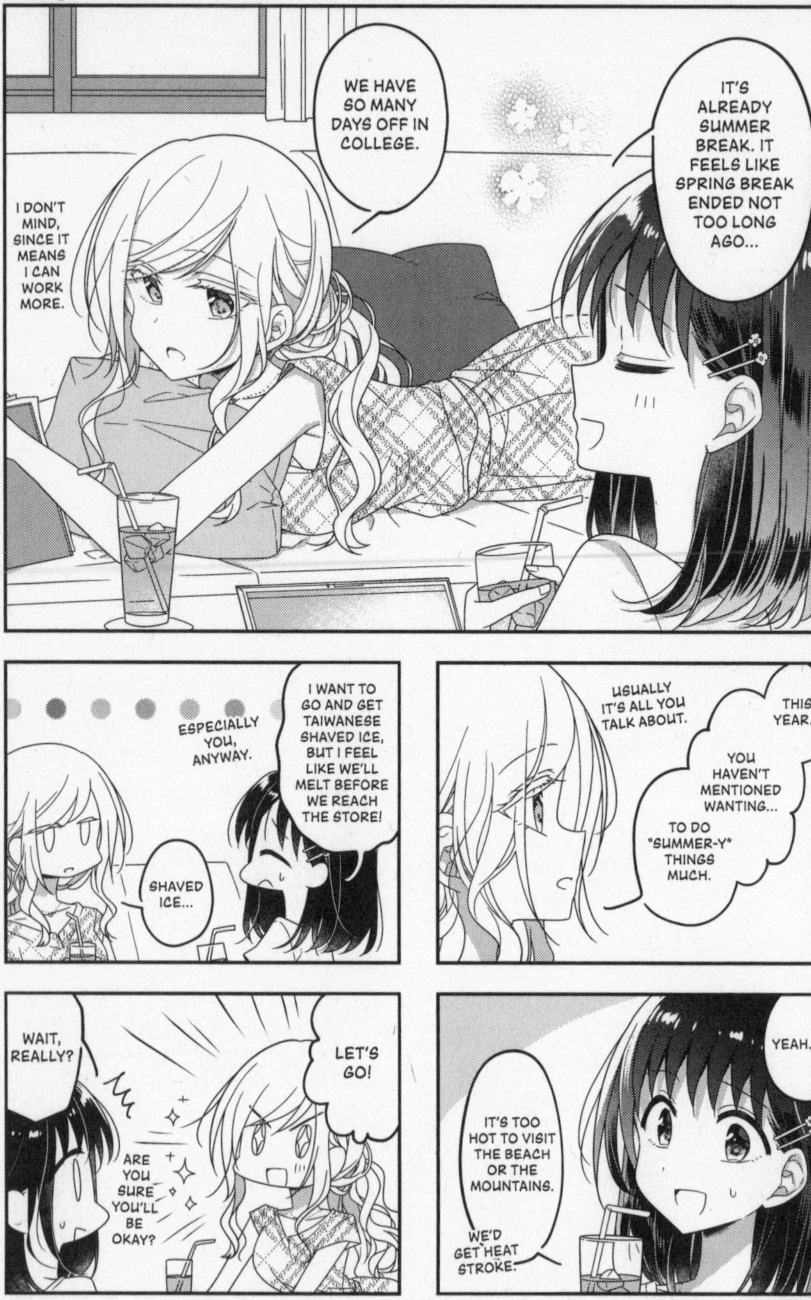
IT'S ALREADY SUMMER BREAK. IT FEELS LIKE SPRING BREAK ENDED NOT TOO LONG AGO...
WE HAVE SO MANY DAYS OFF IN COLLEGE.
I DON'T MIND, SINCE IT MEANS I CAN WORK MORE.
THIS YEAR...
YOU HAVEN'T MENTIONED WANTING...
TO DO "SUMMER-Y" THINGS MUCH.
USUALLY IT'S ALL YOU TALK ABOUT.
I WANT TO GO AND GET TAIWANESE SHAVED ICE, BUT I FEEL LIKE WE'LL MELT BEFORE WE REACH THE STORE!
SHAVED ICE...
ESPECIALLY YOU, ANYWAY.
YEAH...
IT'S TOO HOT TO VISIT THE BEACH OR THE MOUNTAINS.
WE'D GET HEAT STROKE.
LET'S GO!
WAIT, REALLY?
ARE YOU SURE YOU'LL BE OKAY?

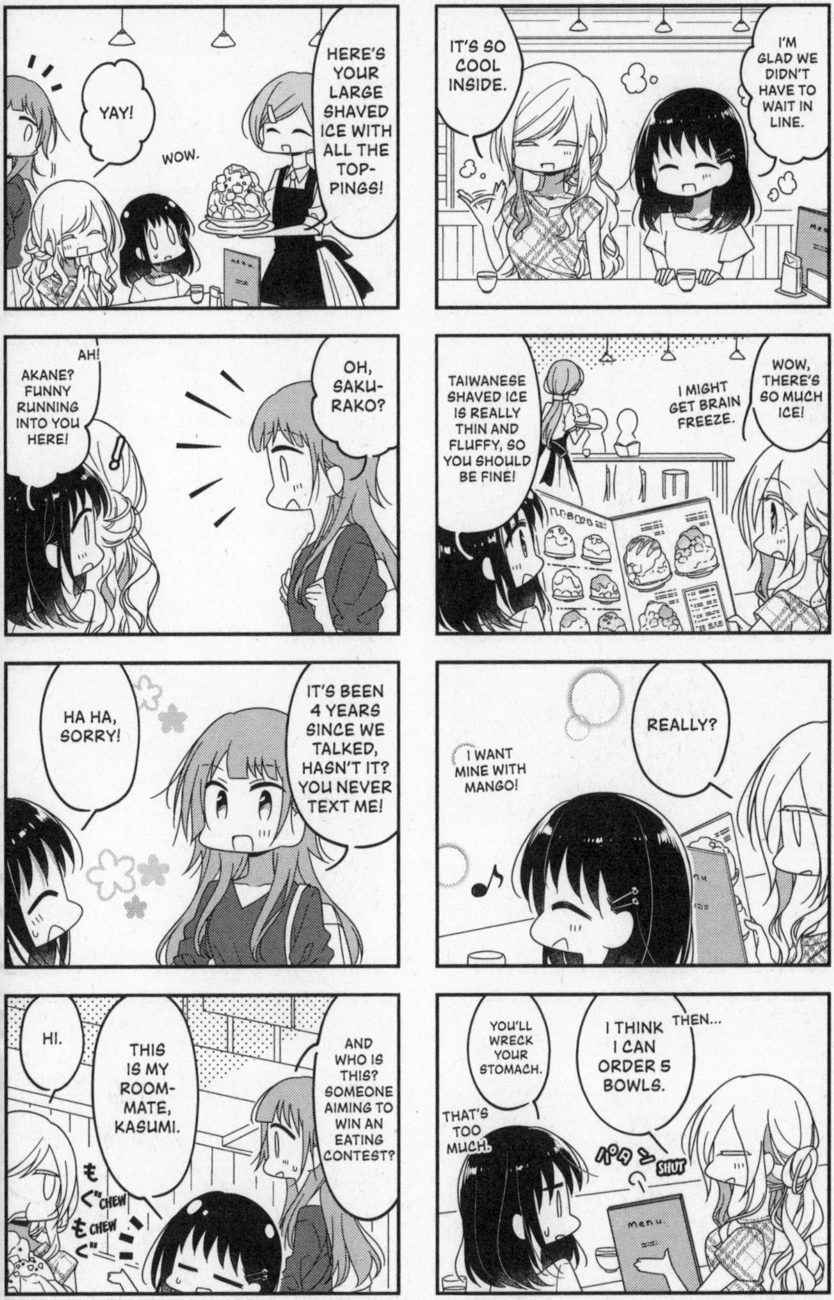
I'M GLAD WE DIDN'T HAVE TO WAIT IN LINE.
IT'S SO COOL INSIDE.
WOW, THERE'S SO MUCH ICE!
I MIGHT GET BRAIN FREEZE.
TAIWANESE SHAVED ICE IS REALLY THIN AND FLUFFY, SO YOU SHOULD BE FINE!
REALLY?
I WANT MINE WITH MANGO!
THEN...
I THINK I CAN ORDER 5 BOWLS.
YOU'LL WRECK YOUR STOMACH.
パタン SHUT
THAT'S TOO MUCH.
HERE'S YOUR LARGE SHAVED ICE WITH ALL THE TOP-PINGS!
WOW.
YAY!
OH, SAKU-RAKO?
AH! AKANE? FUNNY RUNNING INTO YOU HERE!
IT'S BEEN 4 YEARS SINCE WE TALKED, HASN'T IT? YOU NEVER TEXT ME!
HA HA, SORRY!
AND WHO IS THIS? SOMEONE AIMING TO WIN AN EATING CONTEST?
THIS IS MY ROOM-MATE, KASUMI.
HI.
もぐ CHEW もぐ CHEW

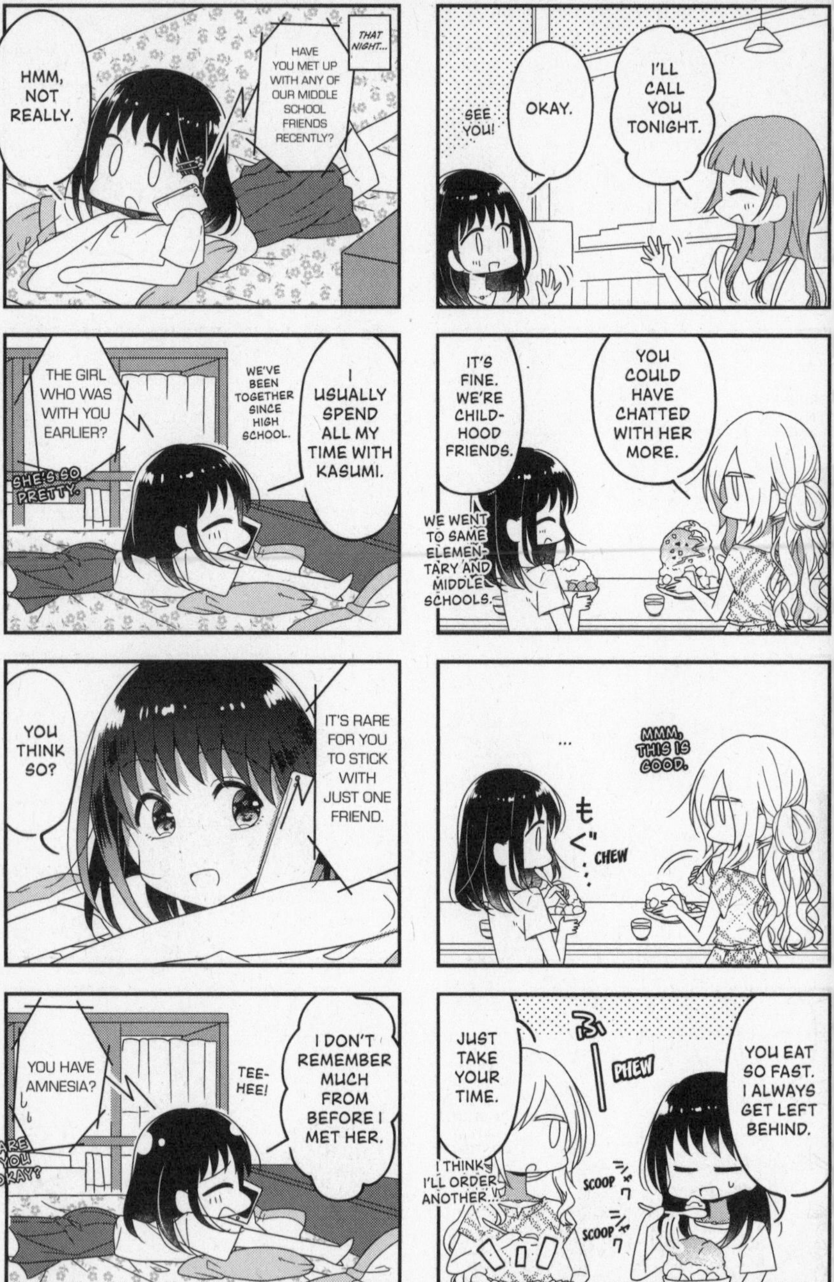

I'LL CALL YOU TONIGHT.
OKAY.
SEE YOU!
YOU COULD HAVE CHATTED WITH HER MORE.
IT'S FINE. WE'RE CHILD-HOOD FRIENDS.
WE WENT TO SAME ELEMEN-TARY AND MIDDLE SCHOOLS.
MMM, THIS IS GOOD.
...
もぐ
CHEW
YOU EAT SO FAST. I ALWAYS GET LEFT BEHIND.
ふー
PHEW
JUST TAKE YOUR TIME.
I THINK I'LL ORDER ANOTHER...
SCOOP
SCOOP
THAT NIGHT...
HAVE YOU MET UP WITH ANY OF OUR MIDDLE SCHOOL FRIENDS RECENTLY?
HMM, NOT REALLY.
I USUALLY SPEND ALL MY TIME WITH KASUMI.
WE'VE BEEN TOGETHER SINCE HIGH SCHOOL.
THE GIRL WHO WAS WITH YOU EARLIER?
SHE'S SO PRETTY.
IT'S RARE FOR YOU TO STICK WITH JUST ONE FRIEND.
YOU THINK SO?
I DON'T REMEMBER MUCH FROM BEFORE I MET HER.
TEE-HEE!
YOU HAVE AMNESIA?
ARE YOU OKAY?

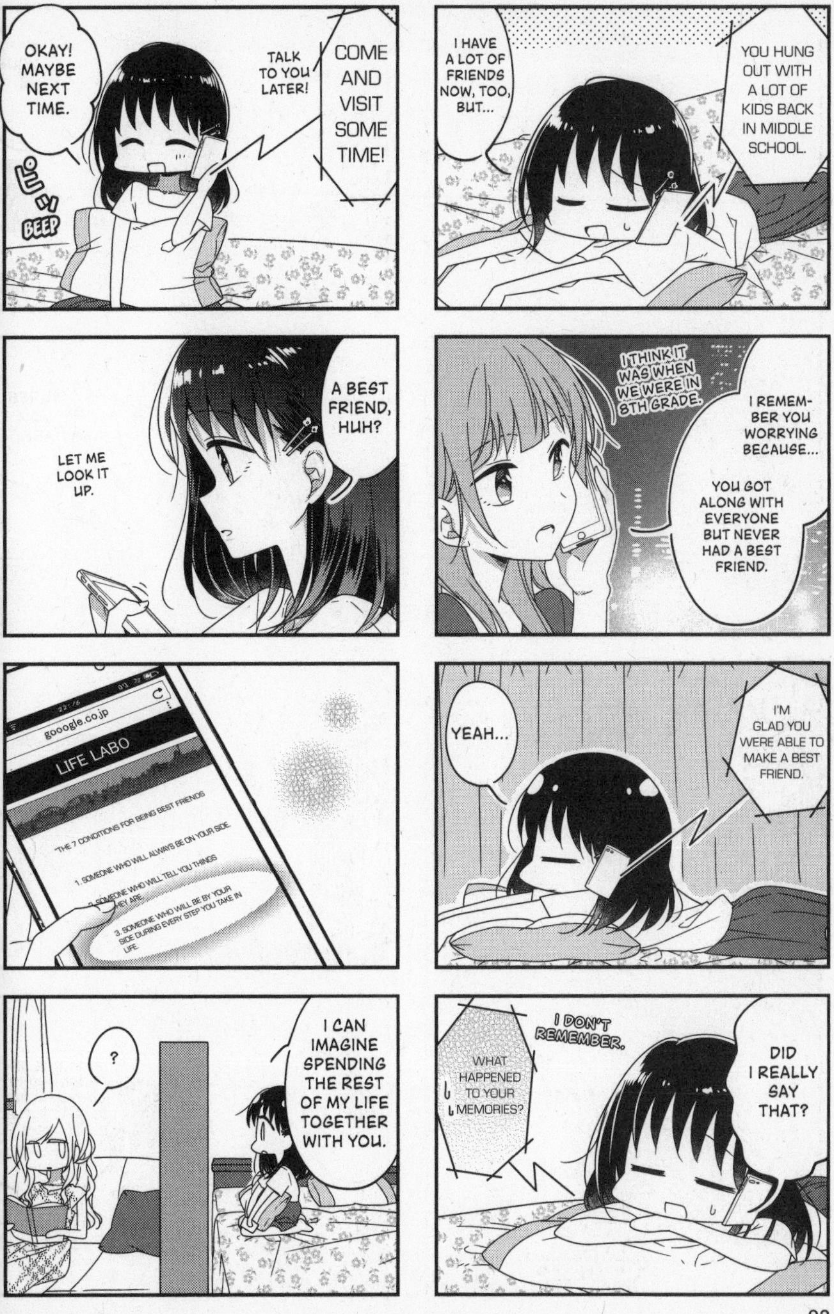
YOU HUNG OUT WITH A LOT OF KIDS BACK IN MIDDLE SCHOOL.
I HAVE A LOT OF FRIENDS NOW, TOO, BUT...
COME AND VISIT SOME TIME!
TALK TO YOU LATER!
OKAY! MAYBE NEXT TIME.
ピッ
BEEP
I THINK IT WAS WHEN WE WERE IN 8TH GRADE.
I REMEMBER YOU WORRYING BECAUSE...
YOU GOT ALONG WITH EVERYONE BUT NEVER HAD A BEST FRIEND.
A BEST FRIEND, HUH?
LET ME LOOK IT UP.
I'M GLAD YOU WERE ABLE TO MAKE A BEST FRIEND.
YEAH...
gooogle.co.jp
LIFE LABO
"THE 7 CONDITIONS FOR BEING BEST FRIENDS
1. SOMEONE WHO WILL ALWAYS BE ON YOUR SIDE.
SOMEONE WHO WILL TELL YOU THINGS
3. SOMEONE WHO WILL BE BY YOUR SIDE DURING EVERY STEP YOU TAKE IN LIFE.
DID I REALLY SAY THAT?
I DON'T REMEMBER.
WHAT HAPPENED TO YOUR MEMORIES?
I CAN IMAGINE SPENDING THE REST OF MY LIFE TOGETHER WITH YOU.
?

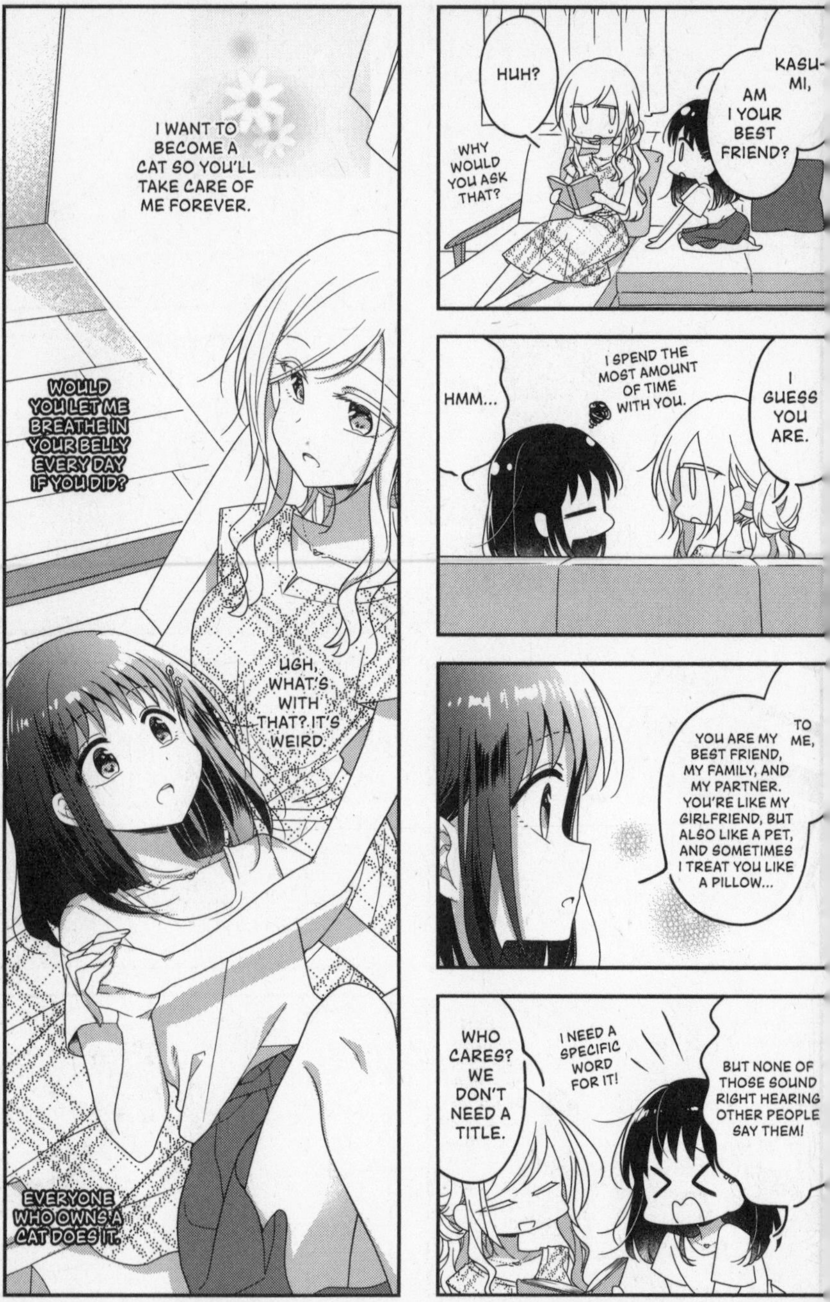
KASU-MI, AM I YOUR BEST FRIEND?
HUH?
WHY WOULD YOU ASK THAT?
I GUESS YOU ARE.
I SPEND THE MOST AMOUNT OF TIME WITH YOU.
HMM...
TO ME, YOU ARE MY BEST FRIEND, MY FAMILY, AND MY PARTNER. YOU'RE LIKE MY GIRLFRIEND, BUT ALSO LIKE A PET, AND SOMETIMES I TREAT YOU LIKE A PILLOW...
BUT NONE OF THOSE SOUND RIGHT HEARING OTHER PEOPLE SAY THEM!
I NEED A SPECIFIC WORD FOR IT!
WHO CARES? WE DON'T NEED A TITLE.
I WANT TO BECOME A CAT SO YOU'LL TAKE CARE OF ME FOREVER.
WOULD YOU LET ME BREATHE IN YOUR BELLY EVERY DAY IF YOU DID?
UGH, WHAT'S WITH THAT? IT'S WEIRD.
EVERYONE WHO OWNS A CAT DOES IT.

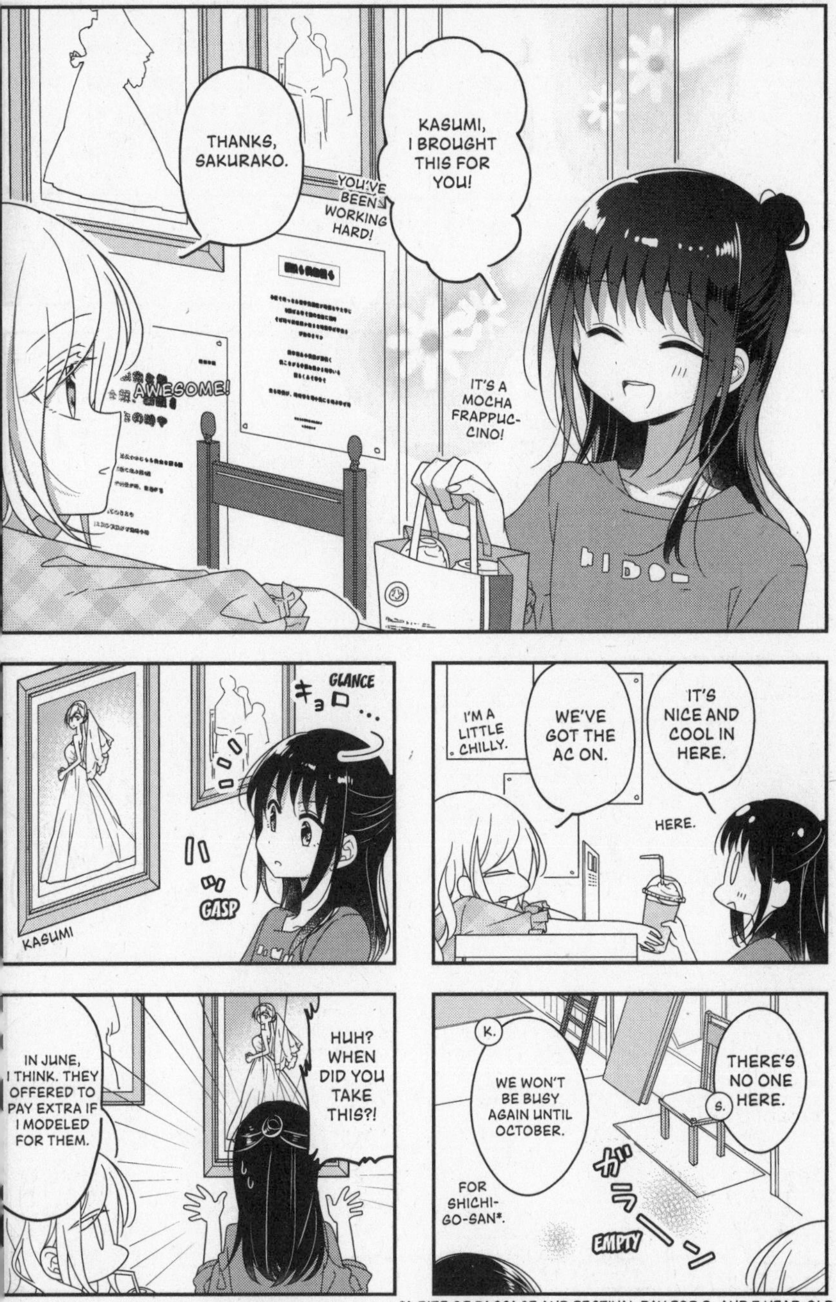
KASUMI, I BROUGHT THIS FOR YOU!
YOU'VE BEEN WORKING HARD!
THANKS, SAKURAKO.
IT'S A MOCHA FRAPPUCCINO!
AWESOME!
IT'S NICE AND COOL IN HERE.
WE'VE GOT THE AC ON.
I'M A LITTLE CHILLY.
HERE.
GLANCE
GASP
KASUMI
THERE'S NO ONE HERE.
S.
K.
WE WON'T BE BUSY AGAIN UNTIL OCTOBER.
FOR SHICHI-GO-SAN*.
EMPTY
HUH? WHEN DID YOU TAKE THIS?!
IN JUNE, I THINK. THEY OFFERED TO PAY EXTRA IF I MODELED FOR THEM.

*A RITE OF PASSAGE AND FESTIVAL DAY FOR 3- AND 7-YEAR-OLD GIRLS AND 5-YEAR-OLD BOYS TO CELEBRATE THEIR GROWTH.

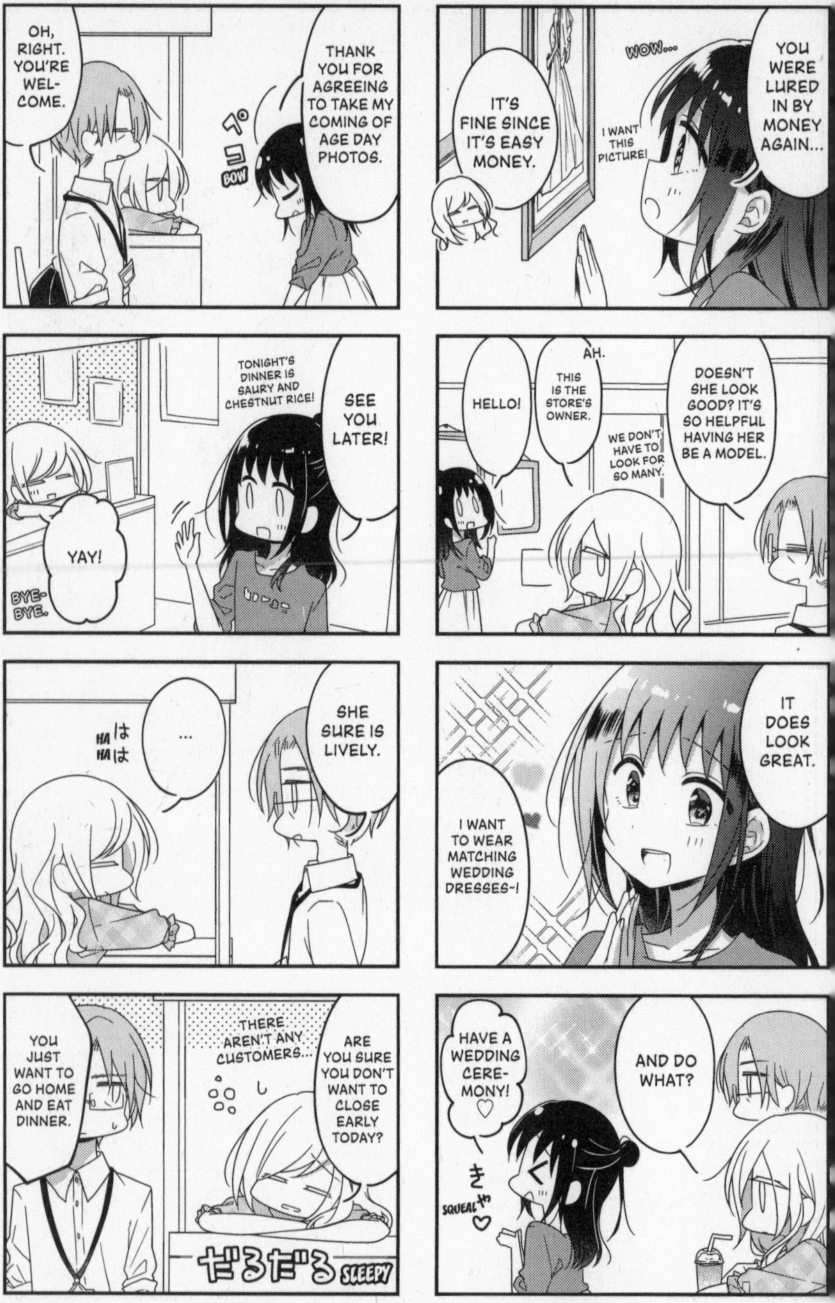
YOU WERE LURED IN BY MONEY AGAIN...
WOW...
I WANT THIS PICTURE!
IT'S FINE SINCE IT'S EASY MONEY.
DOESN'T SHE LOOK GOOD? IT'S SO HELPFUL HAVING HER BE A MODEL.
WE DON'T HAVE TO LOOK FOR SO MANY.
AH.
THIS IS THE STORE'S OWNER.
HELLO!
IT DOES LOOK GREAT.
I WANT TO WEAR MATCHING WEDDING DRESSES~!
AND DO WHAT?
HAVE A WEDDING CERE-MONY! ♡
きゃ♡
SQUEAL
THANK YOU FOR AGREEING TO TAKE MY COMING OF AGE DAY PHOTOS.
ペコ
BOW
OH, RIGHT. YOU'RE WEL-COME.
SEE YOU LATER!
TONIGHT'S DINNER IS SAURY AND CHESTNUT RICE!
YAY!
BYE-BYE.
SHE SURE IS LIVELY.
...
はは
HA HA
ARE YOU SURE YOU DON'T WANT TO CLOSE EARLY TODAY?
THERE AREN'T ANY CUSTOMERS...
YOU JUST WANT TO GO HOME AND EAT DINNER.
だるだる
SLEEPY

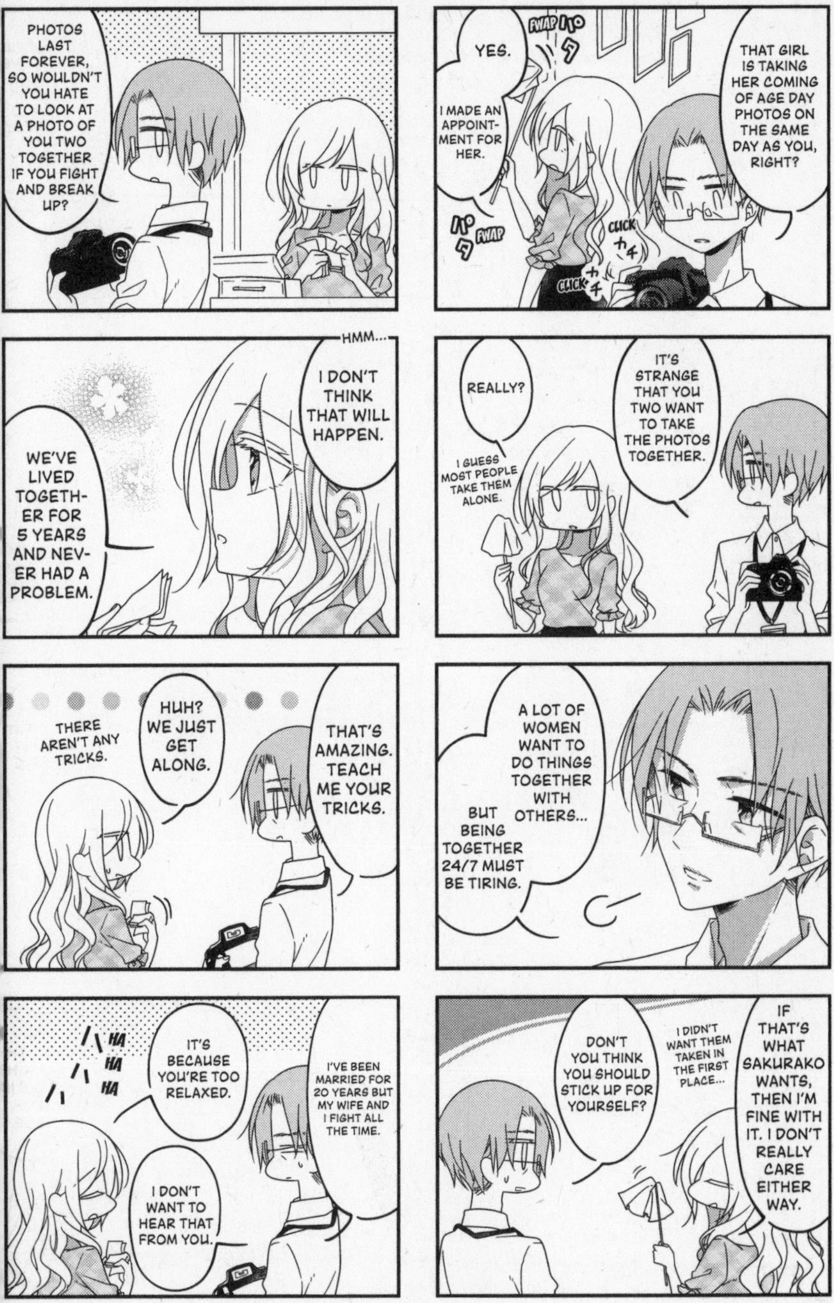
THAT GIRL IS TAKING HER COMING OF AGE DAY PHOTOS ON THE SAME DAY AS YOU, RIGHT?
FWAP パタ
YES.
I MADE AN APPOINTMENT FOR HER.
CLICK カチ
CLICK カチ
パタ FWAP
PHOTOS LAST FOREVER, SO WOULDN'T YOU HATE TO LOOK AT A PHOTO OF YOU TWO TOGETHER IF YOU FIGHT AND BREAK UP?
IT'S STRANGE THAT YOU TWO WANT TO TAKE THE PHOTOS TOGETHER.
REALLY?
I GUESS MOST PEOPLE TAKE THEM ALONE.
HMM...
I DON'T THINK THAT WILL HAPPEN.
WE'VE LIVED TOGETHER FOR 5 YEARS AND NEVER HAD A PROBLEM.
A LOT OF WOMEN WANT TO DO THINGS TOGETHER WITH OTHERS...
BUT BEING TOGETHER 24/7 MUST BE TIRING.
THAT'S AMAZING. TEACH ME YOUR TRICKS.
HUH? WE JUST GET ALONG.
THERE AREN'T ANY TRICKS.
IF THAT'S WHAT SAKURAKO WANTS, THEN I'M FINE WITH IT. I DON'T REALLY CARE EITHER WAY.
I DIDN'T WANT THEM TAKEN IN THE FIRST PLACE...
DON'T YOU THINK YOU SHOULD STICK UP FOR YOURSELF?
I'VE BEEN MARRIED FOR 20 YEARS BUT MY WIFE AND I FIGHT ALL THE TIME.
IT'S BECAUSE YOU'RE TOO RELAXED.
HA HA HA
I DON'T WANT TO HEAR THAT FROM YOU.

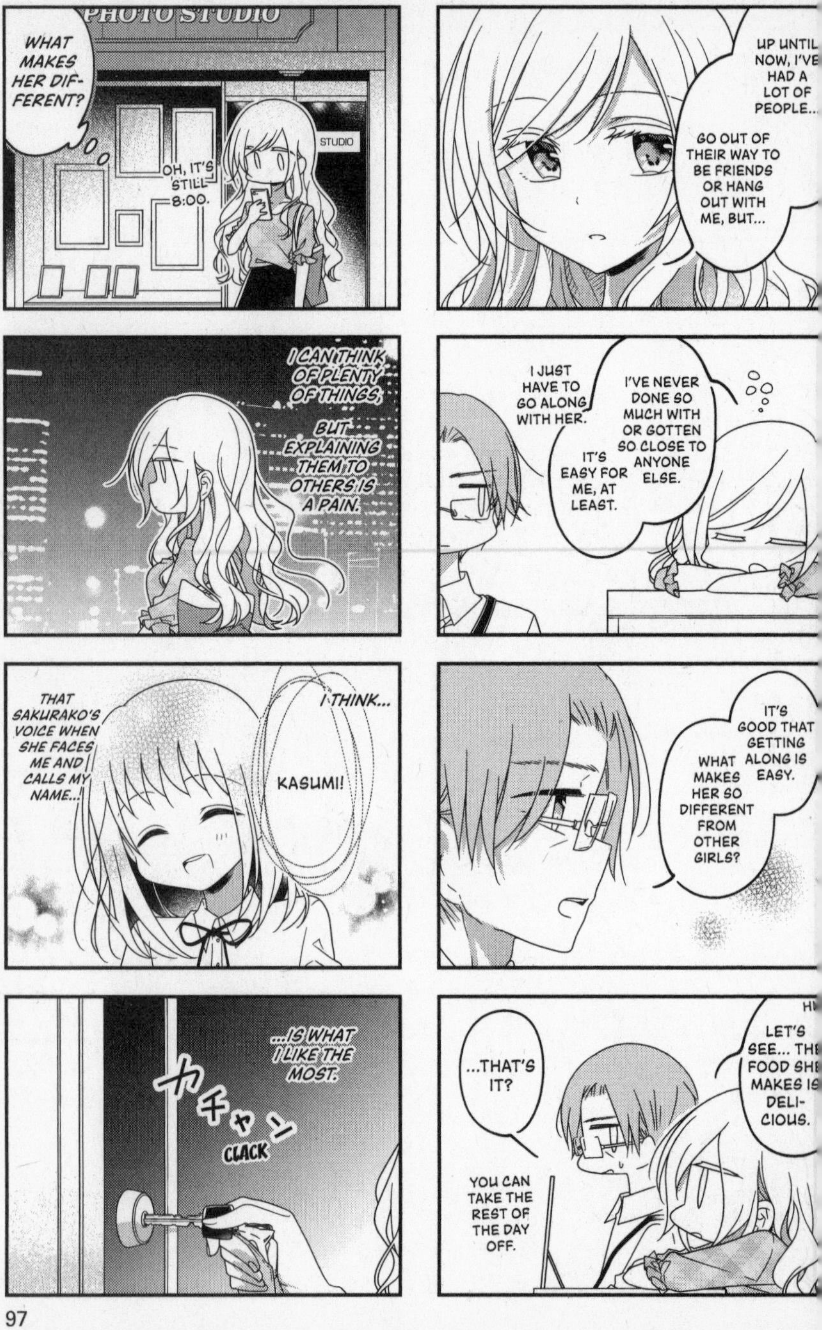
UP UNTIL NOW, I'VE HAD A LOT OF PEOPLE...
GO OUT OF THEIR WAY TO BE FRIENDS OR HANG OUT WITH ME, BUT...
PHOTO STUDIO
WHAT MAKES HER DIF-FERENT?
STUDIO
OH, IT'S STILL 8:00.
I'VE NEVER DONE SO MUCH WITH OR GOTTEN SO CLOSE TO ANYONE ELSE.
I JUST HAVE TO GO ALONG WITH HER.
IT'S EASY FOR ME, AT LEAST.
I CAN THINK OF PLENTY OF THINGS,
BUT EXPLAINING THEM TO OTHERS IS A PAIN.
IT'S GOOD THAT GETTING ALONG IS EASY.
WHAT MAKES HER SO DIFFERENT FROM OTHER GIRLS?
I THINK...
KASUMI!
THAT SAKURAKO'S VOICE WHEN SHE FACES ME AND CALLS MY NAME...
LET'S SEE... THE FOOD SHE MAKES IS DELI-CIOUS.
...THAT'S IT?
YOU CAN TAKE THE REST OF THE DAY OFF.
...IS WHAT I LIKE THE MOST.
CLACK

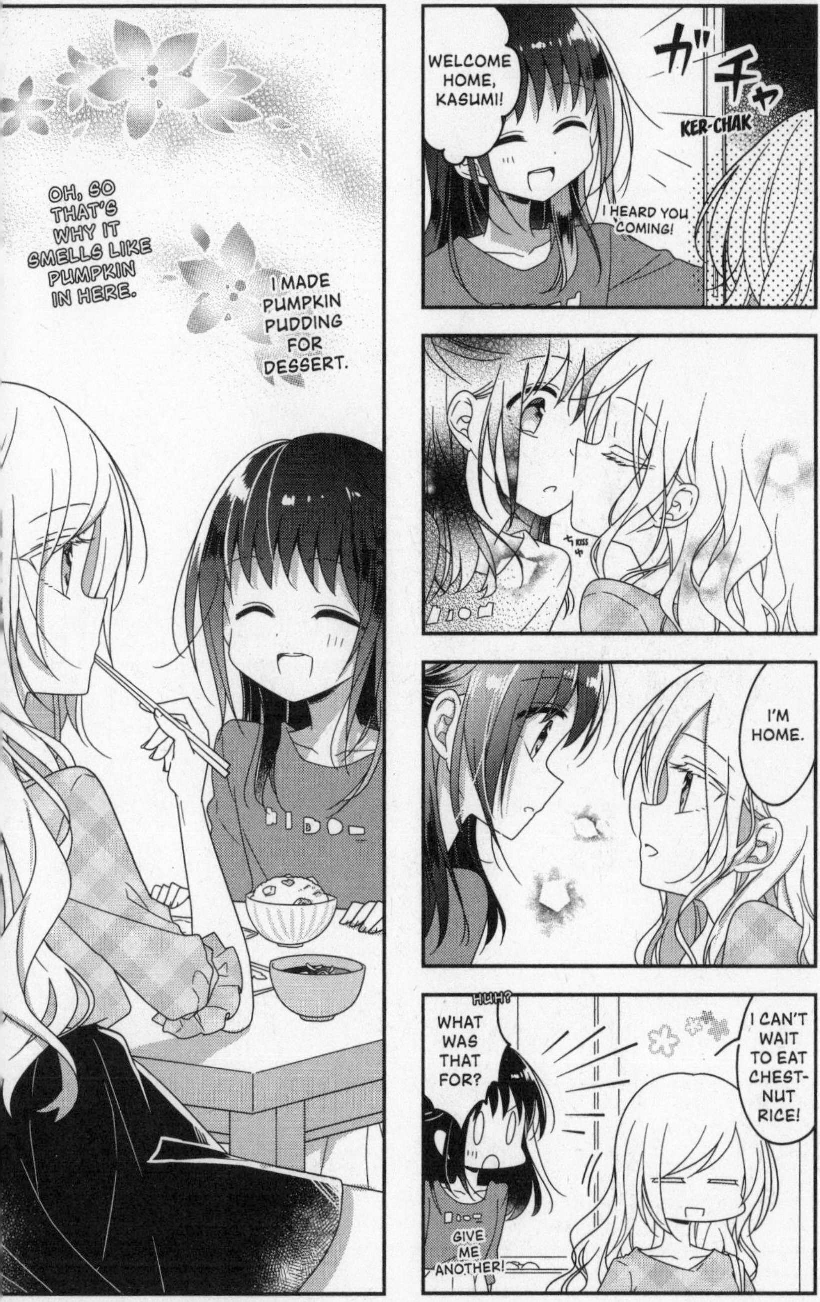
ガチャ
KER-CHAK
WELCOME HOME, KASUMI!
I HEARD YOU COMING!
KISS
I'M HOME.
I CAN'T WAIT TO EAT CHEST-NUT RICE!
HUH?
WHAT WAS THAT FOR?
GIVE ME ANOTHER!
I MADE PUMPKIN PUDDING FOR DESSERT.
OH, SO THAT'S WHY IT SMELLS LIKE PUMPKIN IN HERE.

Illustration gallery of Yukike

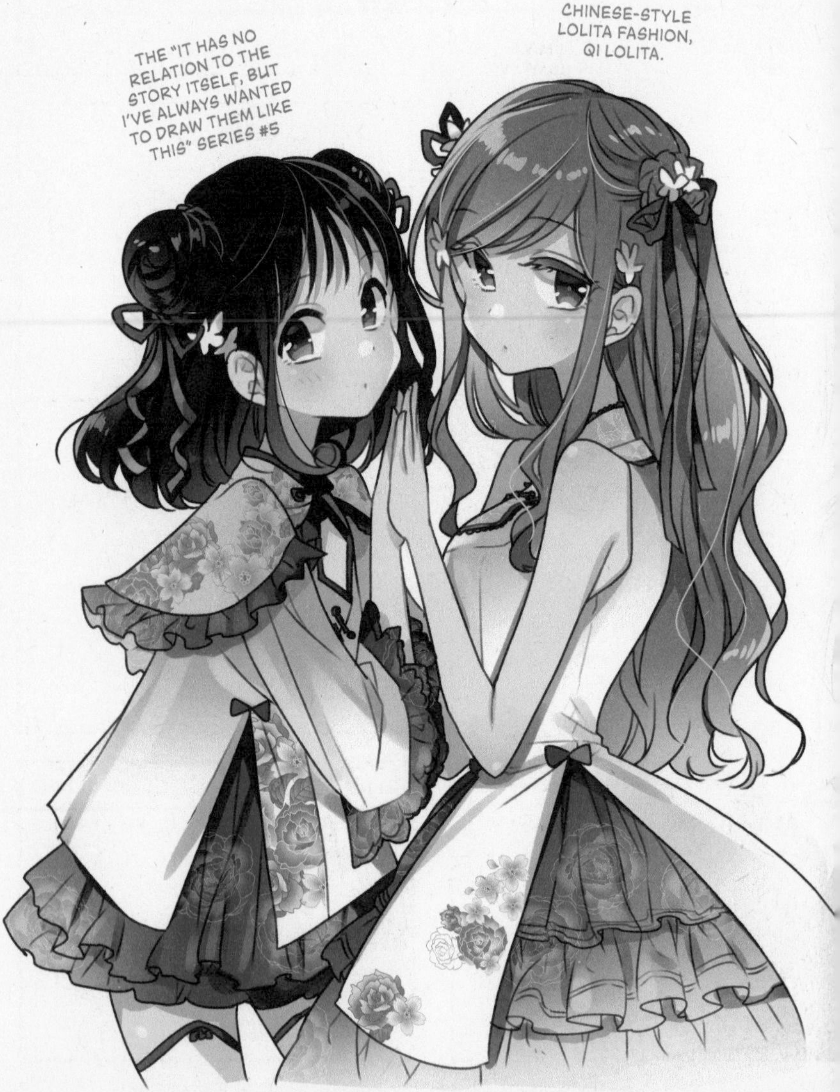

THE "IT HAS NO RELATION TO THE STORY ITSELF, BUT I'VE ALWAYS WANTED TO DRAW THEM LIKE THIS" SERIES #5
CHINESE-STYLE LOLITA FASHION, QI LOLITA.

Futaribeya
A ROOM FOR TWO

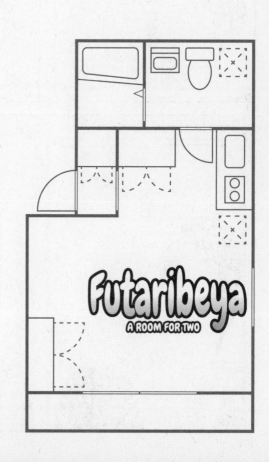

Special Chapter #3 - "Let's Go to Karaoke!"

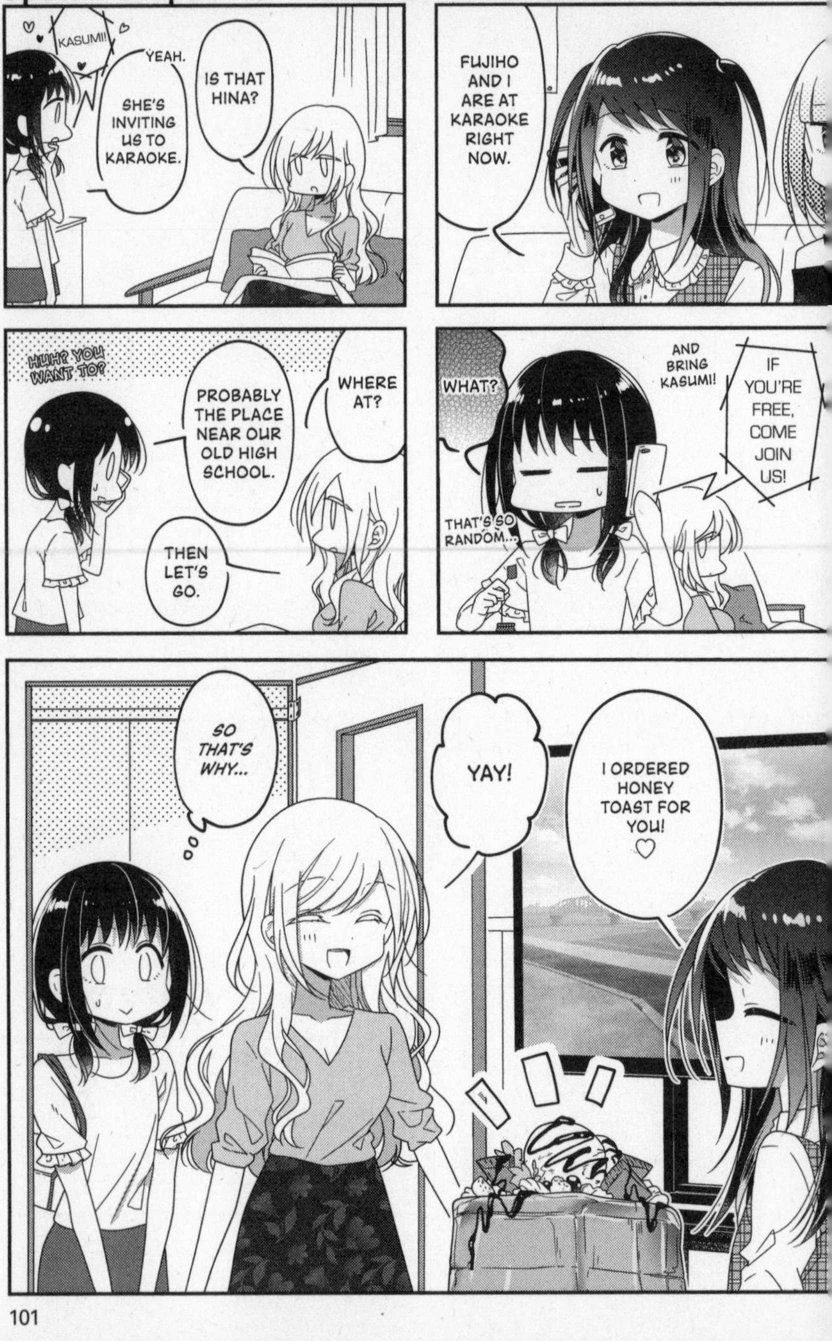
FUJIHO AND I ARE AT KARAOKE RIGHT NOW.
IS THAT HINA?
YEAH. SHE'S INVITING US TO KARAOKE.
KASUMI!!
IF YOU'RE FREE, COME JOIN US!
AND BRING KASUMI!
WHAT?
THAT'S SO RANDOM...
WHERE AT?
PROBABLY THE PLACE NEAR OUR OLD HIGH SCHOOL.
HUH? YOU WANT TO?
THEN LET'S GO.
I ORDERED HONEY TOAST FOR YOU! ♡
YAY!
SO THAT'S WHY...

My Special Privilege

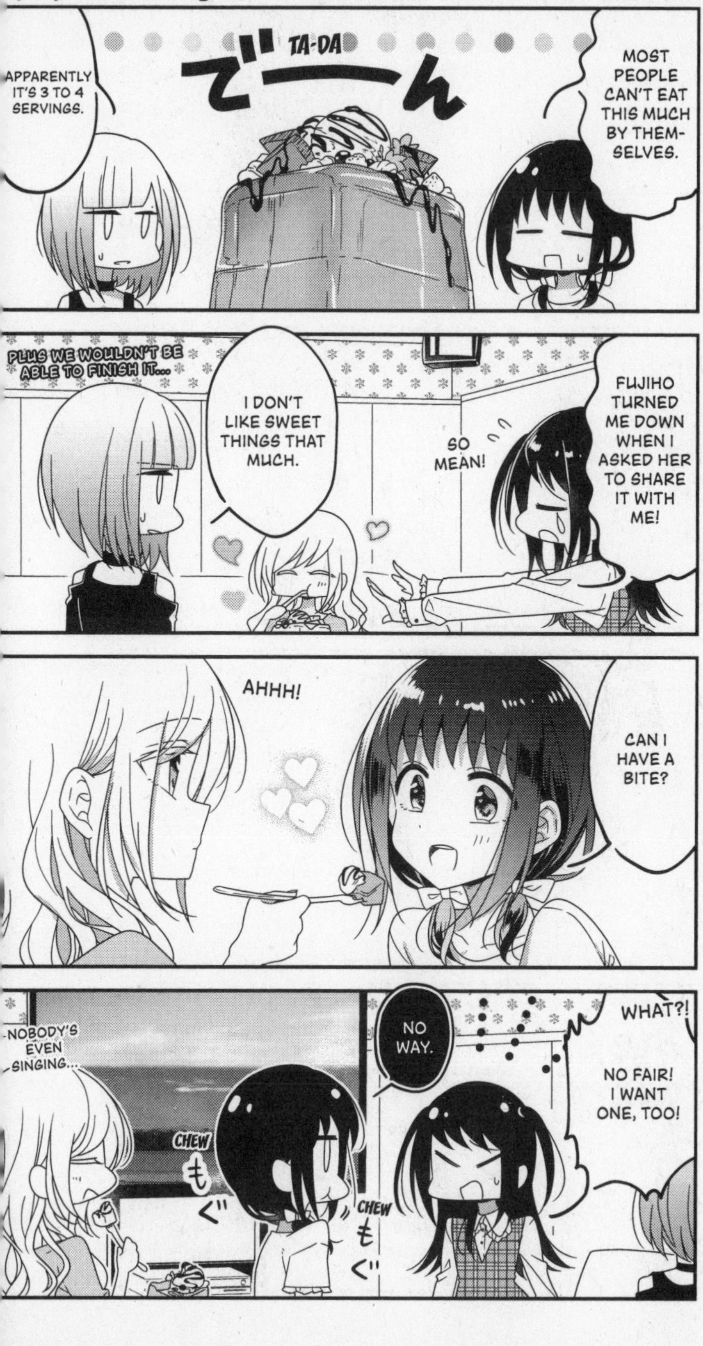
MOST PEOPLE CAN'T EAT THIS MUCH BY THEMSELVES.
TA-DA
でーん
APPARENTLY IT'S 3 TO 4 SERVINGS.
FUJIHO TURNED ME DOWN WHEN I ASKED HER TO SHARE IT WITH ME!
SO MEAN!
I DON'T LIKE SWEET THINGS THAT MUCH.
PLUS WE WOULDN'T BE ABLE TO FINISH IT...
CAN I HAVE A BITE?
AHHH!
WHAT?!
NO FAIR! I WANT ONE, TOO!
NO WAY.
CHEW
もぐ
CHEW
もぐ
NOBODY'S EVEN SINGING...

Not Good at Receiving Compliments

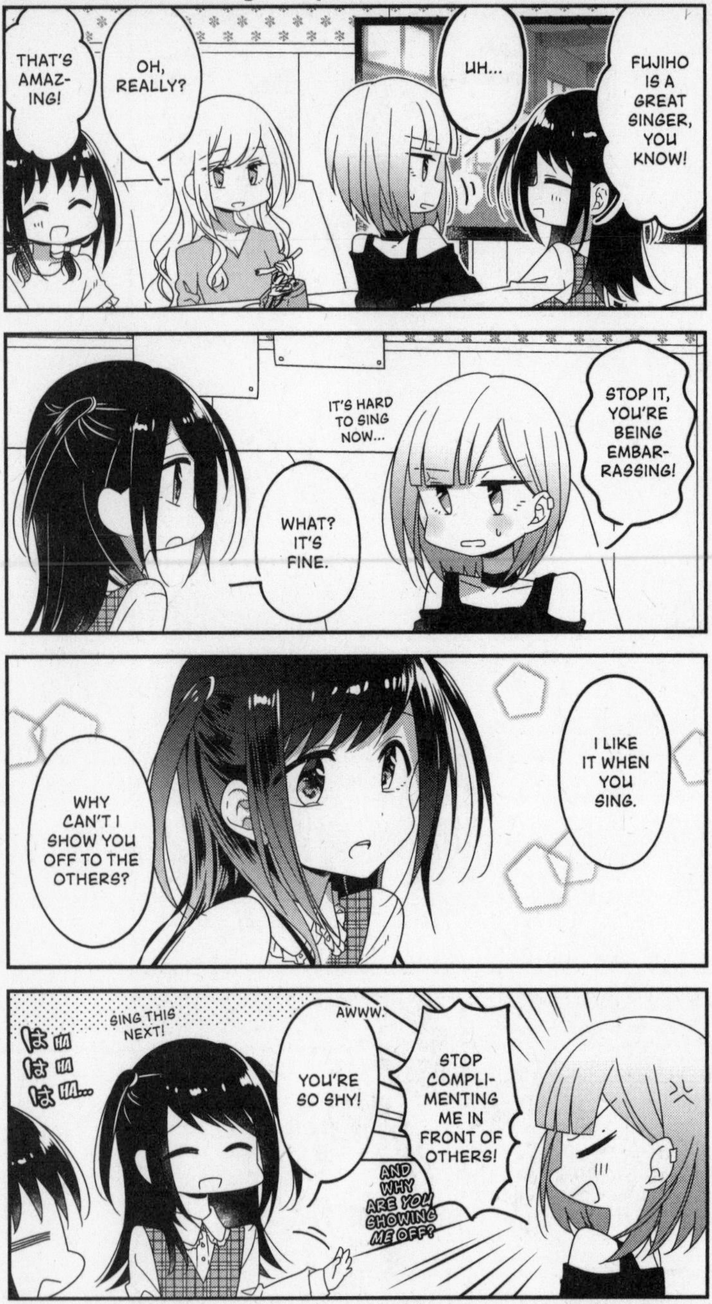
FUJIHO IS A GREAT SINGER, YOU KNOW!
UH...
OH, REALLY?
THAT'S AMAZ-ING!
STOP IT, YOU'RE BEING EMBAR-RASSING!
IT'S HARD TO SING NOW...
WHAT? IT'S FINE.
I LIKE IT WHEN YOU SING.
WHY CAN'T I SHOW YOU OFF TO THE OTHERS?
STOP COMPLI-MENTING ME IN FRONT OF OTHERS!
AND WHY ARE YOU SHOWING ME OFF?
AWWW.
YOU'RE SO SHY!
SING THIS NEXT!
は HA は HA は HA...

My Playlist

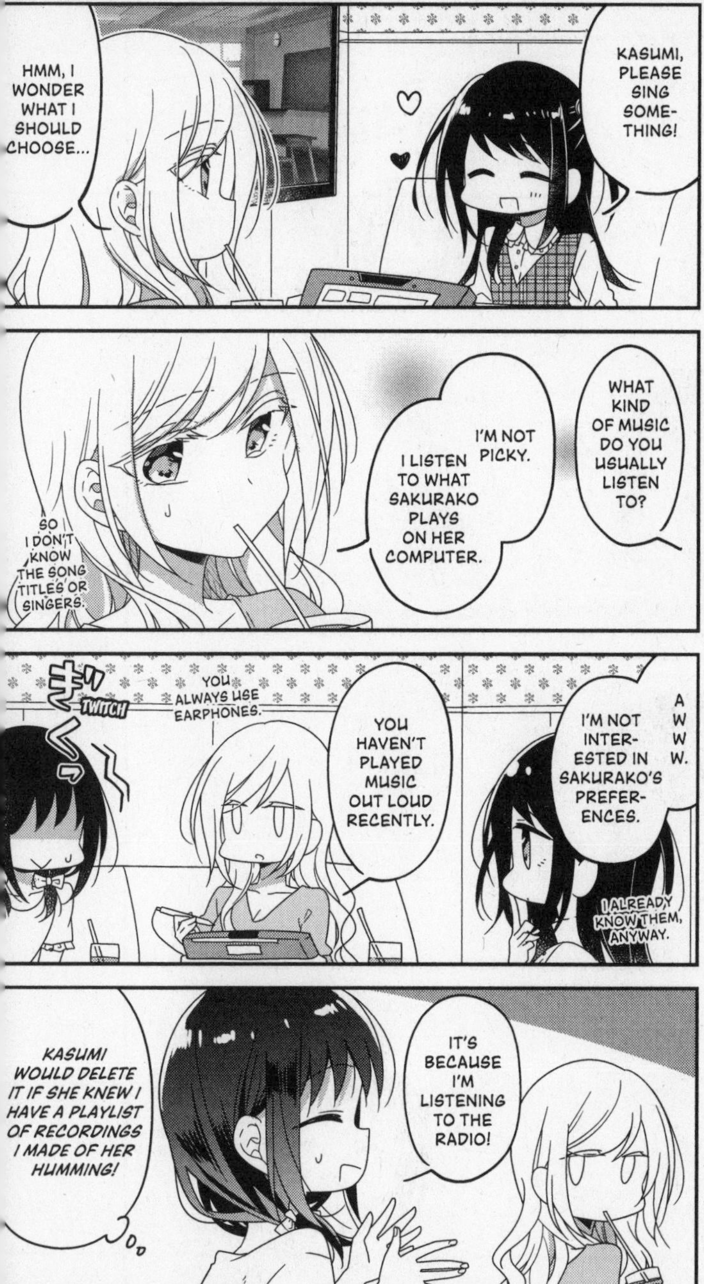

KASUMI, PLEASE SING SOME-THING!
HMM, I WONDER WHAT I SHOULD CHOOSE...
WHAT KIND OF MUSIC DO YOU USUALLY LISTEN TO?
I'M NOT PICKY.
I LISTEN TO WHAT SAKURAKO PLAYS ON HER COMPUTER.
SO I DON'T KNOW THE SONG TITLES OR SINGERS.
AWWW.
I'M NOT INTER-ESTED IN SAKURAKO'S PREFER-ENCES.
I ALREADY KNOW THEM, ANYWAY.
YOU HAVEN'T PLAYED MUSIC OUT LOUD RECENTLY.
YOU ALWAYS USE EARPHONES.
TWITCH
IT'S BECAUSE I'M LISTENING TO THE RADIO!
KASUMI WOULD DELETE IT IF SHE KNEW I HAVE A PLAYLIST OF RECORDINGS I MADE OF HER HUMMING!

Things You Excel At

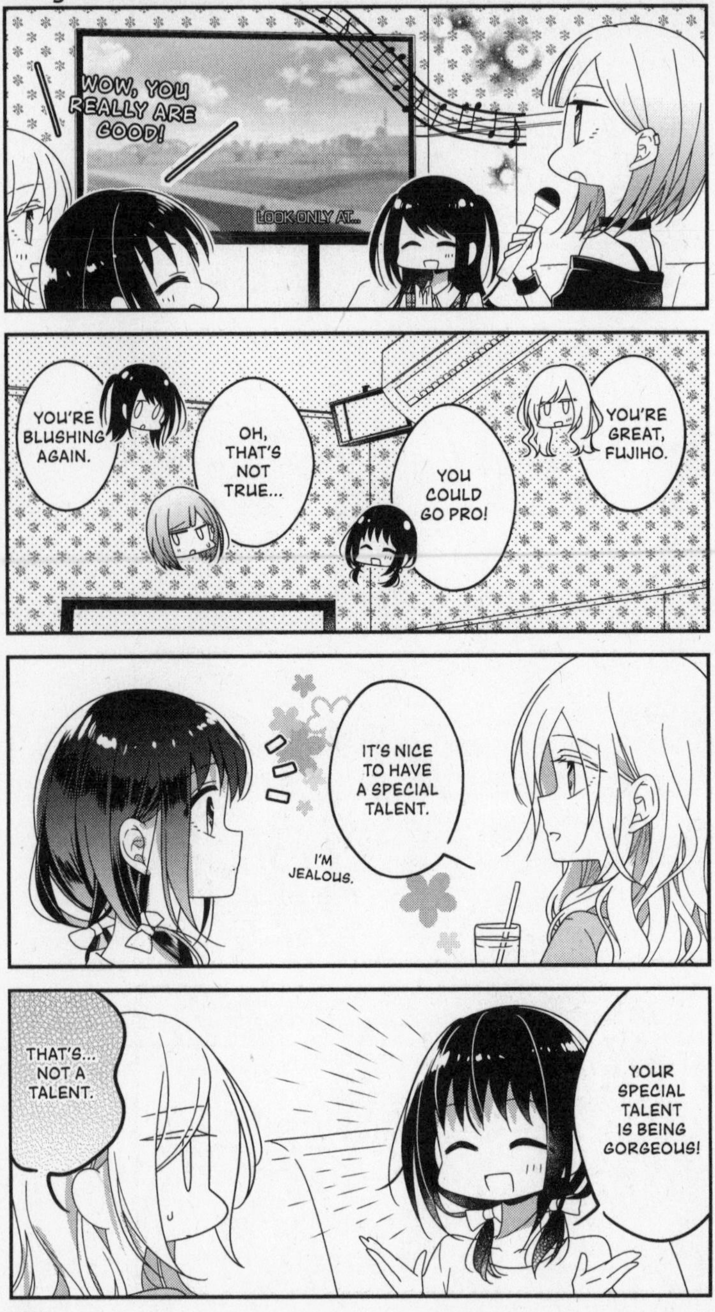

WOW, YOU REALLY ARE GOOD!
LOOK ONLY AT...
YOU'RE GREAT, FUJIHO.
YOU COULD GO PRO!
OH, THAT'S NOT TRUE...
YOU'RE BLUSHING AGAIN.
IT'S NICE TO HAVE A SPECIAL TALENT.
I'M JEALOUS.
YOUR SPECIAL TALENT IS BEING GORGEOUS!
THAT'S... NOT A TALENT.

English Ability

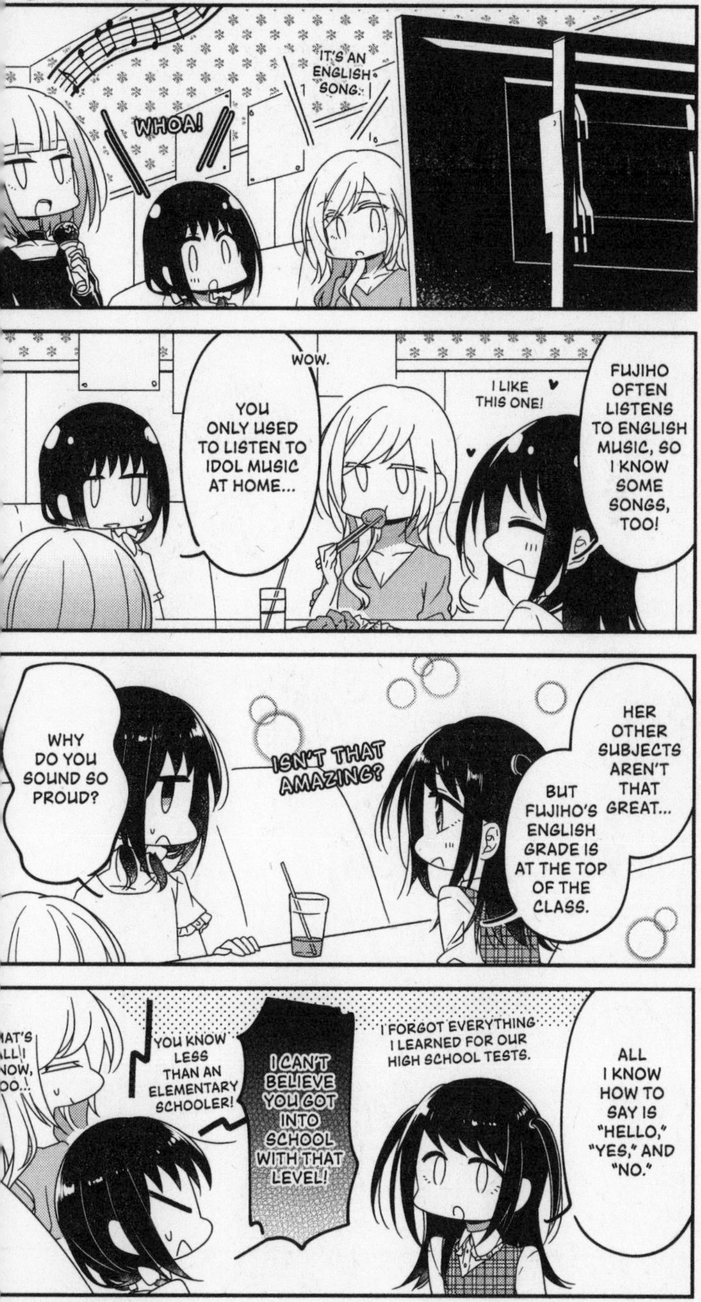
IT'S AN ENGLISH SONG.
WHOA!
FUJIHO OFTEN LISTENS TO ENGLISH MUSIC, SO I KNOW SOME SONGS, TOO!
I LIKE THIS ONE!
WOW.
YOU ONLY USED TO LISTEN TO IDOL MUSIC AT HOME...
HER OTHER SUBJECTS AREN'T THAT GREAT...
BUT FUJIHO'S ENGLISH GRADE IS AT THE TOP OF THE CLASS.
ISN'T THAT AMAZING?
WHY DO YOU SOUND SO PROUD?
ALL I KNOW HOW TO SAY IS "HELLO," "YES," AND "NO."
I FORGOT EVERYTHING I LEARNED FOR OUR HIGH SCHOOL TESTS.
I CAN'T BELIEVE YOU GOT INTO SCHOOL WITH THAT LEVEL!
YOU KNOW LESS THAN AN ELEMENTARY SCHOOLER!
AT'S ALL I NOW, OO...

Lucky Just Being Together

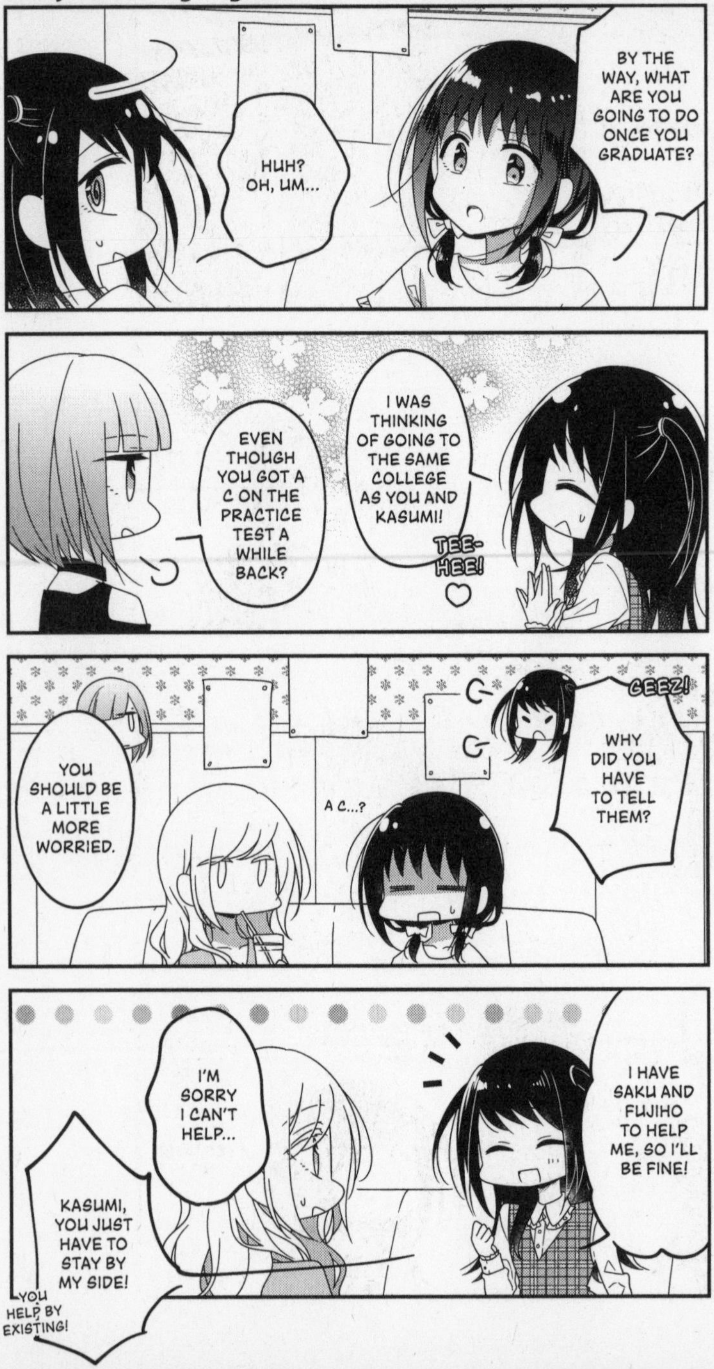
BY THE WAY, WHAT ARE YOU GOING TO DO ONCE YOU GRADUATE?
HUH? OH, UM...
I WAS THINKING OF GOING TO THE SAME COLLEGE AS YOU AND KASUMI!
TEE-HEE!
EVEN THOUGH YOU GOT A C ON THE PRACTICE TEST A WHILE BACK?
GEEZ!
WHY DID YOU HAVE TO TELL THEM?
A C...?
YOU SHOULD BE A LITTLE MORE WORRIED.
I HAVE SAKU AND FUJIHO TO HELP ME, SO I'LL BE FINE!
I'M SORRY I CAN'T HELP...
KASUMI, YOU JUST HAVE TO STAY BY MY SIDE!
YOU HELP BY EXISTING!

The Easy-going Kawawas

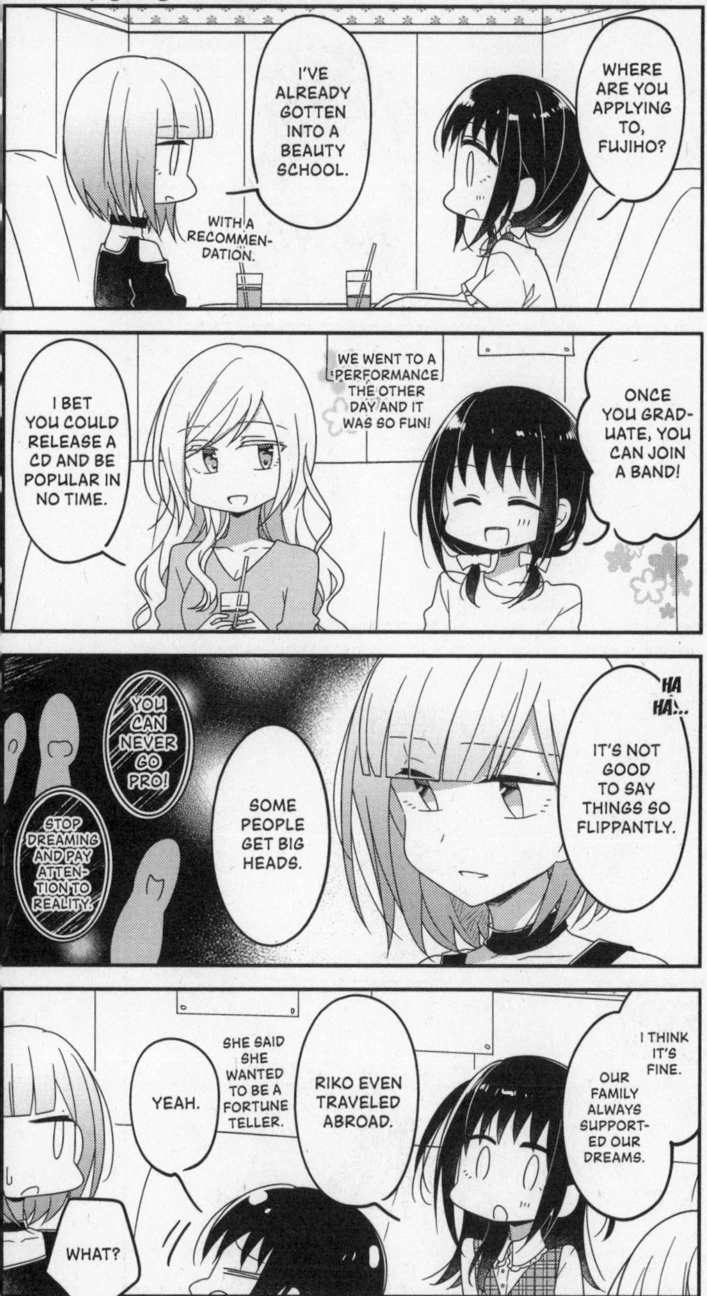

WHERE ARE YOU APPLYING TO, FUJIHO?
I'VE ALREADY GOTTEN INTO A BEAUTY SCHOOL.
WITH A RECOMMENDATION.
ONCE YOU GRADUATE, YOU CAN JOIN A BAND!
WE WENT TO A PERFORMANCE THE OTHER DAY AND IT WAS SO FUN!
I BET YOU COULD RELEASE A CD AND BE POPULAR IN NO TIME.
HA HA...
IT'S NOT GOOD TO SAY THINGS SO FLIPPANTLY.
SOME PEOPLE GET BIG HEADS.
YOU CAN NEVER GO PRO!
STOP DREAMING AND PAY ATTENTION TO REALITY.
I THINK IT'S FINE.
OUR FAMILY ALWAYS SUPPORTED OUR DREAMS.
RIKO EVEN TRAVELED ABROAD.
SHE SAID SHE WANTED TO BE A FORTUNE TELLER.
YEAH.
WHAT?

Not Everything is Okay...

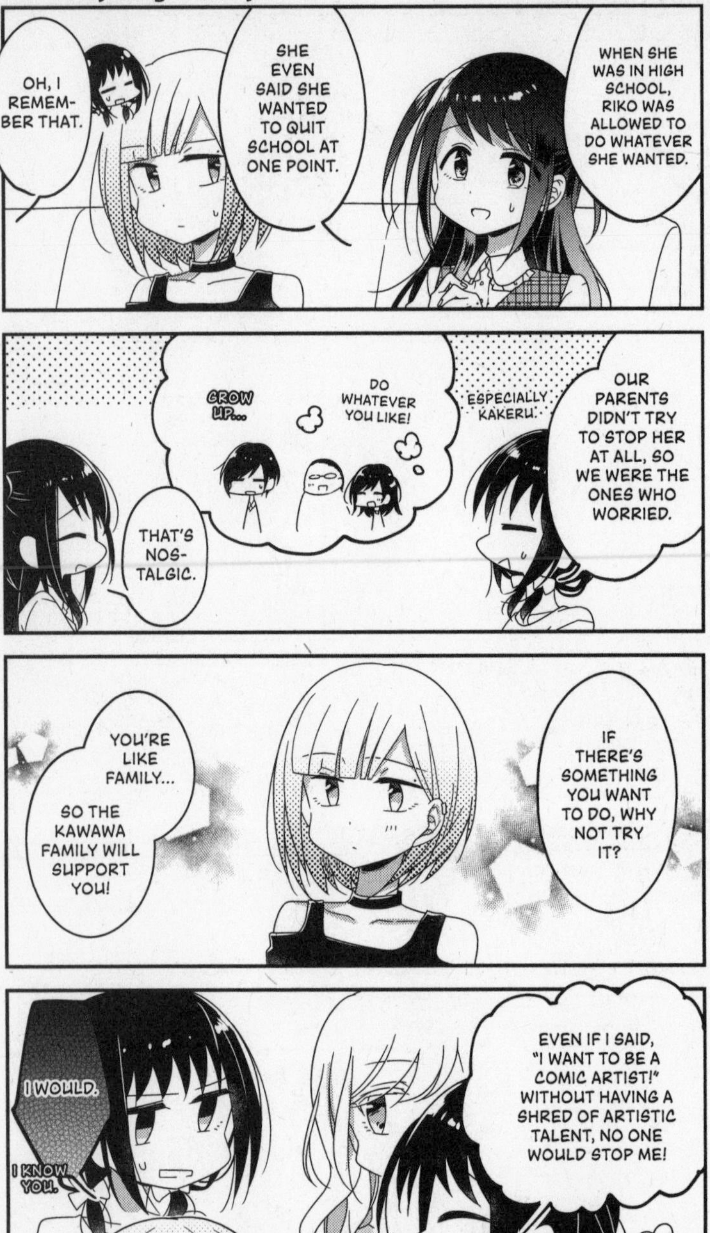

WHEN SHE WAS IN HIGH SCHOOL, RIKO WAS ALLOWED TO DO WHATEVER SHE WANTED.
SHE EVEN SAID SHE WANTED TO QUIT SCHOOL AT ONE POINT.
OH, I REMEMBER THAT.
OUR PARENTS DIDN'T TRY TO STOP HER AT ALL, SO WE WERE THE ONES WHO WORRIED.
ESPECIALLY KAKERU.
DO WHATEVER YOU LIKE!
GROW UP...
THAT'S NOSTALGIC.
IF THERE'S SOMETHING YOU WANT TO DO, WHY NOT TRY IT?
YOU'RE LIKE FAMILY...
SO THE KAWAWA FAMILY WILL SUPPORT YOU!
EVEN IF I SAID, "I WANT TO BE A COMIC ARTIST!" WITHOUT HAVING A SHRED OF ARTISTIC TALENT, NO ONE WOULD STOP ME!
I WOULD.
I KNOW YOU.

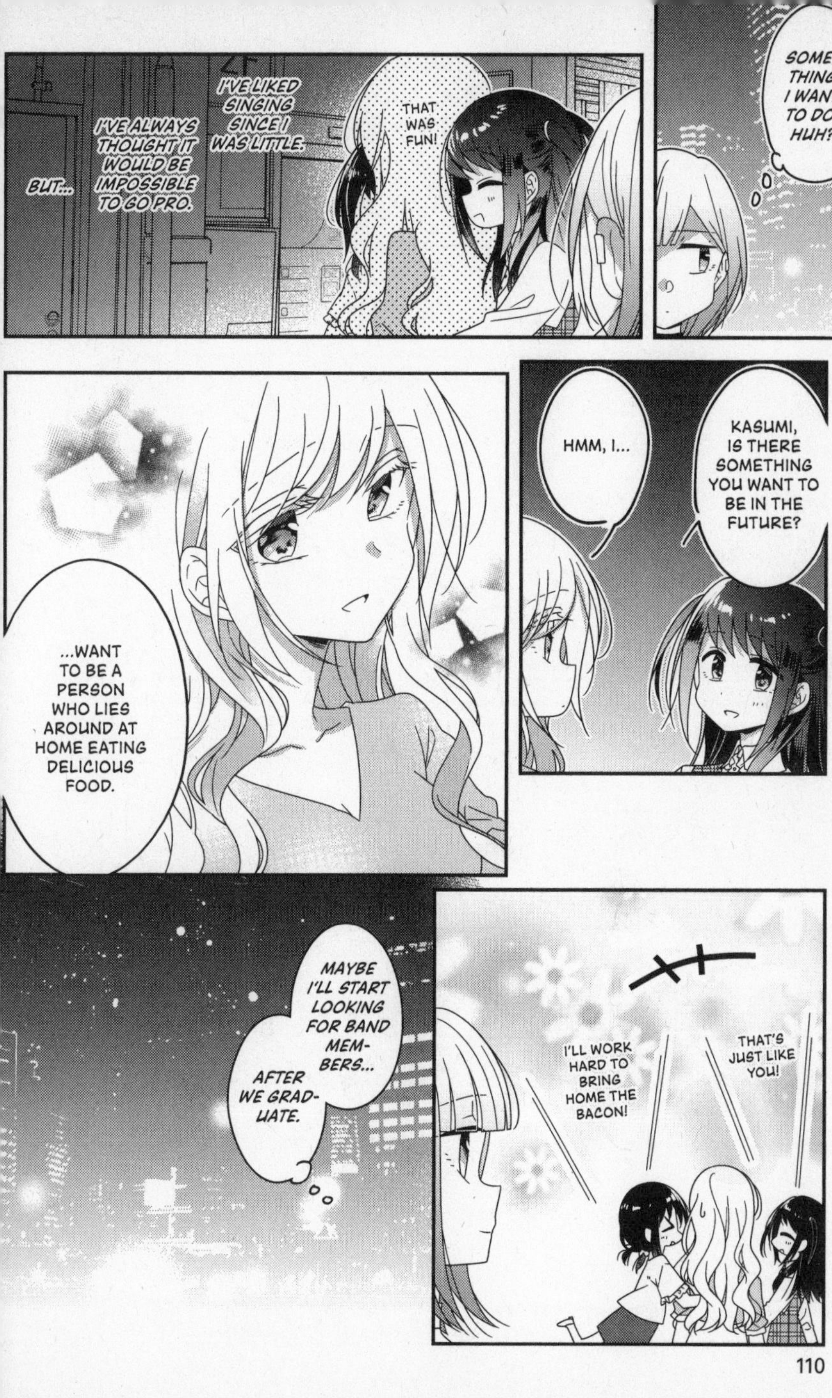
SOMETHING I WANT TO DO, HUH?
THAT WAS FUN!
I'VE LIKED SINGING SINCE I WAS LITTLE.
I'VE ALWAYS THOUGHT IT WOULD BE IMPOSSIBLE TO GO PRO.
BUT...
KASUMI, IS THERE SOMETHING YOU WANT TO BE IN THE FUTURE?
HMM, I...
...WANT TO BE A PERSON WHO LIES AROUND AT HOME EATING DELICIOUS FOOD.
THAT'S JUST LIKE YOU!
I'LL WORK HARD TO BRING HOME THE BACON!
MAYBE I'LL START LOOKING FOR BAND MEMBERS...
AFTER WE GRADUATE.

Illustration gallery of Yukiko

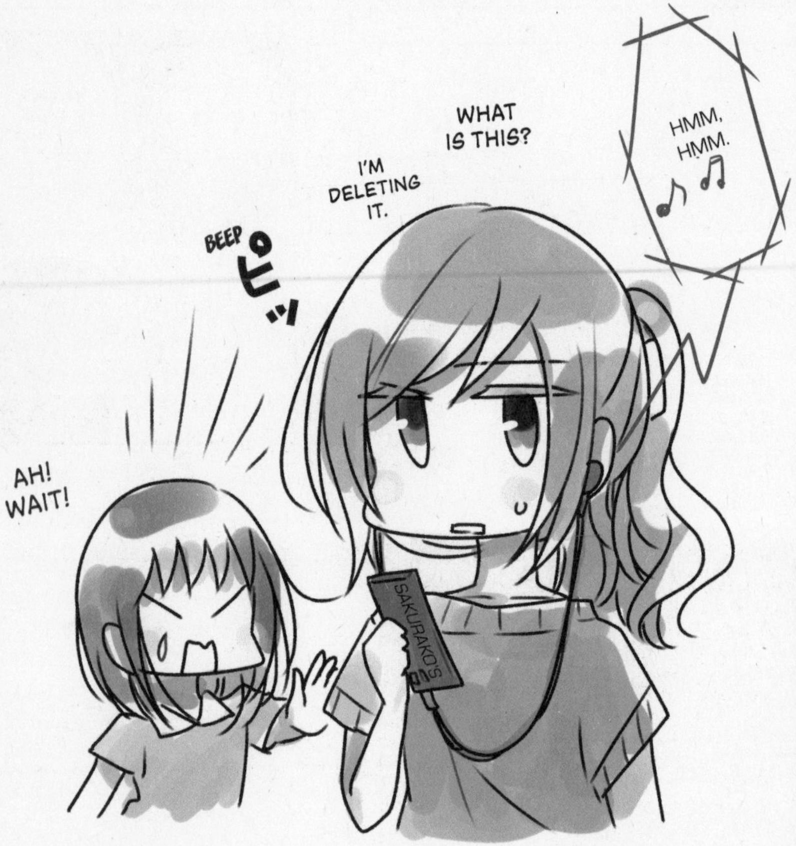
HMM, HMM.
WHAT IS THIS?
I'M DELETING IT.
BEEP
ピッ
AH! WAIT!
SAKURAKO'S

Futaribeya
A ROOM FOR TWO

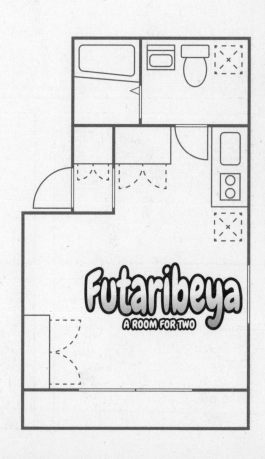

Chapter 54 (Part 1)

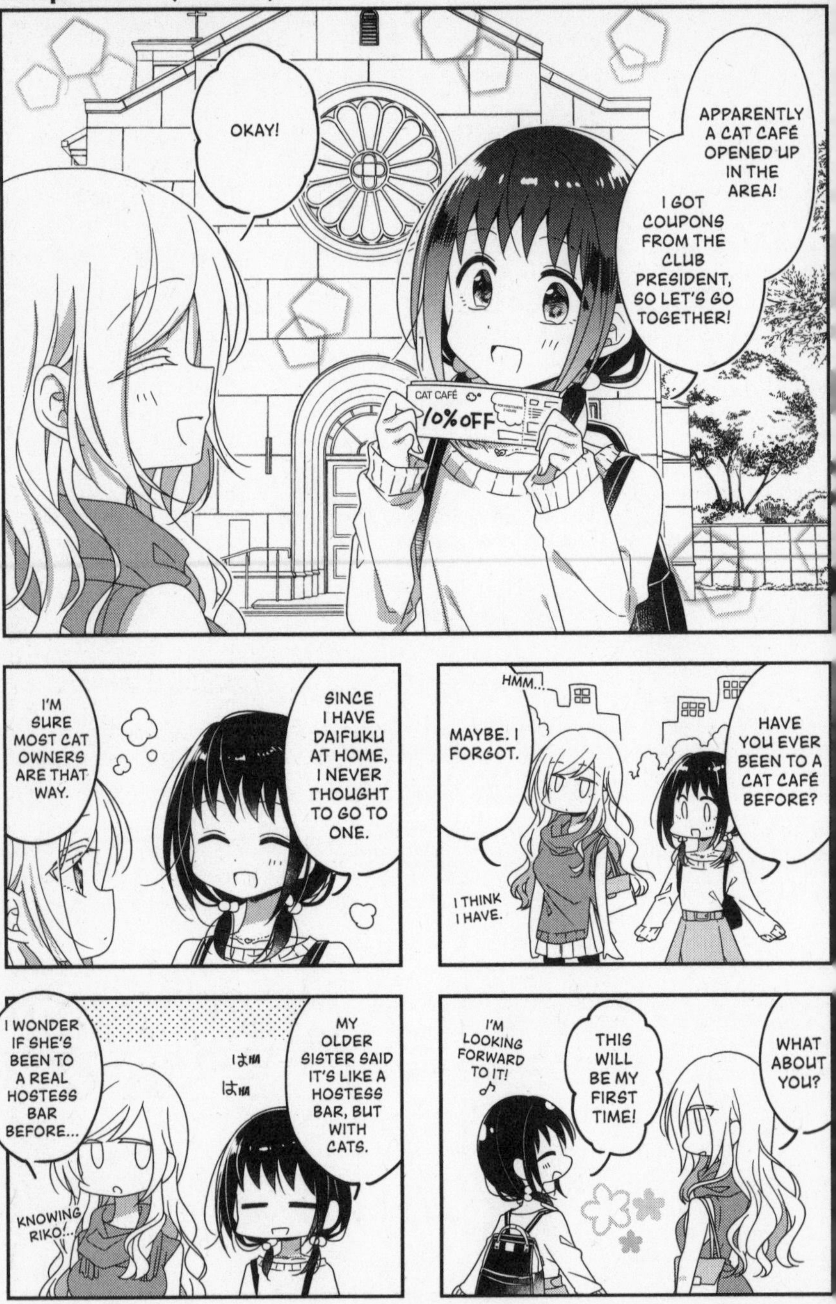
APPARENTLY A CAT CAFÉ OPENED UP IN THE AREA!
I GOT COUPONS FROM THE CLUB PRESIDENT, SO LET'S GO TOGETHER!
CAT CAFÉ
10% OFF
OKAY!
HAVE YOU EVER BEEN TO A CAT CAFÉ BEFORE?
HMM...
MAYBE. I FORGOT.
I THINK I HAVE.
SINCE I HAVE DAIFUKU AT HOME, I NEVER THOUGHT TO GO TO ONE.
I'M SURE MOST CAT OWNERS ARE THAT WAY.
WHAT ABOUT YOU?
THIS WILL BE MY FIRST TIME!
I'M LOOKING FORWARD TO IT! ♪
MY OLDER SISTER SAID IT'S LIKE A HOSTESS BAR, BUT WITH CATS.
I WONDER IF SHE'S BEEN TO A REAL HOSTESS BAR BEFORE...
KNOWING RIKO!...

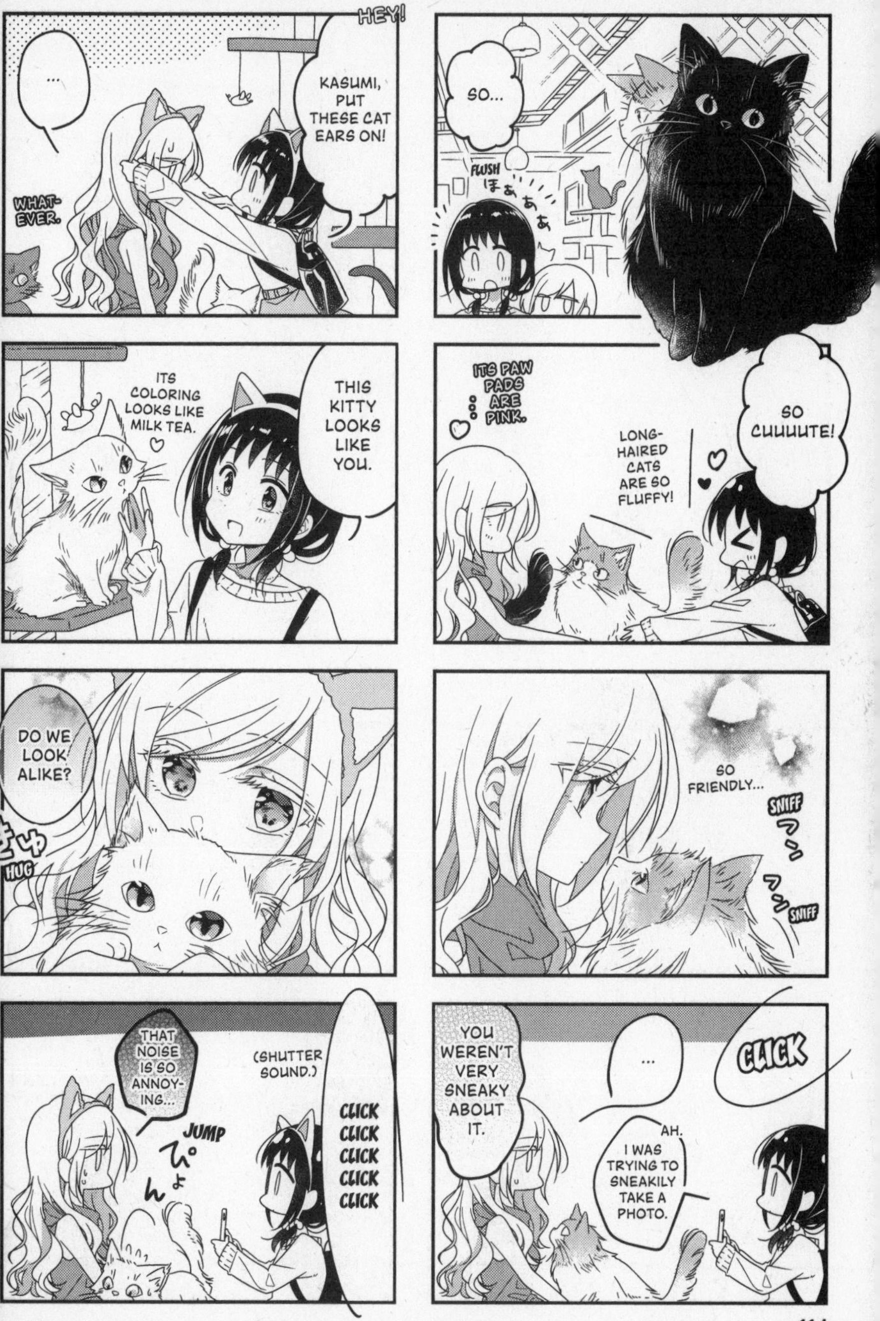
SO...
FLUSH
HEY!
KASUMI, PUT THESE CAT EARS ON!
...
WHAT-EVER.
SO CUUUUTE!
LONG-HAIRED CATS ARE SO FLUFFY!
ITS PAW PADS ARE PINK.
THIS KITTY LOOKS LIKE YOU.
ITS COLORING LOOKS LIKE MILK TEA.
SO FRIENDLY...
SNIFF
SNIFF
DO WE LOOK ALIKE?
HUG
CLICK
...
YOU WEREN'T VERY SNEAKY ABOUT IT.
AH. I WAS TRYING TO SNEAKILY TAKE A PHOTO.
CLICK CLICK CLICK CLICK CLICK
(SHUTTER SOUND.)
THAT NOISE IS SO ANNOY-ING...
JUMP

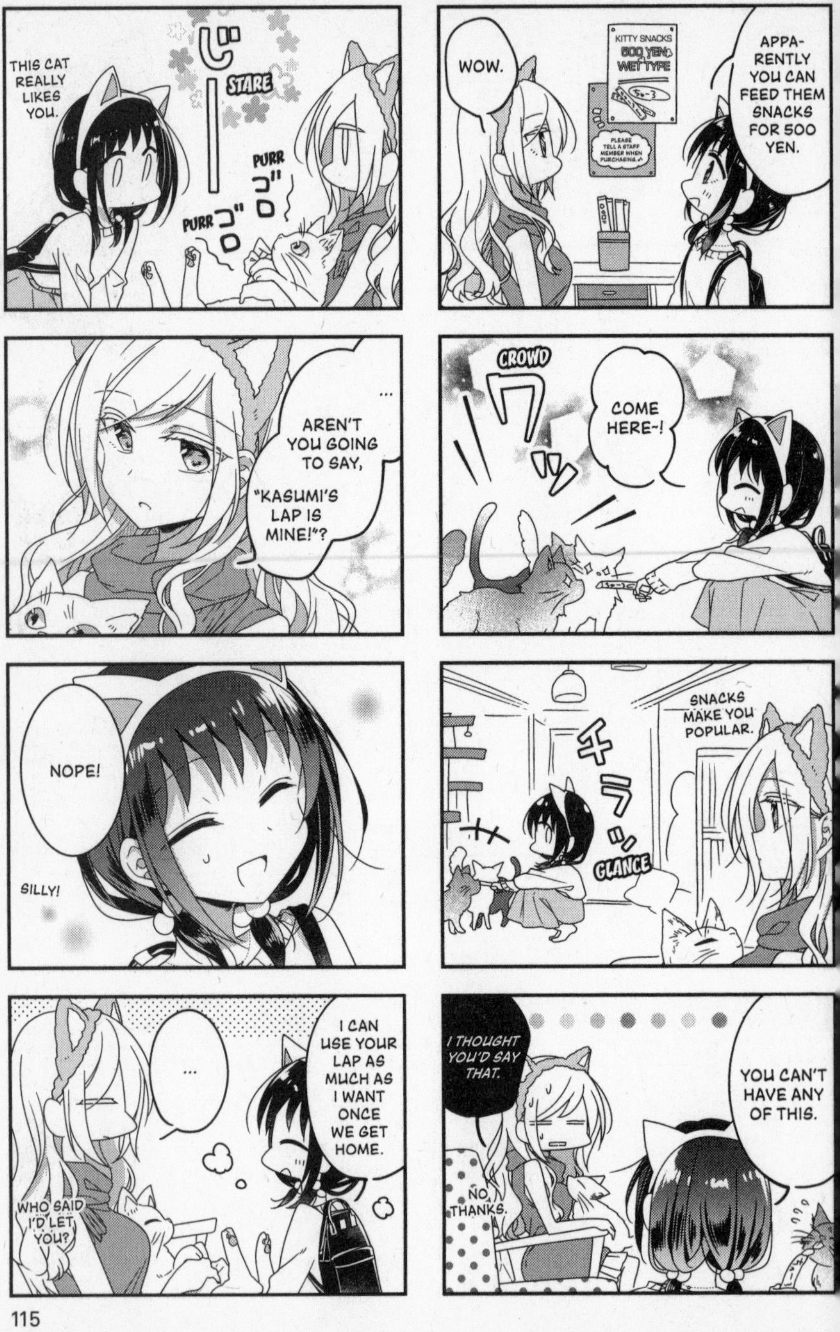
APPARENTLY YOU CAN FEED THEM SNACKS FOR 500 YEN.
KITTY SNACKS
500 YEN WET TYPE
PLEASE TELL A STAFF MEMBER WHEN PURCHASING.♪
WOW.
CROWD
COME HERE~!
SNACKS MAKE YOU POPULAR.
GLANCE
YOU CAN'T HAVE ANY OF THIS.
I THOUGHT YOU'D SAY THAT.
NO THANKS.
THIS CAT REALLY LIKES YOU.
STARE
PURR
PURR
...
AREN'T YOU GOING TO SAY, "KASUMI'S LAP IS MINE!"?
NOPE!
SILLY!
I CAN USE YOUR LAP AS MUCH AS I WANT ONCE WE GET HOME.
...
WHO SAID I'D LET YOU?

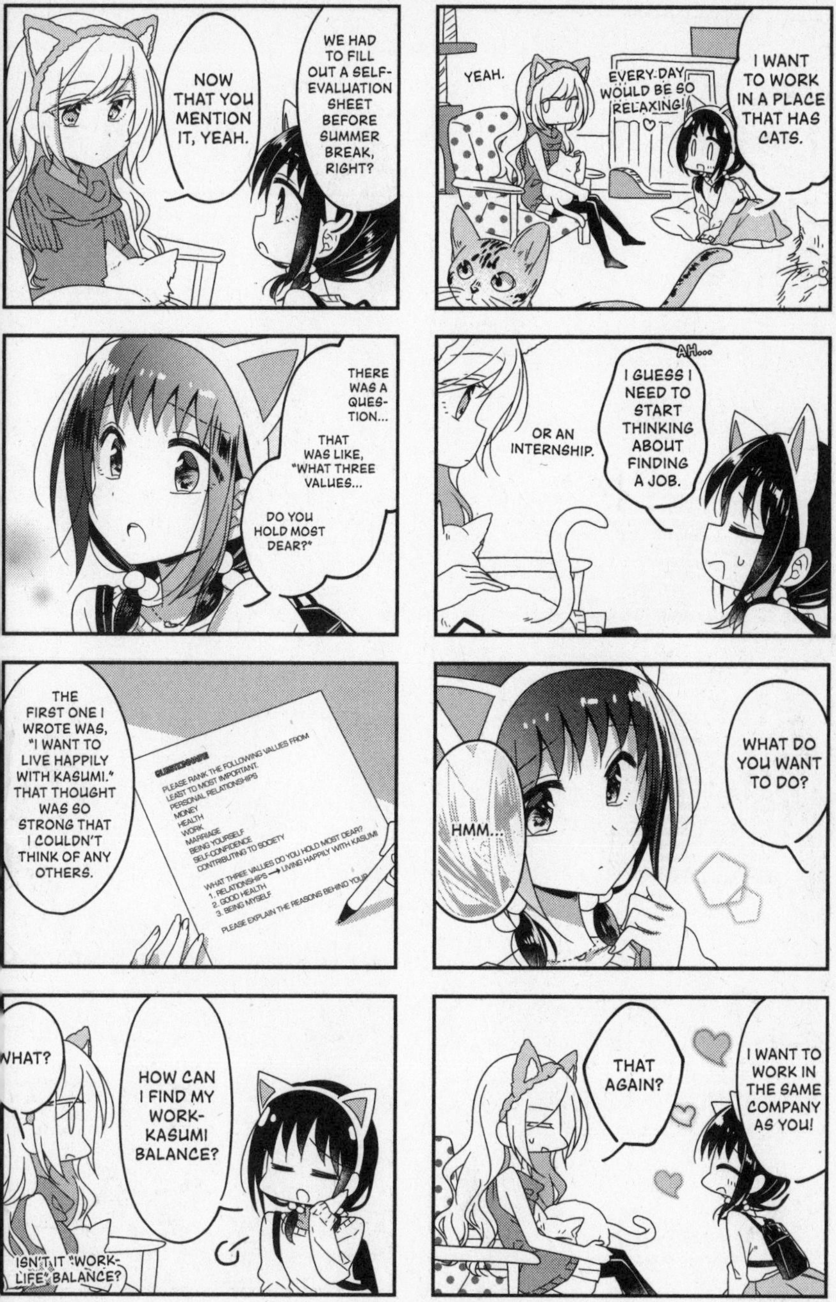
I WANT TO WORK IN A PLACE THAT HAS CATS.
EVERY DAY WOULD BE SO RELAXING!
YEAH.
AH...
I GUESS I NEED TO START THINKING ABOUT FINDING A JOB.
OR AN INTERNSHIP.
WHAT DO YOU WANT TO DO?
HMM...
I WANT TO WORK IN THE SAME COMPANY AS YOU!
THAT AGAIN?
WE HAD TO FILL OUT A SELF-EVALUATION SHEET BEFORE SUMMER BREAK, RIGHT?
NOW THAT YOU MENTION IT, YEAH.
THERE WAS A QUESTION...
THAT WAS LIKE, "WHAT THREE VALUES...
DO YOU HOLD MOST DEAR?"
THE FIRST ONE I WROTE WAS, "I WANT TO LIVE HAPPILY WITH KASUMI." THAT THOUGHT WAS SO STRONG THAT I COULDN'T THINK OF ANY OTHERS.
PLEASE RANK THE FOLLOWING VALUES FROM LEAST TO MOST IMPORTANT.
PERSONAL RELATIONSHIPS
MONEY
HEALTH
WORK
MARRIAGE
BEING YOURSELF
SELF-CONFIDENCE
CONTRIBUTING TO SOCIETY
WHAT THREE VALUES DO YOU HOLD MOST DEAR?
1. RELATIONSHIPS → LIVING HAPPILY WITH KASUMI
2. GOOD HEALTH
3. BEING MYSELF
PLEASE EXPLAIN THE REASONS BEHIND YOUR
HOW CAN I FIND MY WORK-KASUMI BALANCE?
WHAT?
ISN'T IT "WORK-LIFE" BALANCE?

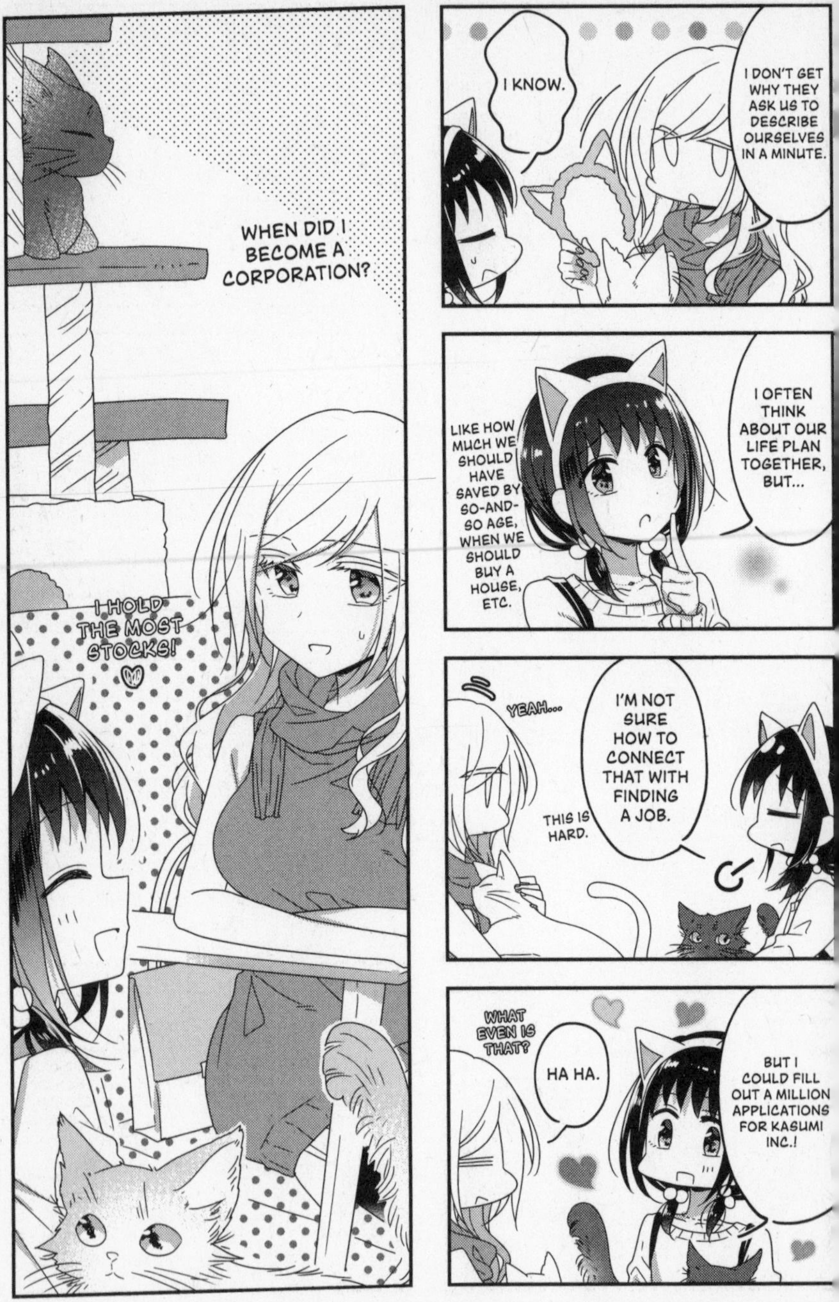
I DON'T GET WHY THEY ASK US TO DESCRIBE OURSELVES IN A MINUTE.
I KNOW.
I OFTEN THINK ABOUT OUR LIFE PLAN TOGETHER, BUT...
LIKE HOW MUCH WE SHOULD HAVE SAVED BY SO-AND-SO AGE, WHEN WE SHOULD BUY A HOUSE, ETC.
I'M NOT SURE HOW TO CONNECT THAT WITH FINDING A JOB.
YEAH...
THIS IS HARD.
BUT I COULD FILL OUT A MILLION APPLICATIONS FOR KASUMI INC.!
HA HA.
WHAT EVEN IS THAT?
WHEN DID I BECOME A CORPORATION?
I HOLD THE MOST STOCKS!

Futaribeya
A ROOM FOR TWO

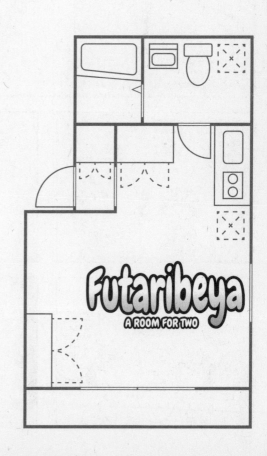

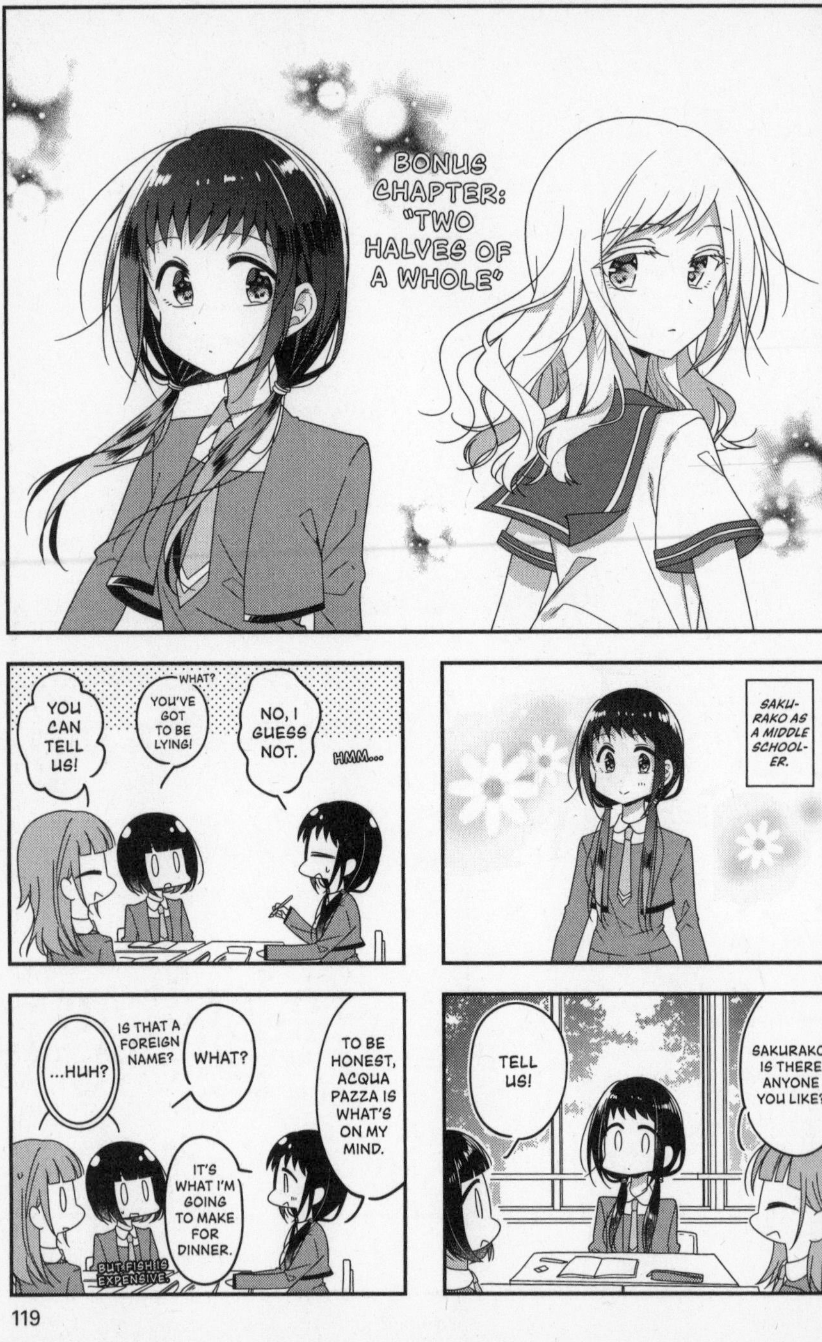
BONUS CHAPTER: "TWO HALVES OF A WHOLE"
SAKURAKO AS A MIDDLE SCHOOLER.
NO, I GUESS NOT.
HMM...
WHAT?
YOU'VE GOT TO BE LYING!
YOU CAN TELL US!
SAKURAKO, IS THERE ANYONE YOU LIKE?
TELL US!
TO BE HONEST, ACQUA PAZZA IS WHAT'S ON MY MIND.
WHAT?
IS THAT A FOREIGN NAME?
...HUH?
IT'S WHAT I'M GOING TO MAKE FOR DINNER.
BUT FISH IS EXPENSIVE.

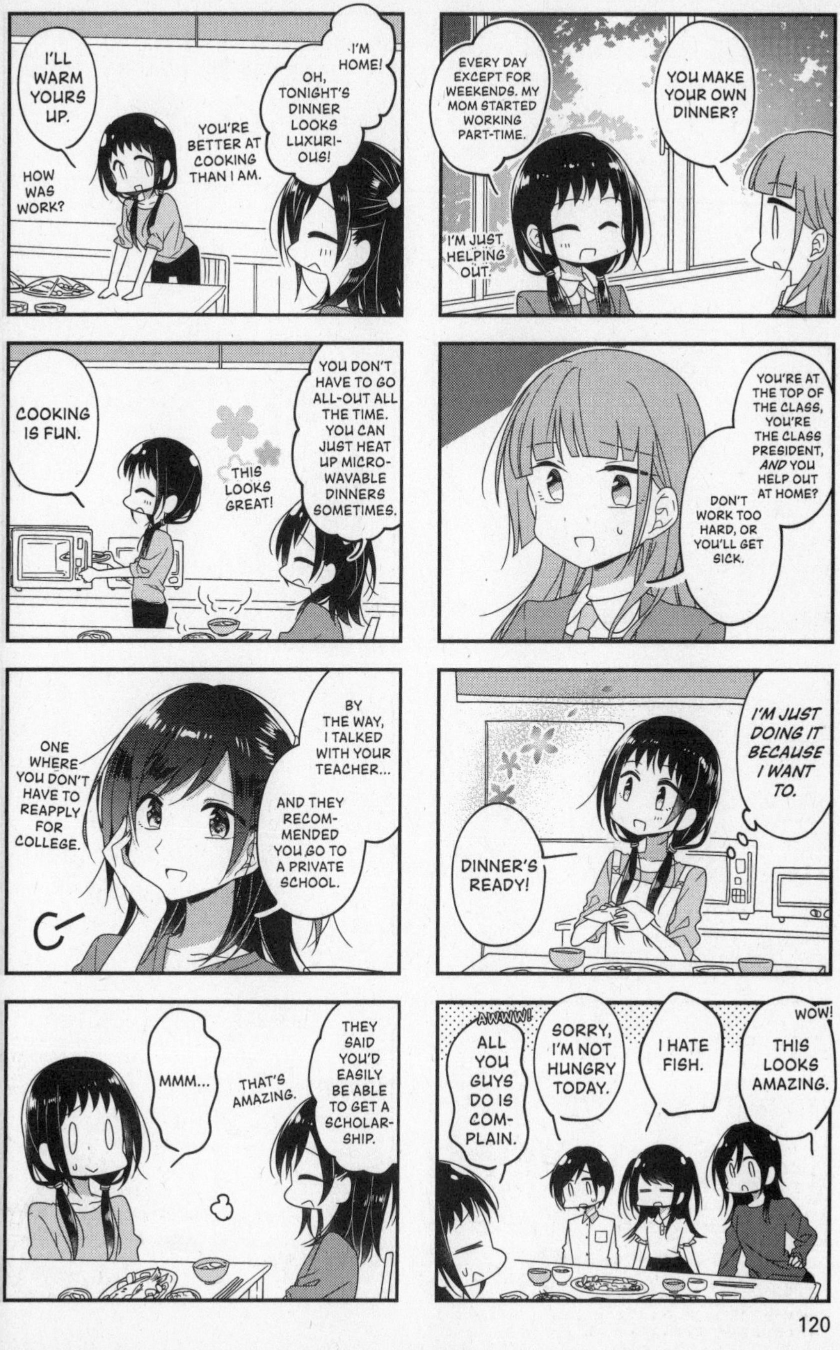
YOU MAKE YOUR OWN DINNER?
EVERY DAY EXCEPT FOR WEEKENDS. MY MOM STARTED WORKING PART-TIME.
I'M JUST HELPING OUT.
YOU'RE AT THE TOP OF THE CLASS, YOU'RE THE CLASS PRESIDENT, AND YOU HELP OUT AT HOME?
DON'T WORK TOO HARD, OR YOU'LL GET SICK.
I'M JUST DOING IT BECAUSE I WANT TO.
DINNER'S READY!
WOW!
THIS LOOKS AMAZING.
I HATE FISH.
SORRY, I'M NOT HUNGRY TODAY.
AWWW!
ALL YOU GUYS DO IS COMPLAIN.
I'M HOME!
OH, TONIGHT'S DINNER LOOKS LUXURIOUS!
YOU'RE BETTER AT COOKING THAN I AM.
I'LL WARM YOURS UP.
HOW WAS WORK?
YOU DON'T HAVE TO GO ALL-OUT ALL THE TIME. YOU CAN JUST HEAT UP MICROWAVABLE DINNERS SOMETIMES.
THIS LOOKS GREAT!
COOKING IS FUN.
BY THE WAY, I TALKED WITH YOUR TEACHER...
AND THEY RECOMMENDED YOU GO TO A PRIVATE SCHOOL.
ONE WHERE YOU DON'T HAVE TO REAPPLY FOR COLLEGE.
THEY SAID YOU'D EASILY BE ABLE TO GET A SCHOLARSHIP.
THAT'S AMAZING.
MMM...

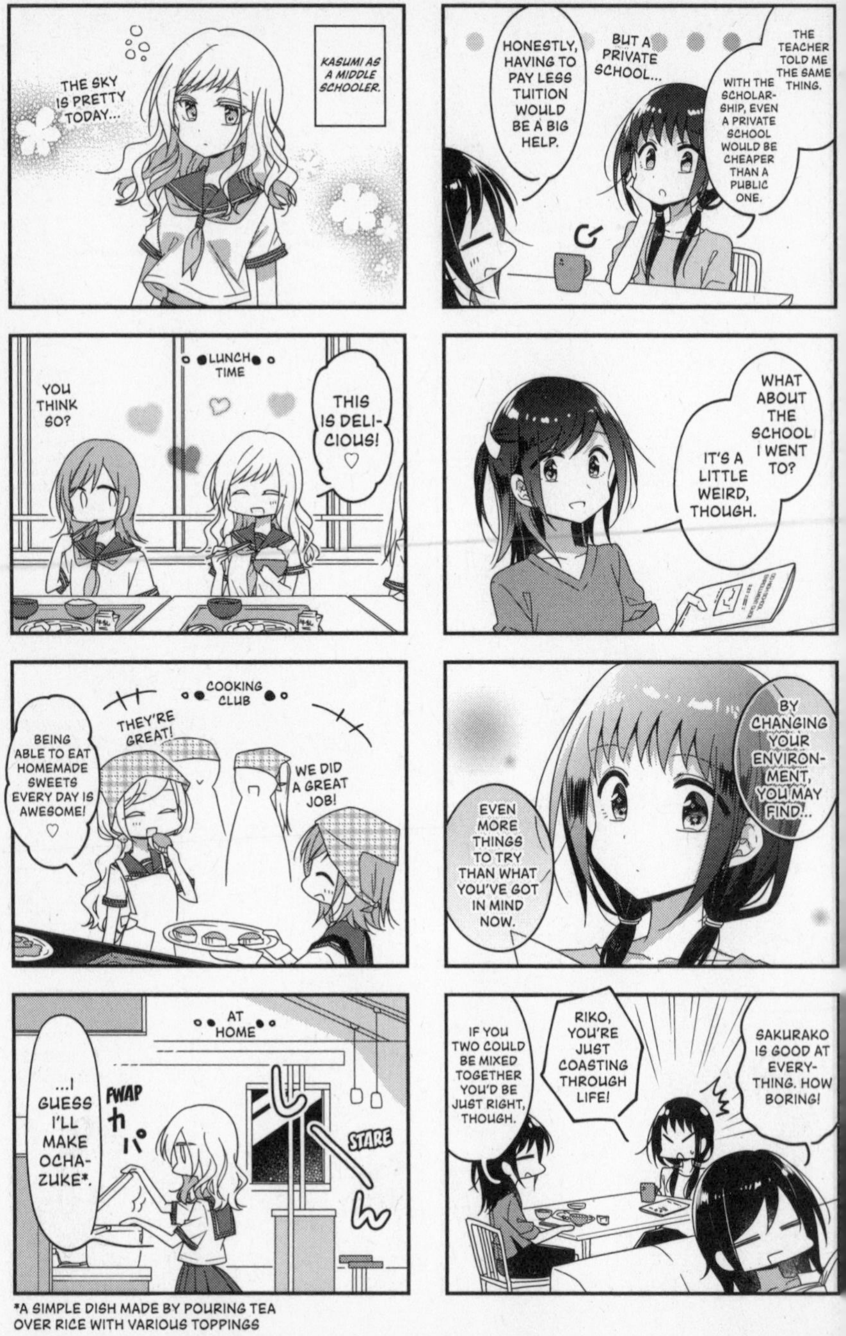
THE TEACHER TOLD ME THE SAME THING.
WITH THE SCHOLARSHIP, EVEN A PRIVATE SCHOOL WOULD BE CHEAPER THAN A PUBLIC ONE.
BUT A PRIVATE SCHOOL...
HONESTLY, HAVING TO PAY LESS TUITION WOULD BE A BIG HELP.
WHAT ABOUT THE SCHOOL I WENT TO?
IT'S A LITTLE WEIRD, THOUGH.
BY CHANGING YOUR ENVIRONMENT, YOU MAY FIND...
EVEN MORE THINGS TO TRY THAN WHAT YOU'VE GOT IN MIND NOW.
SAKURAKO IS GOOD AT EVERYTHING. HOW BORING!
RIKO, YOU'RE JUST COASTING THROUGH LIFE!
IF YOU TWO COULD BE MIXED TOGETHER YOU'D BE JUST RIGHT, THOUGH.
KASUMI AS A MIDDLE SCHOOLER.
THE SKY IS PRETTY TODAY...
LUNCH TIME
THIS IS DELICIOUS! ♡
YOU THINK SO?
COOKING CLUB
WE DID A GREAT JOB!
THEY'RE GREAT!
BEING ABLE TO EAT HOMEMADE SWEETS EVERY DAY IS AWESOME! ♡
AT HOME
STARE
FWAP
...I GUESS I'LL MAKE OCHAZUKE*.

*A SIMPLE DISH MADE BY POURING TEA OVER RICE WITH VARIOUS TOPPINGS

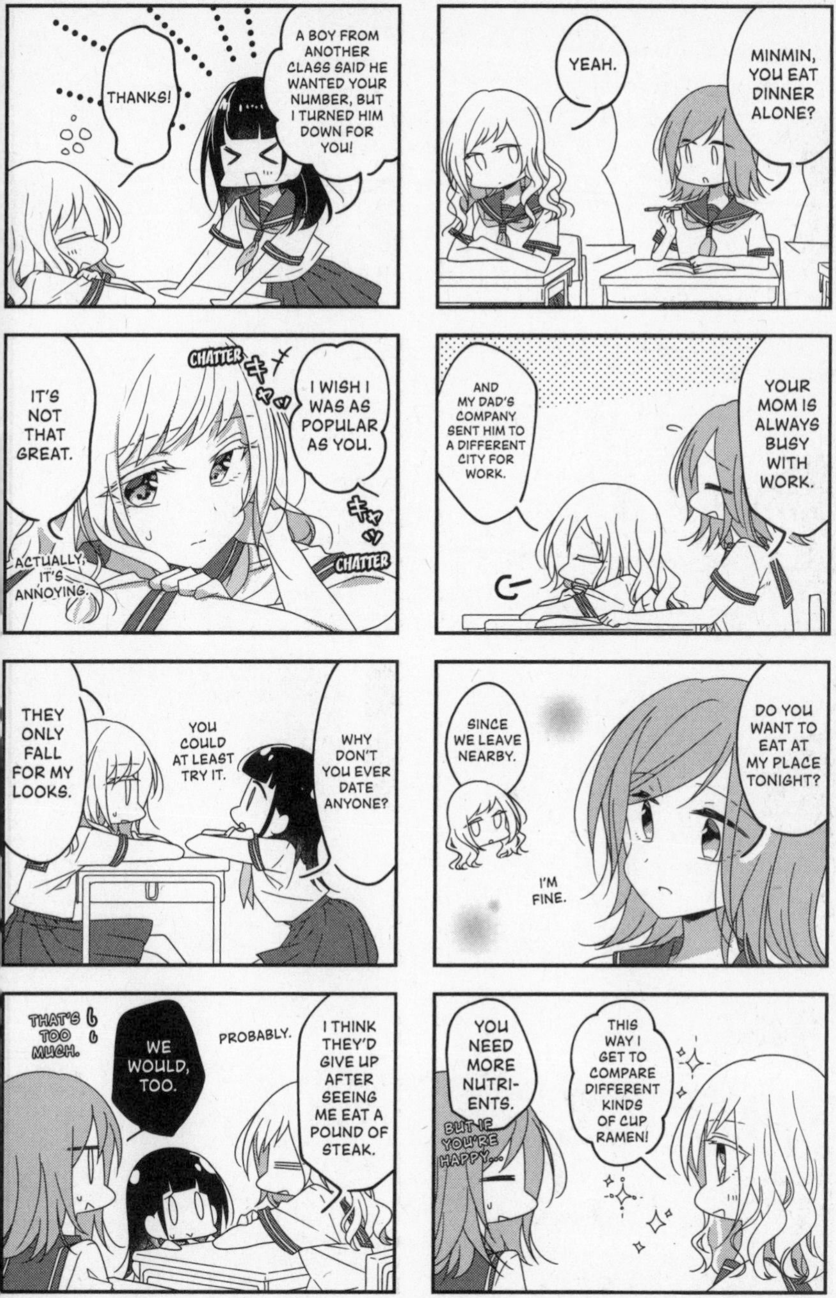
MINMIN, YOU EAT DINNER ALONE?
YEAH.
YOUR MOM IS ALWAYS BUSY WITH WORK.
AND MY DAD'S COMPANY SENT HIM TO A DIFFERENT CITY FOR WORK.
DO YOU WANT TO EAT AT MY PLACE TONIGHT?
SINCE WE LEAVE NEARBY.
I'M FINE.
THIS WAY I GET TO COMPARE DIFFERENT KINDS OF CUP RAMEN!
YOU NEED MORE NUTRI-ENTS.
BUT IF YOU'RE HAPPY...
A BOY FROM ANOTHER CLASS SAID HE WANTED YOUR NUMBER, BUT I TURNED HIM DOWN FOR YOU!
THANKS!
I WISH I WAS AS POPULAR AS YOU.
CHATTER
CHATTER
IT'S NOT THAT GREAT.
ACTUALLY, IT'S ANNOYING.
WHY DON'T YOU EVER DATE ANYONE?
YOU COULD AT LEAST TRY IT.
THEY ONLY FALL FOR MY LOOKS.
I THINK THEY'D GIVE UP AFTER SEEING ME EAT A POUND OF STEAK.
PROBABLY.
WE WOULD, TOO.
THAT'S TOO MUCH.

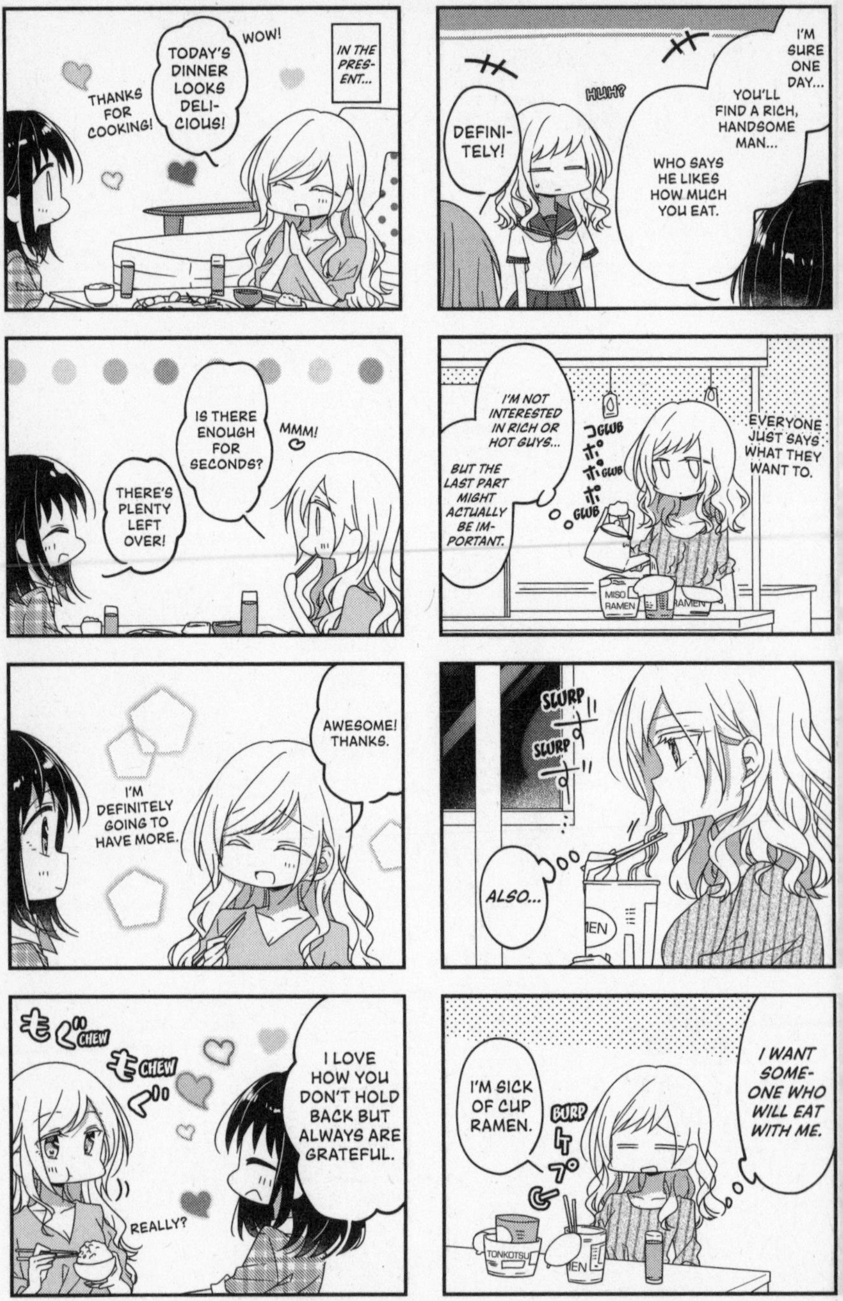
I'M SURE ONE DAY... YOU'LL FIND A RICH, HANDSOME MAN... WHO SAYS HE LIKES HOW MUCH YOU EAT.
HUH?
DEFINITELY!
EVERYONE JUST SAYS WHAT THEY WANT TO.
GLUB
GLUB
GLUB
I'M NOT INTERESTED IN RICH OR HOT GUYS... BUT THE LAST PART MIGHT ACTUALLY BE IMPORTANT.
MISO RAMEN
RAMEN
SLURP
SLURP
ALSO...
I WANT SOMEONE WHO WILL EAT WITH ME.
BURP
I'M SICK OF CUP RAMEN.
TONKOTSU
IN THE PRESENT...
WOW!
TODAY'S DINNER LOOKS DELICIOUS!
THANKS FOR COOKING!
MMM!
IS THERE ENOUGH FOR SECONDS?
THERE'S PLENTY LEFT OVER!
AWESOME! THANKS.
I'M DEFINITELY GOING TO HAVE MORE.
I LOVE HOW YOU DON'T HOLD BACK BUT ALWAYS ARE GRATEFUL.
CHEW
CHEW
REALLY?

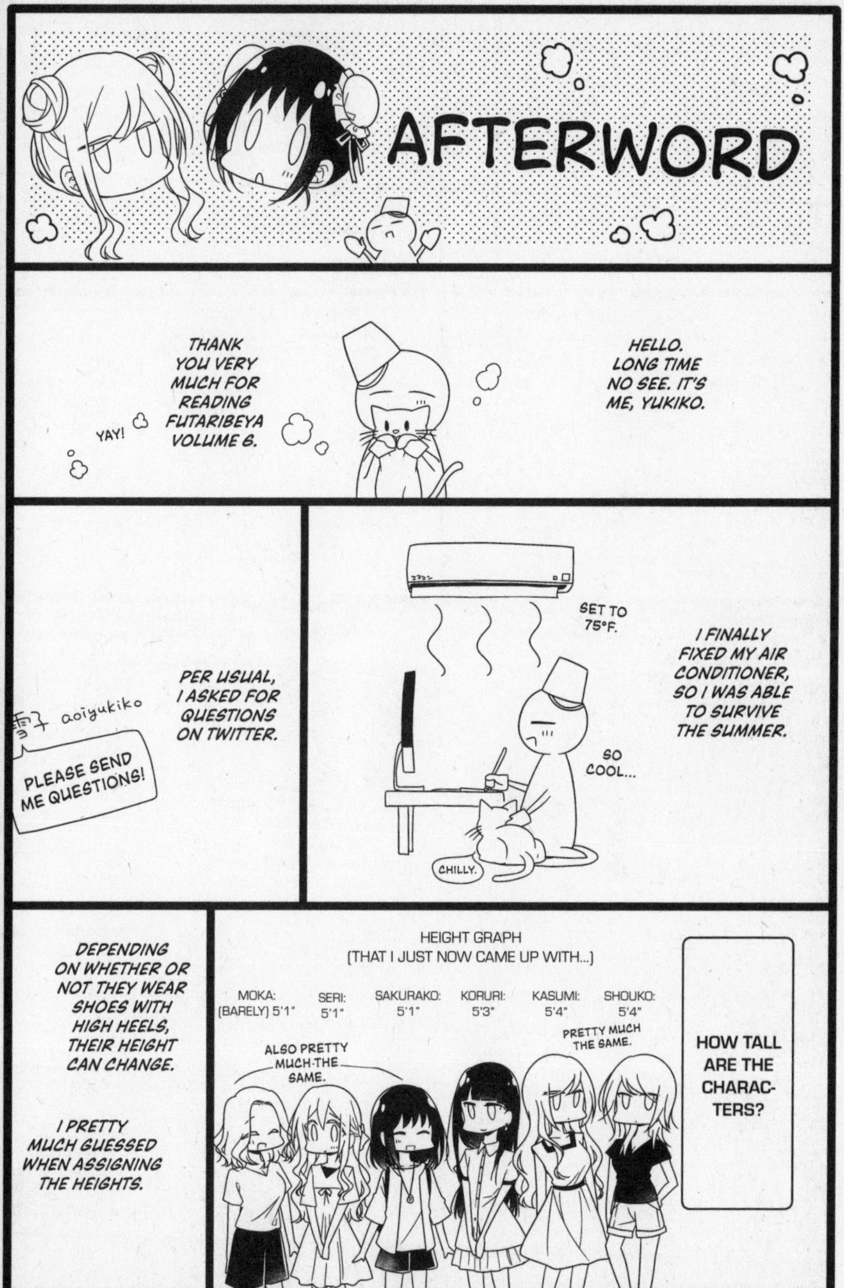
AFTERWORD
HELLO. LONG TIME NO SEE. IT'S ME, YUKIKO.
THANK YOU VERY MUCH FOR READING FUTARIBEYA VOLUME 6.
YAY!
I FINALLY FIXED MY AIR CONDITIONER, SO I WAS ABLE TO SURVIVE THE SUMMER.
SET TO 75°F.
SO COOL...
CHILLY.
PER USUAL, I ASKED FOR QUESTIONS ON TWITTER.
雪子 aoiyukiko
PLEASE SEND ME QUESTIONS!
HOW TALL ARE THE CHARAC-TERS?
HEIGHT GRAPH
(THAT I JUST NOW CAME UP WITH...)
SHOUKO: 5'4"
KASUMI: 5'4"
KORURI: 5'3"
SAKURAKO: 5'1"
SERI: 5'1"
MOKA: (BARELY) 5'1"
PRETTY MUCH THE SAME.
ALSO PRETTY MUCH THE SAME.
DEPENDING ON WHETHER OR NOT THEY WEAR SHOES WITH HIGH HEELS, THEIR HEIGHT CAN CHANGE.
I PRETTY MUCH GUESSED WHEN ASSIGNING THE HEIGHTS.

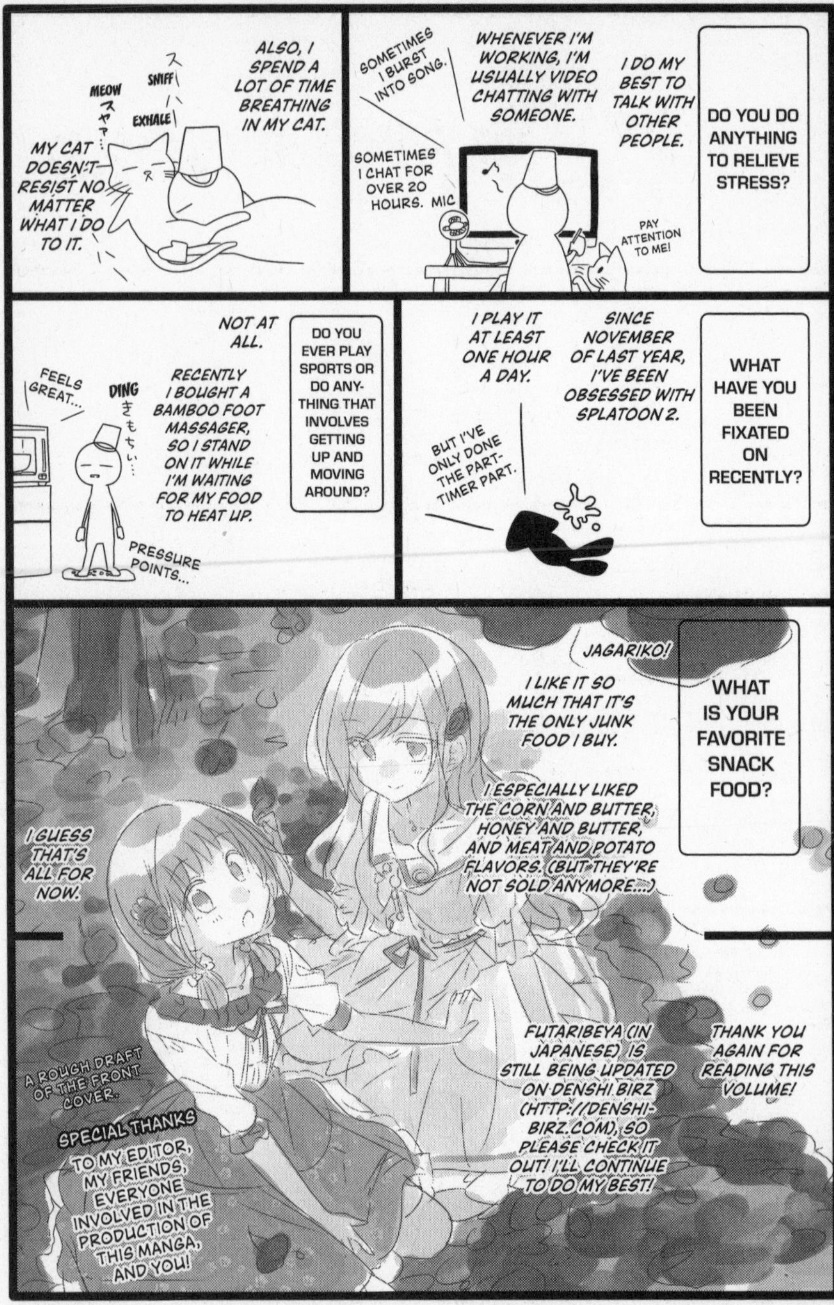
DO YOU DO ANYTHING TO RELIEVE STRESS?
I DO MY BEST TO TALK WITH OTHER PEOPLE.
WHENEVER I'M WORKING, I'M USUALLY VIDEO CHATTING WITH SOMEONE.
SOMETIMES I BURST INTO SONG.
SOMETIMES I CHAT FOR OVER 20 HOURS.
MIC
PAY ATTENTION TO ME!
ALSO, I SPEND A LOT OF TIME BREATHING IN MY CAT.
スー SNIFF
ハー EXHALE
MEOW スヤァ…
MY CAT DOESN'T RESIST NO MATTER WHAT I DO TO IT.
WHAT HAVE YOU BEEN FIXATED ON RECENTLY?
SINCE NOVEMBER OF LAST YEAR, I'VE BEEN OBSESSED WITH SPLATOON 2.
I PLAY IT AT LEAST ONE HOUR A DAY.
BUT I'VE ONLY DONE THE PART-TIMER PART.
DO YOU EVER PLAY SPORTS OR DO ANYTHING THAT INVOLVES GETTING UP AND MOVING AROUND?
NOT AT ALL.
RECENTLY I BOUGHT A BAMBOO FOOT MASSAGER, SO I STAND ON IT WHILE I'M WAITING FOR MY FOOD TO HEAT UP.
DING
FEELS GREAT... きもちぃ…
PRESSURE POINTS...
WHAT IS YOUR FAVORITE SNACK FOOD?
JAGARIKO!
I LIKE IT SO MUCH THAT IT'S THE ONLY JUNK FOOD I BUY.
I ESPECIALLY LIKED THE CORN AND BUTTER, HONEY AND BUTTER, AND MEAT AND POTATO FLAVORS. (BUT THEY'RE NOT SOLD ANYMORE...)
I GUESS THAT'S ALL FOR NOW.
THANK YOU AGAIN FOR READING THIS VOLUME!
FUTARIBEYA (IN JAPANESE) IS STILL BEING UPDATED ON DENSHI BIRZ (HTTP://DENSHI-BIRZ.COM), SO PLEASE CHECK IT OUT! I'LL CONTINUE TO DO MY BEST!
A ROUGH DRAFT OF THE FRONT COVER.
SPECIAL THANKS
TO MY EDITOR, MY FRIENDS, EVERYONE INVOLVED IN THE PRODUCTION OF THIS MANGA, AND YOU!

Futaribeya
A ROOM FOR TWO

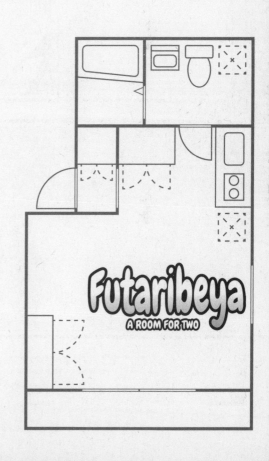

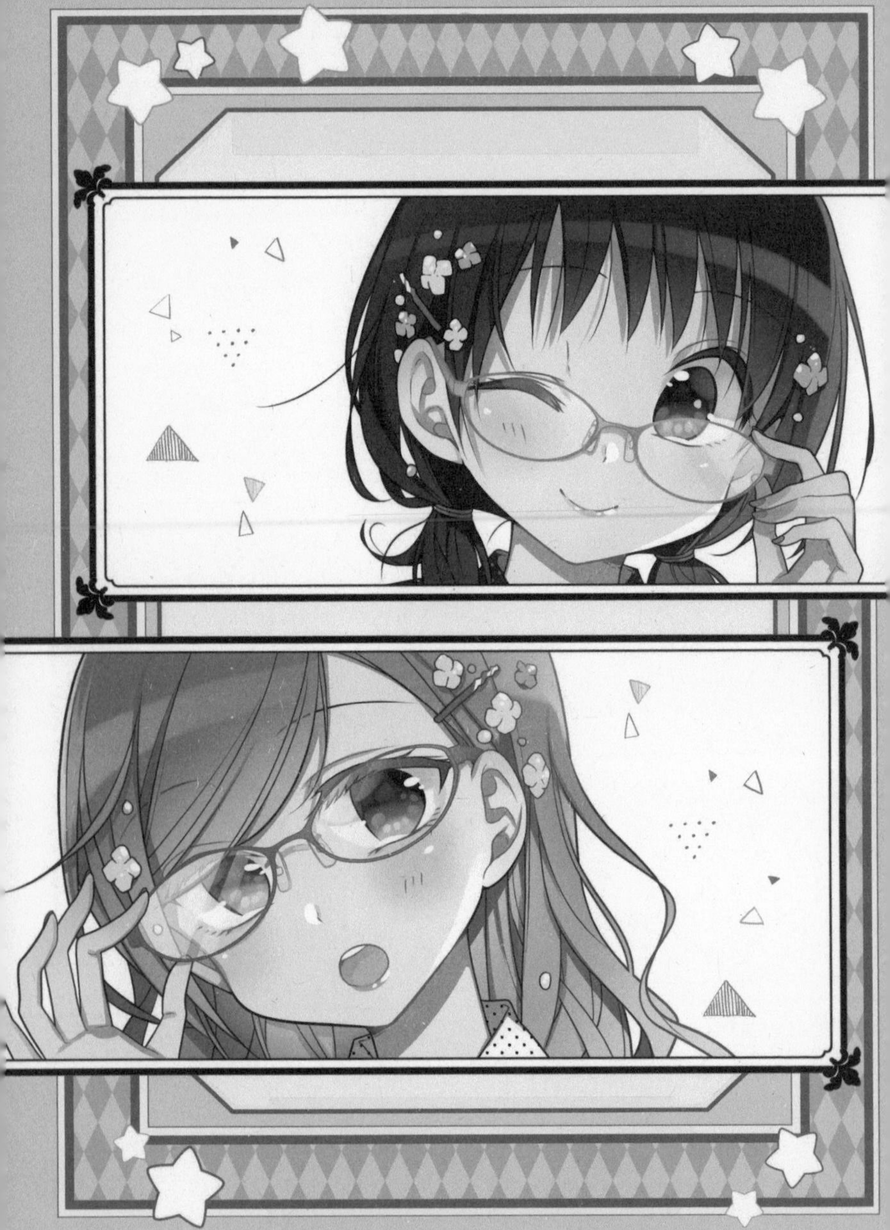

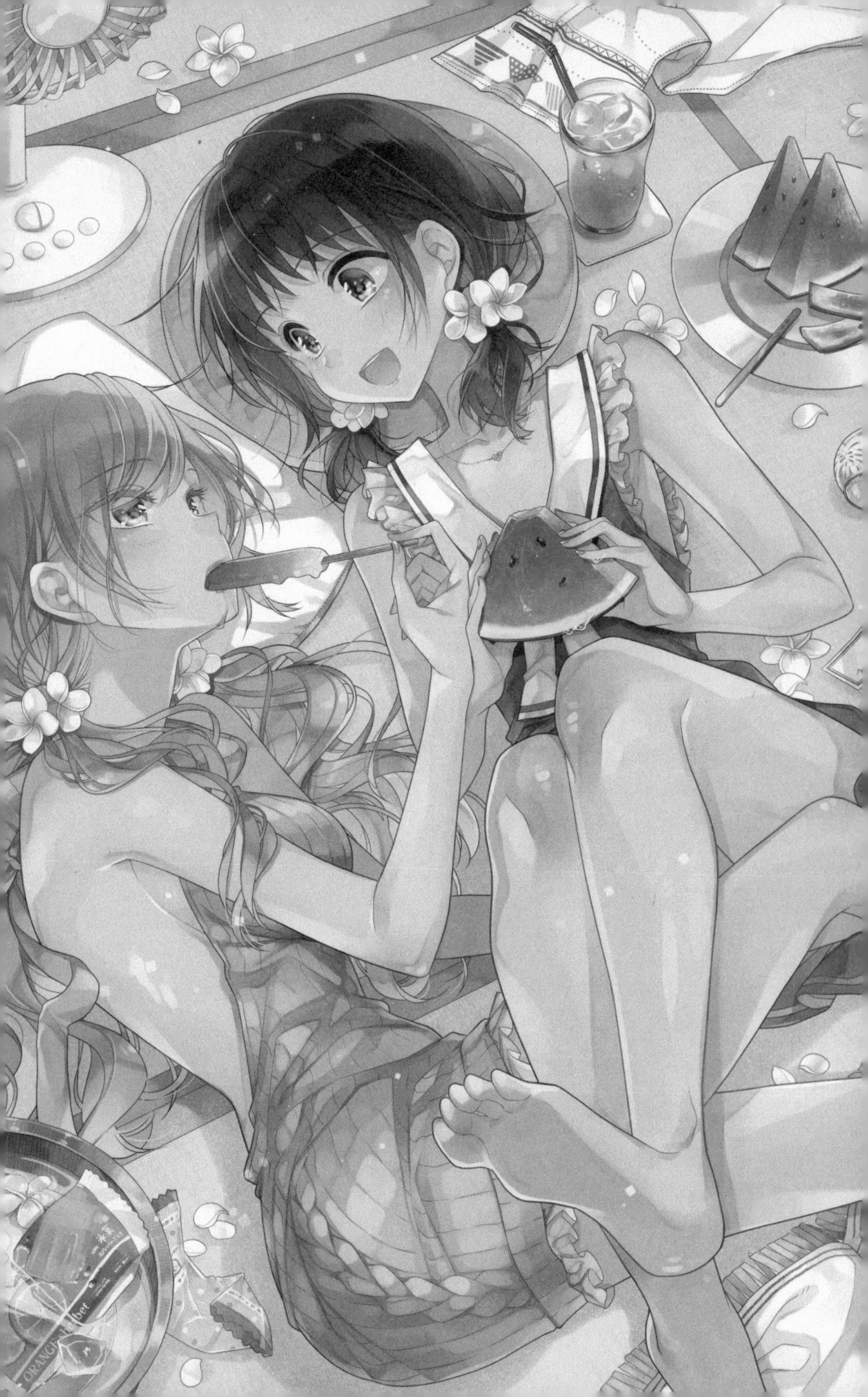